Praise for
Managing Leadership Transition for Nonprofits

"Leadership transition is one of the greatest challenges and opportunities faced by an organization. Leaders know that leaving well is the last great gift a leader can give to the organization. *Managing Leadership Transition for Nonprofits* is an indispensable guide for leaders across the sector."

—Frances Hesselbein, President and CEO, Leader to Leader Institute

"Invaluable guidance on the most neglected topic in nonprofit management— leadership changes at the top. A trio of very successful practitioners—with deep experience in the full range of nonprofit roles—provides a highly readable and useful conceptual framework and practical tools, with a focus on the essential responsibilities of nonprofit board members. A distinctive strength of this book is that it provides advice on both how to avoid common problems and also on how to seize the positive opportunities that are presented by leadership transitions."

—Rob Hollister, Dean, Jonathan M. Tisch College of Citizenship and Public Service, Tufts University

"*Managing Leadership Transition for Nonprofits* demonstrates the importance of leadership continuity. As the baby boomers retire and relinquish the reins to a new generation, the process is as critical to the continued strength of the organization as are the leadership qualities of the successor. There is a crisis afoot in America's nonprofits, and this book identifies the solution."

—Vicki Donlan, author, *Her Turn: Why It's Time for Women to Lead in America*

"Transitions of leadership are often scary and volatile moments in an organization's history. Yet, they can also be used as strategic moments to bring clarity to the organization, reinforce direction, and align a new leader with the organization for the next chapter of growth and social impact. This book captures not just the steps in a transition, but the overall strategy to keep an organization vibrant and healthy over the long term. It is a guide for building the foundation of a leadership culture that will position organizations toward healthy and natural CEO transitions."

—Ned Rimer, Co-Founder and formerly Executive Director, Citizen Schools; and Founder & Executive Director, Chronic Care Community Corps, EDC

"The number one responsibility of a Board either for profit or nonprofit is managing risk, and the number one risk is transition of leadership at the top. The authors have done an excellent job in identifying a major issue for all companies and present a roadmap that is logical, thorough, and a good approach to succession planning for directors to follow."

—Bud Bergren, President and CEO, The BonTon Stores, Inc.

"*Managing Leadership Transitions for Nonprofits* is a highly readable, comprehensive, thoughtful, and realistic guide to the critical issue of leadership transition in nonprofit organizations—a topic that will become even more timely as the current generation of nonprofit leaders retires. Authors Dym, Egmont, and Watkins each bring important and diverse experiences and perspectives to this topic based on years of advising and running nonprofits. In particular, they do not shy away from discussing some of the real challenges of managing a charitable organization and transitioning to new leadership. And yet they do this while also giving a sense of how rewarding and how special the work of a nonprofit CEO can be. The book's focus on the role of nonprofit boards and strategy development is especially important, and the inclusion of specific sample tools that can be used in a change process are an added plus."

—Beth Smith, Executive Director, Hyams Foundation

"*Managing Leadership Transitions for Nonprofits* is about much more than the mechanics of the transition process. It goes deep into what effective nonprofit leadership looks like—for the board, for the CEO, and for the board/CEO partnership. It nicely champions the moment of CEO turnover as a special opportunity for a nonprofit to refresh its strategic vision and renew its commitment to the leadership excellence needed to pursue that vision."

—Tim Wolfred, Senior Project Director, CompassPoint Nonprofit Services

"During the next two decades, the challenge of leadership transition will be among the most important in the nonprofit world. *Managing Leadership Transitions for Nonprofits* is the perfect companion to those transitions. It clarifies the problems and provides a step-by-step guide for taking advantage of the great opportunity: to select and align new leadership with organizational strategy and objectives. And, by the way, it offers an excellent general blueprint for good governance and good management. This is an important book for nonprofit boards, leaders, and staff."

—Pat Brandes, Executive Director, Barr Foundation

"The long-term success of all nonprofits is directly tied to the selection and on-boarding of CEOs. As the time between transitions gets shorter and the role of the Board of Directors becomes more complicated, a full understanding of the complexities of CEO transitions is essential. *Managing Leadership Transition for Nonprofits* provides an exceptional roadmap toward success. It should find a place on the must-read list for current and aspiring CEOs and for all who serve on nonprofit boards."

—Jan Verhage, Chief Operating Officer, Girl Scouts of the USA

"Having experienced transitional situations described in the book, I found myself saying an AMEN to the analysis of problems as well as the how-to steps that can be taken to construct an organization to achieve their objectives—and how to bridge from the 'old' to the 'new' to sustain organizational effectiveness. The information, direction, and guidance provided is not theoretical, but definitive and clear in the approach to passing the torch and is on target in diagnosing problems and challenges involved in leadership transition. The specifics provided in creating a management plan is an invaluable blueprint."

—Sandy Kautz, Nonprofit Management Consultant

Managing Leadership Transition for Nonprofits

Managing Leadership Transition for Nonprofits

Passing the Torch to Sustain Organizational Excellence

Barry Dym
Susan Egmont
Laura Watkins

Vice President, Publisher: Tim Moore
Associate Publisher and Director of Marketing: Amy Neidlinger
Executive Editor: Jeanne Glasser
Editorial Assistant: Pamela Boland
Operations Manager: Gina Kanouse
Senior Marketing Manager: Julie Phifer
Publicity Manager: Laura Czaja
Assistant Marketing Manager: Megan Colvin
Cover Designer: Sandra Schroeder
Managing Editor: Kristy Hart
Senior Project Editor: Lori Lyons
Copy Editor: Gill Editorial Services
Proofreader: Water Crest Publishing
Indexer: Lisa Stumpf
Senior Compositor: Gloria Schurick
Manufacturing Buyer: Dan Uhrig

Publishing as FT Press
Upper Saddle River, New Jersey 07458
FT Press offers excellent discounts on this book when ordered in quantity for bulk purchases or special sales. For more information, please contact U.S. Corporate and Government Sales, 1-800-382-3419, corpsales@pearsontechgroup.com. For sales outside the U.S., please contact International Sales at international@pearson.com.

Company and product names mentioned herein are the trademarks or registered trademarks of their respective owners.

Printed in the United States of America
First Printing March 2011
ISBN-10: 0-13-704765-7
ISBN-13: 978-0-13-704765-9
Pearson Education LTD.
Pearson Education Australia PTY, Limited.
Pearson Education Singapore, Pte. Ltd.
Pearson Education North Asia, Ltd.
Pearson Education Canada, Ltd.
Pearson Educación de Mexico, S.A. de C.V.
Pearson Education—Japan
Pearson Education Malaysia, Pte. Ltd.
Library of Congress Cataloging-in-Publication Data
Dym, Barry, 1942-
 Managing leadership transition for nonprofit : passing the torch to sustain organizational excellence / Barry Dym, Susan Egmont, Laura Watkins.
  p. cm.
 Includes bibliographical references and index.
 ISBN 978-0-13-704765-9 (hardback : alk. paper)
 1. Nonprofit organizations—Management. 2. Leadership. 3. Chief executive officers. I. Egmont, Susan, 1953- II. Watkins, Laura, 1950- III. Title.
 HD62.6.D963 2011
 658.4'06—dc22
                    2010031612

We would like to thank the many, many leaders, managers, staffers, board members, and other volunteers who have dedicated so much of their lives to bringing to life the values and objectives of nonprofit organizations.

To my grandchildren, Molly, Jake, and Eli: May they carry the torch of practical idealism and fight the good fight in this very confusing world of ours.
—Barry

To Bill Bolling, who invited me into the nonprofit world, Badi Foster who encouraged me to pursue my dream of consulting, and to Westy, my partner in work and life.
—Susan

To Girl Scouting, which taught me to lead; and to my family, who taught me to love and honor community action.
—Laura

Contents

About the Authors

Barry Dym, PhD, is Founder and Executive Director of the Institute for Nonprofit Management and Leadership. During his wide-ranging career, Dr. Dym has been an organization development consultant, executive coach, psychotherapist, entrepreneur, author, researcher, and teacher. Currently, Dr. Dym is the Executive Director of the Institute for Nonprofit Management at the Boston University School of Management.

As a consultant, Dr. Dym specializes in executive coaching and team building; strategic planning and implementation; aligning strategic direction with organizational capabilities; and the management of change and key organizational transitions.

He has founded and directed three other organizations—The Family Institute of Cambridge, The Boston Center for Family Health, and WorkWise Research and Consulting—and a journal, *Family Systems Medicine*. He has served on and advised many boards of directors.

Dr. Dym has written four books—*Leadership in Nonprofit Organizations*, *Leadership Transitions*, *Couples*, and *Readiness*, and *Change in Couple Therapy*—and many articles, including "Utilizing States of Organizational Readiness" (*OD Practitioner*), winner of the Larry Porter Prize as the best article on organizational development, 1998–1999, "Resistance in Organizations: How to Recognize, Understand and Respond to It," "Integrating Entrepreneurship with Professional Leadership," and "Forays: The Power of Small Changes."

Dr. Dym received his A.B. and his Ph.D. from Harvard University, where he received a Woodrow Wilson Fellowship and a Harvard Five-Year Prize Fellowship.

Susan Egmont is principal of Egmont Associates, an executive search firm for nonprofit organizations and for corporations, foundations, and academic centers with nonprofit interests. She has more than 30 years of experience in nonprofit management, including youth development, education, workforce development, healthcare, children's issues, the arts, and in organizations fighting hunger and poverty. Susan's passion is excellence in nonprofit management and matching vital organizations with effective leaders. Her clients include foundations, academic institutions, peace and justice organizations, socially responsible investment companies and nonprofits, human service groups, community health providers, environmental coalitions, arts organizations, education reform efforts, and other nonprofits.

In addition to executive transition work, Susan has consulted extensively with nonprofit organizations in board development, strategic planning, human resource issues, and program development.

Susan was formerly Executive Director of Blue Cross and Blue Shield of Massachusetts' foundation for children's health and Deputy Director of the Boston Private Industry Council. She was the director of a contemporary dance company and spent eleven years in management at the Atlanta Community Food Bank.

Susan holds an MBA from Emory University and is a Certified Association Executive and Certified Fund Raising Executive. She served on the founding boards of directors of the Alliance for Nonprofit Management, the national professional association for nonprofit consultants and management assistance centers, Massachusetts Nonprofit Network, the statewide association, and Atlanta's Nonprofit Resource Center (now Georgia Center for Nonprofits).

Laura Watkins is principal of Dovetail Associates, a consulting firm which provides integrated services to nonprofit organizations with a focus on strategic planning and organizational development, senior leadership transition, and executive coaching. Laura's passion is to build a nonprofit sector to sustain a healthy democracy. Her clients include organizations of all sizes, regional and national coalitions, and nonprofit boards of directors seeking to reorganize operations to achieve their mission.

Dr. Watkins works with organizations to develop coalitions around shared strategic visions. The outcomes of these strategic alliances have ranged from shared facilities and administrative staff to collective purchasing, and integrated programming and training to developing joint grants and fundraising initiatives.

Laura was formerly the Chief Executive Officer of Patriots' Trail Girl Scout Council in Boston, Massachusetts. She has worked in the nonprofit sector for thirty years. She has served on the board of directors of Leadership America, the Children's Trust Fund, the Chamber of Commerce, Charles River Museum, and the National and Community and Service Commission.

Dr. Watkins received her B.S. from the University of Missouri, MPA from George Williams College, MBA from Illinois Benedictine College, and Doctor of Philosophy in Organizational Development from the Union Institute. She has directed nonprofit organizations across the country during her career. Dr. Watkins has given innumerable seminars to nonprofit organizations and taught courses in Non-Profit Management at Suffolk University and Northeastern University.

Introduction

There is a crisis of leadership in our country. We idealize and revile leaders with equal passion. We welcome them as saviors and boot them out as scoundrels. The crisis, however, may reside as much in our confusing expectations as in the leaders' ineffectuality. There may be better ways to identify, introduce, support, and monitor our leaders that will enhance rather than undermine their performance.

That is the subject of this book: how to manage the change from one leader to the next in a way that gives leaders and the organizations they serve the best possible chance to succeed.

Leadership transitions are among the most important activities in the lives of organizations. Some people believe, for instance, that George Washington's stepping down after two terms in office set the stage for American democracy. Through his action, he rejected monarchy, even his own, and announced the imperative of orderly succession. So it is with organizations: Orderly succession announces the preeminence of an ongoing collective, not personal, agenda.

This is not always easy. Succession often follows conflict and confusion or, as in Washington's case, the departure of a beloved and trusted steward. How, we wonder, will we trust anyone else? But, of course, we must. And the way we guide that transition—the manner of our management itself—is the key to assuring our stakeholders that the continuity of purpose and activity will be preserved.

Managing Leadership Transition for Nonprofits: Passing the Torch to Sustain Organizational Excellence presents an analysis of the problems that lead to frequent leadership turnover and the mismanagement of transitions. Ours is an aspirational portrait of how to construct organizations to achieve their objectives and how to transition management in a way that forms a sturdy bridge between the departure of the old leadership and the introduction of new.

The Crisis of Transition

For many people, the question of leadership turnover and transition is relatively minor and obscure—nothing to particularly concern them-selves about. The scale of the problem along with the importance and complexity of the cure fly well below the radar. Some think a few profes-sional consultants should pay attention, but not themselves even if they work or volunteer or serve on the boards of nonprofits. But for all of us who care about nonprofits, the conduct of leadership transitions is a big problem with a big upside if we learn to do it right. Transitions are deserving of a great deal of our attention.

What initially drew our attention to transitions were reports of the frequent, repetitive, and destructive turnover of leadership in the non-profit world. Our work in executive education, executive search, and organization development consulting put us inescapably in the path of the storm. More formal research filled out our understanding.

Here's what we learned.

At any given time, there be as many as 20 to 25 percent of executive directors (called CEOs throughout this manuscript) in or near transition. According to various sources, as many as 34 percent of organizations have already had two or more executives in the past five years, and within five years more than 70 percent of CEOs expect to leave their current positions. Nearly 75 percent of all nonprofit executives will reach retire-ment age over the next two decades (Annie Casey Foundation).[1] Accord-ing to Bridgespan, by 2016, the nonprofit sector will need to add an average of 80,000 senior managers every year. These are astounding numbers!

Depending on who is measuring, the average tenure of nonprofit leaders is between three and five years. This leaves hardly enough time to build programs, put together effective teams, and achieve financial viability and credibility. Whatever progress leaders make in their adopted organizations is often undermined by rapid turnover, which inevitably proves costly and destabilizing to the organizations and to their own confidence. With the diminishment of credibility and resources, each new start becomes more difficult than the one before. It becomes harder and harder to convince funders, staff, and community leaders that this time will be different.

A Problem of Significant Proportion

And the scale of the problem is growing. Currently, a huge proportion of nonprofits are led by members of the baby boom generation who will be retiring during the next decade. Tens of thousands of new leaders will be selected by tens of thousands of boards of directors, managing millions of staff people and serving many millions of clients.

Some of the turnover, then, is natural: people aging, retiring, and giving way to a new generation of younger executives. But in many, even the majority, the displaced leaders are not older and ready for the next stage of life, and there is little about their departure that is natural, peaceful, or productive. Many depart on a sour and dispirited note. They have been fired or eased out, or, seeing the handwriting on the wall, they leave while they can still command good letters of recommendation— not necessarily given because board members believe in these recommendations but because boards would like to see a "peaceful" transition before circumstances get really bad.

Some CEOs are poor stewards, naïve about finance, marketing, and program development and poor managers of their staff. Or, at their worst, they are scoundrels who have embezzled money or betrayed the hope and dreams with which they had been entrusted. For their part, CEOs flee situations that they realize are untenable: unrealistic goals married to limited resources; demanding, micromanaging boards who raise few funds and provide fewer connections to those who have the resources; helter-skelter programs in search of any stray foundation dollar; and poorly paid staff with limited experience or ability.

There are also times when long-standing leaders depart with dignity, when illness makes leadership impossible, or when a bigger, better job looms on the horizon—when leadership "dies of natural causes." But, more often than not, the actual turnover follows periods of contention, behind-the-scenes rumors, wrangling, and accusations that divide and debilitate the nonprofits. Transitions don't generally begin with clear, rational decision making and at clearly marked times. Rather, they build and seethe over time. One of the problems with "rapid transitions" is that they really take place over long periods, during which ill will and organizational ineffectuality build.

Much can be lost in transition. Transitions absorb time and energy from boards and staff. They are costly. Credibility may be sacrificed. Funders and partners wonder if the organization has lost its way, whether it will have the ability to carry out programs, and whether it is trustworthy. Program development tends to slow or stop, awaiting the approval and guidance of the new leader. Staffs may grow indecisive or contentious without a leader to guide. Organizational memory can be lost.

During the transition period, conflict and chaos can sometimes be so unrestrained that the growth of the organization is seriously impaired for years to come. High turnover and poorly managed transitions all too often mean that organizations develop neither stable, experienced leadership nor the opportunity to grow in the planned and steady way that optimizes their potential. Perhaps worst of all, some organizations may fall into a downward spiral of events, precipitated by poorly managed leadership transitions, and move unavoidably toward dissolution.

Some leadership trajectories play out differently. In arenas like community health and legal services, leadership tends to be long lived; some would say it's too long, because the length of tenure clogs the pipeline of fresh younger minds and talents. Turnover in these stable organizations generally follows retirement. After 20 or 30 years with one leader, these organizations can be so set in their ways that it isn't chaos but stagnation that threatens. And it is hard to step into the shoes of the legendary people who founded and shepherded their organizations through so many good and bad times.

These days, however, frequent turnover is more often the rule. Downward spirals are created that go something like this. The organization experiences difficulties. Someone must be blamed; the leader is nominated, putting her under increased scrutiny and pressure and cutting into the trust and credibility that is her prime capital. As a result, she grows less effective, fueling the inevitable movement to replace her. As disappointed as the staff, board of directors, and funders may be in the leader, however, they are equally anxious about life without her, and they hurry to find a replacement. In their worry and hurry, they choose too quickly—a smart person, an articulate person, but one who may be not quite right for this particular organization. Then they place an exaggerated amount of hope in the new leader and her ability to rescue the organization. Almost invariably, she does not live up to the hype—maybe only by a small margin—but staff and board react as though she has betrayed their trust. The downward spiral continues.

There are about 1.4 million nonprofits in the United States today. Every year another 40,000 nonprofits are created. In many cities, they represent between 10 to 15 percent of a region's economy, including an important percentage of jobs and many distinctive services. Collectively, these organizations provide a huge array of services from which local, state, and federal governments have withdrawn in recent years. They are the source of many of the most innovative ideas in social services, environmental advocacy, and the arts, and they are the proving grounds for these ideas before governmental agencies, corporations, and society as a whole adopt them on a major scale. Nonprofit organizations represent both an advanced guard and a sustained voice for social justice. Ever since the nineteenth century, when Alexis de Tocqueville celebrated America's "voluntary societies," nonprofits have been the signature and one of the great bastions of our free society. Allowing them to weaken would be a national disaster.

At the same time, the proliferation of nonprofits during the past couple of decades has created problems. The majority, for example, are small, with revenues between $50,000 and $250,000 and staffs of two to six. They provide limited resources with which CEOs can build programs, staff, or infrastructure. It is hard to succeed in these organizations whose boards tend either toward a "rubber stamp" approach—"friends of Sarah"—with little accountability from the CEO or toward operational boards. Founding boards, for example, often have to roll up their sleeves to stuff envelopes, market services, and manage staff and are reluctant to yield control to anyone, including the CEO. In such cases, control problems naturally arise. Inexperience on the part of both boards and CEOs can exacerbate these control problems. They don't know what responsibility belongs to whom. They haven't lived and worked their ways through crises. They don't know what an effective relationship between the board and the CEO looks like.

The clash of inexperienced, not-so-confident forces—board presidents and CEOs—can provide a flammable mix. Without experience, each event, each challenge can take on a magnified appearance. In the best of situations, CEOs and board presidents balance and complement one another. Problems arise, and in the worst of situations, one person's anxieties fuel the other's anxieties, and one person's criticism leads to defensive responses from the other.

With relatively green CEOs and board presidents, there is a good likelihood of escalating levels of concern and conflict. Our research findings, then, should come as no surprise: Conflict between these two pivotal players may be the most influential cause of leadership turnover. If no lessons are learned with the first transition, this result is likely to repeat itself—the downward spiral mentioned previously. As a result, much too little leadership capital is built.

One hidden but significant victim of the trend toward rapid leadership turnover is leadership itself. There is little time for leadership to grow and ripen. It is rare that skilled leadership emerges full blown. There are those rare beings that had "it" from the start. They were presidents of the homerooms and high school classes—centers of attention in any room they entered. But most people take time to build the skills, confidence, maturity, or even self-image to lead others in effective and sustained ways.

During workshops with people currently in leadership positions, we have asked for a show of hands on who frequently feels like an impostor. Almost everyone raises their hands, expressing more relief at the company than embarrassment at being found out. At the Institute for Nonprofit Management and Leadership at Boston University, whose students are already practicing nonprofit executives, the biggest gain they report is in their level of confidence. Even when these executives are skilled—say in the creation and management of budgets—they tend to feel insecure in their knowledge.

Unlike business leaders who have taken the MBA path, many leaders of small to medium-sized nonprofits have had few objective standards by which to measure themselves. Although an increasing number of nonprofit executives do have MBAs, many are self-taught or taught by others like them. They have "built their ships while they sailed" and may not fully trust the lessons they have learned. They are often extraordinary people who have made do with much less than their corporate counterparts or even than their peers in large nonprofits. But they don't always know how talented they are, and they don't always have the specific training to help realize their talent.

Peter Drucker, a father of management theory and practice, sang the praises of nonprofit leaders—at the same time, tweaking arrogant corporate executives—when he called Frances Hesselbein, the then-CEO of Girl Scouts of the USA, the best leader in America. Bridgespan, the nonprofit consulting organization created out of Bain Consulting and Harvard Business School, implies the same when it says that nonprofit management is more complicated than corporate management. Corporations have only to please their customers and thereby their stockholders. Nonprofits have very different types of customers: the people they serve and the funders they have to woo with equal or even greater zeal. Top-notch nonprofit leaders who are able to manage both markets would be top of the line in any field. But this does not hold for all nonprofit leaders. Many find the complexity and extent of their work daunting.

The same is true for the volunteer leaders who form the boards of small to middle-sized nonprofits and are inexperienced and uneducated in the work of boards. Many have never served on boards before. Individual members might have experience and skills in management, but program or financial management is different from board leadership. Few have chaired boards, with their complex and demanding charge that minimally includes fiduciary oversight, strategy, and policy formation along with hiring, firing, and managing the CEO. Board presidents raise money themselves, connect CEOs to people of influence and wealth, and generally serve as all-purpose advisors to CEOs. It can be and often is a 15 to 30 hour a week job on top of their day job. And, even more than CEOs, many board presidents conduct their job by feel, with little to no formal education in mentoring or coaching to help them. As a result, they may lack clarity and confidence.

Collective leadership on boards is another kind of animal altogether. In fact, it is often the inability of boards to act in concert, to provide coordinated guidance to CEOs, that creates problems that weaken leadership. CEOs, for instance, often enough get caught between differing or conflicting board factions. Some boards drive CEOs crazy through their micromanagement—insisting on attention to and participation in the smallest details. Others act the role of loyal supporters: "Whatever Tom thinks is right is right by me." In the first case, control struggles tend to emerge. In the second, lax program and financial management is over-looked until crises occur. It is the combustible mix of inexperienced CEOs and their boards that leads most often to leadership turnover.

Boards During Transition

During transition periods, boards take on a more direct leadership role. They write the job description for the next CEO. What, after all, is an executive job description—or what should it be—but a statement of the organization's objectives and strategies and how the board expects the new leader to carry them out? At the same time, boards must manage senior staff so that programs continue as smoothly as possible and financial accountability is maintained so that staff can feel secure enough to perform their job in the absence of executive leadership. And boards have to create effective communications with all the organization's stake-holders—clients, staff, funders, community supporters—assuring all that the organizational agenda will survive and thrive despite the departure of the current leader.

The more we focused on the critically important role of boards during the transition process and throughout, the more we realized that our book is largely about volunteer leadership: how to work effectively during the transition stage and how to be effective through what we call the *cycle of leadership*. By that, we mean the stages leaders pass through, from the honeymoon to vulnerability to a kind of mature confidence.

Even among relatively experienced people, leadership capacity in any single organization takes time to develop. New CEOs have to understand the levers of power. They have to create alliances with stakeholders to build programs and raise money. To make these alliances, new leaders have to figure out how to fit into the organizational culture. They have to build trust and credibility to have people come along on the journey—particularly in nonprofits, where financial incentives (high salaries and performance bonuses) are largely absent. It takes time to be a truly effective nonprofit leader. Rapid turnover robs leaders and organizations of that time, ultimately creating stagnation. From one transition to the next, organizations too often tread water instead of reaching toward their potential.

The absence of sufficient leadership development in the nonprofit sector is no secret. Almost all the foundations that invest in nonprofits acknowledge the dilemma. Sometimes they wring their hands in anguish but don't quite know what to do about it, suggesting, for example, that organizations merge so that scale will produce opportunity for leadership development. They also know that boards of directors often represent part of the problem. They willingly fund board development training, which sometimes proves extraordinarily effective but more often trends toward interventions with too little "dosage."

There are few sustained or substantial programs for board leaders, although their skills and knowledge essentially make or break the effectiveness of leadership transitions. Ironically, they are the neglected element in the leadership transition. In many ways, this book is for them. The transition period is the one in which they are front and center. They must shine. They must set the stage for all that follows.

Keeping Pace

This is the dramatic problem that brought us to the subject of leadership transition. The more we looked, however, the more we saw rapid turnover and poorly managed transitions as manifestations of more general problems in nonprofit leadership, both professional and volunteer. And, because frequent turnover broadly stunts the stable development of leadership, we believe the whole nonprofit sector cannot grow as strong as it might without the emergence of skillful, experienced leaders.

All too often, the management approach to leadership turnover is rushed, remedial, and reactive. As an antidote, we will propose an approach that is careful, strategic, and forward looking. We emphasize the transformational potential of professionalizing the transition process. We are talking about good leadership, in general, not just good transition leadership. The model we have built for leadership transition, then, extends beyond the transition period and throughout the lifetime of a leader's tenure.

As we noted, nonprofit organizations have been proliferating at such a rapid rate that it has been impossible for leadership capacity to keep pace. The primary source of feedback to CEOs should be boards of directors. After all, their mandate is threefold. First is fiduciary responsibility: holding the executive accountable and providing feedback in the management of organizational finances. Second is policy and strategy—that is, the framing of the organization's mission, vision, and strategy and holding executives accountable for executing the strategic plans. Third, boards hire, fire, *and* manage the executive. This includes yearly performance reviews, but more importantly, it includes an ongoing dialogue on how well the organization, under the executive's leadership, is meeting its objectives.

Reconceiving Leadership Transition and Its Management

Organizations traditionally view leadership transition from a linear short circuited perspective. It is assumed that a leader can transition in or out of the organization without creating holistic change throughout the organization. When a board receives a resignation from a CEO, most often the transition is seen as a finite task. They attempt to find the right person to replace the CEO as quickly and efficiently as possible. The board then hopes that this person can be inserted into the organization without impact on systems, volunteers, or the larger community. In reality, the transition of leadership is a catalyst for seismic changes throughout every aspect of the "living, breathing organism" we know of as "the organization." The new leader has to come to an understanding of the organization's strengths, weaknesses, and strategic perspectives. They have to weave their leadership into the collective roles of the leadership team while honoring or negotiating around the organization's culture. The new leader has to earn the right to be trusted by the board, the staff, volunteers, and the community, to name a few of the tasks that create an effective transition. In this section we describe a shift in thinking from the linear task-oriented transitions currently used by organizations; and we broaden the transition process to include a continuous growth process for the leadership and the organization. Process takes time and attention at all levels of the community.

The Problem with Current

The mismanagement of leadership transitions has tended to compound and exacerbate the problems that have led to them. Why? Because management generally takes a narrow, remedial view, often in the mood of crisis. More often than not, leadership transitions focus almost exclusively on the search process, not enough on the direction they want the organization to move and the style in which they want to move it. They tend to rush, correctly nervous about all that can be lost during the transition but, rather than manage the transition to preserve the organization and separately take time with the search, they rush to find a savior.

Participation in the search process is often confined to a few people. When that is so, information is limited and lost, and communication is poor. Staff, clients, and funders grow nervous within the vacuum of information, make up stories, and pass them around. Rumors abound, creating fires that have to be put out.

Then, once the new leader is chosen, the organization is handed off like a colicky baby—"Here, you take her!" The search process may have lasted longer than expected. The board is exhausted and feeling out of its depth, almost irritated that the new leader has taken so long to enter the scene. In this scenario, boards often act like neglectful parents, failing to exercise even the minimum of oversight. Alternatively, they are so pleased with their choice that they confidently hand off the organization to their knight in shining armor, fully expecting that she will repair what has been lost and bring the organization back to lost glories.

Now a honeymoon stage begins, generally, with little accountability between boards and new leaders—and with equally little support. With time, the exuberance and optimism begin to ebb. Cracks emerge: Financial reports are not as positive as they might be; program development is slower than expected; fundraising is uninspired. The board, who had put too much faith in the leader, then tends to overreact. It grows critical, pulls in the reins too hard, and speculates about the need for new leadership. Mistrust and conflict build.

In other words, the downward spiral that we mentioned at the beginning of the chapter is virtually built in from the beginning of the new leader's tenure. It is built in because inadequate attention is paid to the period that follows the introduction of the new leader. The cycle leading to the need for another transition is built into the beginnings.

The Opportunity

In spite of and often because of all the *sturm und drang* that surrounds leadership turnover and transition, it also presents a unique opportunity for organizations. It may be the only time—except during an extensive and creative strategic planning project—that organizations not only have the opportunity but are charged with the task of reviewing their mission and objectives, their strategy and capacity, their resources and standing in the world. To select a new leader, organizations must ask: to do what? How best might a leader succeed within the constraints and the opportunities presented by this organization? In this market? Who is the best kind of leader for us? How should we relate to this leader?

In effect, leadership transitions present both the opportunity and the requirement for getting one's house in order. How can you select a new leader without knowing where you want that person to lead or what resources are available? The type of resources—people, finance, infrastructure, partnerships—you have tells you a great deal about the kind of leader you should pick. If you are poor, for example, you may want to choose someone who can do with less, an improvisational person, an unspoiled person, a person who can turn around declining staff morale. Or you may select a relatively unambitious leader, someone with not so much to prove, someone who is happy to be the steward of a stable organization and doesn't need to build a giant. The opposite is also true. If resources are plentiful and the will is there, you might look for a leader who has built organizations before, who can seize the moment to rapidly take you to the next level. What a tremendous intervention it can be to select just the right person for this moment in the organization's history.

Transition as Crisis

Leadership transition means replacing one seemingly irreplaceable person with another, a move that requires everyone else to reorient their work, thinking, and relationships to adjust to this change. As a result, all leadership transitions can be considered crises. Organizations in crisis are temporarily off balance, understandably confused, and somewhat disorganized. They make us uncomfortable, and we almost never seek them out. But, they are a fact and a force of nature, as much a part of our personal and professional lives as the births and deaths, the unfulfilled yearnings of adolescence, and the broken hips of old age. And as much as we try to avoid these crises, they often enough leave us in a better place.

The tendency in times of crisis is to pull in, to maintain, and to protect what you've got. It is the rare person or organization who sees the opportunity in crisis, and rarer still is the person who intentionally takes advantage of the confusion—the disorganization, the grasping for solutions—as the catalyst to move on, to improve, to take the next big step. Rarest of all are those who organize themselves so that they are nimble enough to regularly adapt to change in positive ways.

Incremental change is possible without crisis, improving a little here, a little there. But major change requires the loosening of bonds that generally hold us tight. It requires us to be off-kilter so that we must seek some fundamental new balance. It requires us to lose something basic— a leader—to seek not just a replacement but someone who will move us in directions we really wanted to move in the first place.

Our book's purpose is to lay out a map for the intrepid traveler who believes there is great value in sailing through the rough weather of leadership transitions.

There are three types of crisis. In our approach to leadership transition, we must respond to each and take advantage of each.

Disequilibrium

By definition, crises create confusion and disorganization. The technical word used for such a state is disequilibrium. Although painful, disequilibrium also creates opportunities. As the physicist Ilya Prigogine observed, systems in disequilibrium are vulnerable to change. Everyone who has tried his hand at changing people and organizations knows how difficult it normally is. People are stuck in their ways, skeptical or fearful of change. Most of the time, systems resist change, but during crisis, their resistance is lowered. There is a loosening in the patterns of thought and behavior. There is an urgency that pushes people out of their comfort zone and into innovative approaches to old problems.

Usually these innovations don't last long; people fall back into habitual ways of thinking and doing things. But if these innovations are buttressed by solid and sustained management practices, by creating formal structures and processes that institutionalize the innovations, lasting change is possible.

With this potential in mind, we need to put aside our normal anxieties and embrace the change potential that is inherent in leadership transitions. When new ideas, now solutions, emerge during the transition period—say the value of a strong executive team, long dormant during the reign of an autocratic leader, or the introduction of more regular financial reporting to keep abreast during the potentially chaotic time—they can be grasped and institutionalized. As the saying goes, we must seize the day.

Even more importantly, a transition team has the opportunity to assess whether an organization's programs really do stand a good chance of realizing the mission, whether the financial model is adequate, and whether the type of leader you have had is the best fit for the current organization. So many basic questions come to the fore—if the transition team permits them to.

As we suggested, the tendency during crisis is to minimize damage, to plug the hole left by the departing leader, and to bring the interim confusion to an end as quickly as possible. But if you can establish a trusted transition management process and it takes time to really assess what the organization needs, you have a chance to take advantage of opportunities provided by the disequilibrium that has been created.

Part 2, Chapters 3 through 6, describes the fundamentals of effective leadership: the clarification of mission, vision, objectives, and strategies; good governance; and how to align all resources in the service of mission and strategy. As new ideas burst forth and potential leaders appear during the transition period, we need ways to assess whether they are in keeping with our values and whether they will move us in the direction we have chosen. We need a picture of our future to guide our present search.

Trouble and Pain

Even in the best of situations, change creates anxieties. There is fear of the unknown and the loss of the well known. Even when the past has been difficult, it is hard to give up. Dramatic transitions due to the death or illness or impropriety of leaders jolt those whose lives are intimately connected with organizations. Sustained failure and conflict create their own form of internal havoc and employees and volunteers who show the symptoms of traumatic stress disorders: general anxiety, overreaction to small events that trigger old fears, and inappropriately dramatic behavior.

There are two requirements for managing these stressful situations. First, there is a need for strong, consistent management and clear communication to eliminate the fear of strange things happening behind closed doors. During extended transitions, people always fear that their interests won't be protected. They fear that deals will be struck behind their backs or that chaos will reign. All of this can be addressed by solid, transparent management by teams composed of boards of directors and senior staff or a wise and experienced interim director. There should be teams to search for the new CEO and to manage the everyday operations of the organization. Both need to communicate regularly on both progress and difficulties to reassure, to maintain credibility, and to sustain an optimistic view.

If distress is high and trust is low among stakeholders, it is important to create a transition management process that is more inclusive, one that provides a regular forum for people to ask questions, express their concerns, and share their fears. This kind of openness may not come naturally to the people who serve on boards. They may be more accustomed to keeping financial information private—the domain of the inner few. They are likely to believe that the search process will be best served by minimizing complications. They may fear that clients and community members can't handle too much information. Although all of these concerns may be well grounded, a well-managed, inclusive process will answer them. If communication is clear and as assuring as the facts will bear, both distress and disorganization will decrease instead of escalate. Equally important, the inclusiveness of transition management will have strengthened and broadened a constituency to support the incoming leader.

Five chapters, 7 through 11, are dedicated to professionalizing transition management to provide order and clarity during this potentially difficult period.

Developmental Crises

There is a third type of crisis to consider: the developmental crisis. Organizations, like people, pass through recognizable stages: for example, from start-up, grass roots, or entrepreneurial to managerial and on to a synthesis of entrepreneurial and managerial. Transitions from one stage to another are rarely smooth. Often the developmental shift is both signaled and facilitated by the introduction of new leadership. To protect their investment venture, capitalists traditionally maintain at least

51 percent of board votes so they can replace the founding entrepreneur with an experienced manager at a strategic time. This is a conscious way to facilitate a developmental transition.

This kind of planned transition is rare among nonprofits, but it points the way. The core idea is this: to treat transitions not as a way to repair the old but instead as the main instrument for moving an organization into its next, more effective stage of development.

At their most productive, developmental crises bring forward the best of who we are and help us let go of what is no longer appropriate. The resolution of the adolescent crisis, for example, requires young people to let go of much that had been charming in childhood to bring into the foreground more of the independent, reasonable decision maker. When adolescents cannot move through this developmental conundrum, they remain mired in internal conflict, unnervingly shifting between childish and counter-dependent modes of behavior. Organizations caught in the vicious cycle of poor transition management are like adolescents caught in cartoonish expressions of themselves—and remaining stagnant at best.

The implications of the developmental view are twofold. We will ask our transition team to determine what the next developmental stage will be and what kind of leadership will best move them in that direction. Second, we will ask the team to support the new leader through the stages of development that each leader goes through.

As our prior mention of a honeymoon period suggests, we also believe that the quality of leadership and the relationship between volunteer and professional leaders move through recognizable stages. Leadership tenure usually begins with a sense of great, often exaggerated promise. As reality sets in, there is a tendency toward disillusionment. And, if people don't act precipitously on their sense of disillusionment, a third stage emerges in which good and bad qualities of leadership, together, prove acceptable. Each stage presents its own challenges. Managing well through all these stages represents the best chance of sustained and effective organizational leadership. Chapter 12, "Succession Planning," presents a model for managing the (developmental) cycle of leadership.

An Expanded Sense of Time

Earlier, we criticized the hurried, narrow style of transition management that we have found too common to nonprofits. This approach almost makes sense if you think of transitions as beginning with the departure of the old and ending with the entry of the new leader. Within that time frame, there is a straightforward task to be done, and it is best to do it as expeditiously as possible.

If, however, you believe that the build-up to the departure holds important information for the selection of the new leader, and if you believe that positioning the new leader well counts, you must consider a much lengthier transition process. We think of transitions as beginning with the first strong signs of trouble with the current CEO or, in the case of effective leaders, the first strong signs that they will leave. The period does not end when the new leader is hired but when the new leader has her feet on the ground—that is, when the new leader can act effectively as a leader. The build-up to departure may take years, and it certainly tends to span many months. The period between the announced departure and the introduction of the new leader can vary. It can be brief—a few months—but counting on that is wishful thinking. It is more likely to be 6 to 9 months, especially when the process is deliberate and thoughtful. And it can be up to 18 months, when, for instance, the selection process brings out schisms among the board, leading to indecision.

We are now talking about a period that encompasses between one and three years—the same length of time as the tenure of many, current nonprofit leaders.

By expanding the time understood to be under transition management, we can expand the scope of the management. Instead of focusing almost exclusively on the selection of the new CEO, the management team can prepare the organization so that the new leader can succeed. If, for example, one faction in a divided board had clashed with a CEO, we know that we must bring the board together on key issues—before hiring a new leader. If the board had served as a rubber stamp for a founder, an arrangement that had worked when the organization was small enough to work with the founder's skills but failed to hold the leader accountable when the organization grew larger and more complex, it is vital to restructure the board. It should be more demanding, requiring more information to evaluate movement toward objectives. And, for this new stage of organizational development, the board should create a little distance between itself and the new leader to maintain perspective.

On either end of this spectrum of time—one and three years—we see an extended period in which the board of directors must play an active governing role and, for periods, an active role in the management of the organization. With the expanded time comes the possibility—the necessity—of managing a much more extensive set of challenges.

As crisis managers, for example, the board must establish a reassuring solidity, beginning with the notice of the CEO's departure and ending with the grounding of the new one; and the board must communicate to all stakeholders that this is what the team intends. To communicate about such an extensive process, the transition team must imagine where the organization is going and by what strategic means it will get there. Then the team must find and hire a leader capable of realizing the strategic plan, charge the new leader with this challenge, and help position her to succeed.

An Expanded Sense of Who and What Must Be Transitioned

Leaders work in context: organizations, communities, financial markets, and so on. So must boards and transition teams. To manage well, boards need to understand their organizations much more deeply than they ordinarily do. They must ask, for example, what came before the departure? What led to contentious or drawn-out departures? Or, if it is a long-standing and much-loved CEO, what kind of culture was built around her? How did people prepare, both formally and informally, for her departure? What kind of expectations, positive and negative, were built in anticipation of the new leader? Transition teams need to ask about the market the new leader will enter: for example, the market for clients, and the competition; the market for funding, and the competition; the market for employees, and the competition. It is within these markets that the new leader will succeed or fail.

There are many dimensions of organizational culture, structure, and processes that provide valuable information about what kind of leadership will succeed, and it is up to the transition team to learn about them—and to be honest with themselves. It's a terrible mistake, for example, to bring an ambitious leader into an organization with potentially ambitious goals when it is clear the resources will be scarce for the next few years. It might be equally disastrous to bring an African American leader into an organization consisting primarily of Latino staff in a Latino community that feels itself at odds with the neighboring African American community. There has to be an alignment among the board's ambitions, its willingness and capacity to raise funds, the stated objectives of an organization, the community it serves, and the type of leadership it seeks.

Self-reflection is the byword here. To select a leader well, organizations have to understand themselves. What is its organizational culture, for example? Let's suppose it had been built around a charismatic founder who made almost all important decisions and to whom people, out of respect and admiration, ceded that right. Let's say that this worked out well for almost ten years, until she left. At that point, believing no one could replace her and that her major lieutenants could collectively lead, a kind of plutocracy was established. This leadership group, however, never gained a full legitimacy. Many other staff people didn't accept their leadership and felt unfairly excluded from the decision-making process. In effect, the group never achieved the legitimacy needed to lead an organization. The absence of leadership legitimacy contributed to both conflicts and a lack of productivity that had brought the organization to a perilous financial position.

Perhaps the organization could move further along toward a participatory culture in which responsibility and decision making were even more broadly shared. If the transition team believed that this would work well for the staff, and if the board believed it could hold even a broad-based leadership accountable, it would seek a leader able to work in this mode. If, on the other hand, the board believed that the culture still yearned for and performed best under a more authoritative leader, it might hire one who could also be extremely respectful and consultative with staff, thus achieving a synthesis of the first two forms of leadership.

The greatest opportunity of leadership transition is to hire a leader who is both aligned with the organizational culture *and* seemingly able to perform superbly in the service of the organization's objectives. This may seem obvious, but it is not so obvious to many search processes, which emphasize either cultural fit or goal alignment to the exclusion of the other.

A Renewed Focus on Objectives

Most importantly, we want to know how well organizations under the departing leadership were achieving their objectives, how and why they were succeeding, and how and why they were coming up short. Unless and until we have a hypothesis about what worked in the old leadership, we can't accurately determine what we need in the new. This is critical. All too often, boards evaluate CEOs based on their personality and forget to focus on objectives. If the organization is moving effectively toward achieving objectives, the leader is succeeding, even if she doesn't look good in doing so. Shifting board and public perception away from show and charisma to results would be of immense value. It would be crucial to the selection of new leadership, crucial to communications to stakeholders about the selections, and crucial to the way the new leader is supported during the first year.

Many a CEO have fallen to the style and personality axe. It is said that they don't fit. They are too autocratic, too democratic, too assimilated, too ethnic—whatever. When boards focus on these and other process variables—the CEO doesn't know how to manage teams or women or the younger generation—they often lose sight of their own objectives. The leadership transition process represents a moment when boards can and, in fact, must refocus on their objectives: to clarify and affirm them; to keep them front and center during the search and selection process; to hire the leader who is most able to achieve them. That's why Chapters 3 and 4 provide guidelines for the development or review of mission, vision, and strategy in organizations.

We believe that the fundamental challenge of leadership is to align all organizational resources in the service of its mission, vision, and strategies. Hiring a new leader without some clarity about strategic direction is asking him to fly blind. It is asking for the disaster that usually takes place a little after the initial honeymoon stage in the form of a struggle between the disillusioned board and floundering CEO. Developing at least a rough agenda for the organization's future to serve as the new leader's guide star is a vital part of successful transitions.

Back to crisis management. The uncertainty of the moment lends itself to a clarification of purpose. The opportunity to clarify one's mission and strategy and to hire primarily based on the new leader's ability to realize them is the principle advantage of leadership transition. The opportunity to refocus the organization on objectives, even before the selection of a new leader, presents an opportunity of almost equal magnitude.

The Centrality of Boards During Transitions

During leadership transitions, the challenge and the opportunity for boards of directors is to figure out who they must be to guide and constrain the kind of leader best suited for the upcoming years. There, in fact, is the irony. Although the board is supposedly focused on the search and selection of a new CEO, it cannot perform this job well unless the members can perform in an optimal way. So they must focus equally on rules and activities of good governance. They must focus, first, on themselves.

We know that boards conduct searches, but most of us don't exactly see the implications of that observation: Boards of directors govern. Essentially, governance consists of three activities: fiduciary responsibility, setting policy, and hiring and managing the CEO. Boards have these responsibilities all the time, but during transitions, their governance is more visible. Strengths and weaknesses show themselves more vividly, which is not all bad. It provides the opportunity for self-reflection.

One of the key challenges during the transition period is self-governance: How can the board improve itself? How can it prepare itself to govern better during the tenure of the incoming CEO?

Improved functioning is particularly important during the first six months to a year of the new CEO's tenure: finding the right balance between guidance and giving the new leader room to lead is key. Often a separate "kitchen cabinet" is helpful to keep mission, vision, and strategy front and center; to encourage the CEO to find her own way of realizing organizational objectives; to connect the new CEO to staff, funders, and community leaders; and if a geographic move is required, to introduce the leader and her family to the community.

Because poor board functioning is often a primary cause of leadership turnover, board transformation must be a primary goal of leadership transition. Before selecting a CEO, boards should evaluate themselves as individuals and as a collective entity. They should determine what kind of board will be most effective during the next stage of organizational development. It isn't only CEOs who must shift focus from stage to stage. Founding boards, often with their loose structure and processes and willingness to roll up their sleeves, are different from more mature boards that operate within more formal rules and structures and with different core functions in mind.

Imagine, for example, a young organization that is primarily supported by foundation grants. Here, fundraising is largely a staff function. As the organization grows, it determines that public funding and individual donor contributions are necessary. The staff doesn't have sufficient connections with individual philanthropists and government figures. Now the board must take on a major role in fundraising. But a founding board may also lack connections. The composition of the board must change for the organization to continue growing. Simultaneously, the transition team must be looking into a CEO and a board that can dedicate skillful attention to public funding and to building an individual donor base.

The Importance of the Board-CEO Partnership

Organizations are built on relationships as much as they are on individuals. The effectiveness of the CEO depends very much on her relationships with the financial officer, program and development directors, and the board president. In that sense, the history of these relationships provides critical information about the selection and integration of new leaders. This is particularly true of the board-CEO relationship, which our research suggests is the key to the retention and success of organizational leadership.

CEOs come and go—as they should. So, too, board presidents and board members. As a result, the partnerships between boards and CEOs may shift several times during the tenure of a single CEO. As each new board president comes into the picture—often every two, three, or four years—new relationships have to be established. Each new board president tends to set his own tone rather than seek continuity with the past and to act as though he, not the whole board, is in charge. As he does so, the CEO has to adjust—or, as often happens, appear to adjust. When the reality behind appearances comes clear, differences between board presidents and CEOs have to be reconciled.

Over the long haul, these periods of reconciliation and compromise appear with some regularity. Boards have to assess their ability to manage these regular, predictable changes. They need to ask themselves whether they have developed the habit of candid, open conversation and conflict resolution.

Even more important, boards must learn to exercise self-discipline. When a board member, for example, speaks to the CEO, who is he representing? Has the president checked his board to determine support—or lack of support—for positions he takes with the CEO? Can a board succeed in maintaining more continuity than discontinuity from one president to the next? Without doing so, it may confuse, alienate, and anger the CEO and set the ground for conflict. This is one of the key subjects we address in Chapter 5, "Good Governance."

Managing the Cycle of Leadership

We might have called our book *Board Management* because much of it focuses on the role that boards play in setting direction, managing CEOs, and holding whole organizations accountable to achieving their objectives. We have focused on a specific period in the life of the board—the transition from one CEO to another—but the job doesn't start and stop there. The best way for boards to minimize unwanted leadership turnover is to manage well throughout what we call the cycle of leadership. Chapter 12 describes this process in full.

Here's what we mean by managing the whole cycle. We have identified a regular sequence of challenges faced by all leaders and board-director partnerships. Each stage in the sequence presents particular challenges. When these challenges are met proactively and rigorously, continuity and quality are sustained.

During the transition period, we highlight four activities:

- Maintain a well-functioning transition team.
- Create job descriptions and strategic plans.
- Sustain honest, positive communication with all stakeholders.
- Conduct a highly competent professional search and selection process.

Following the selection of a new CEO, there are four key challenges:

- Introduce the new leader with expectations in proportion.
- Position the leader with key stakeholders.
- Charge the new person with a clear sense of objectives and strategies—"Manage these well and we will consider you a success."
- Disband the transition team, leaving the CEO fully in charge of the organization's operations.

A period of relative stability should follow assuming the introduction goes well. When leadership is stable and at least relatively effective, boards and CEOs relax; they often don't want to think about the future. But this may be the most important phase of the cycle. Here are the particular management challenges during this phase:

- **Assessment**—Make sure that the organization is on track: true to its mission and strategies; operationally effective; financially sound; functioning with up-to-date systems, providing adequate support to the CEO; and nurturing the partnership between the board and the CEO. The assessment can be managed internally or with the assistance of a consultant.
- **Strategic planning**—Every several years, the organizational assessment should be part of a strategic planning process that clarifies the mission, vision, and strategies and realigns the organization in the service of those core values. The plan's implementation also serves as the essential job description for current and future leaders.
- **Annual performance review**—This is for both the CEO and the board president (and regularly for the full board).
- **Succession planning**—This is for both emergencies and regular leadership transition.

Because you cannot guarantee stability and success, it helps to plan for times of difficulty. These times will crop up as regularly as others. To prepare, we suggest two steps. First, develop the habit of conversation and problem-solving between the CEO and the board. Second, identify an outsider—a trusted community member or a professional consultant—who is familiar with the organization and ready to help when regular problem-solving approaches fail.

Ultimately there will be another decision by the CEO to depart since every leader reaches an end to her tenure. To anticipate expected and unexpected departures, it helps to prepare a transition plan, identify a potential transition team, and build a communication plan.

The transition of the board president is a similar process. Because board presidents come and go with regularity, it is vital to create a plan for volunteer leadership transitions. The major challenges to address include these:

- **Clarifying the mission, objectives, and strategies**—In effect, the board president is charged with monitoring the CEO's implementation of strategy, and a new president must be on board with the existing plan.
- **Training or orienting the new president**—For example, there may be a six-month period of shadowing the current president.
- **Clarifying roles and expectations between the CEO and the president**—Whether it is the CEO or the president who is new to this partnership, there is a period of coming to agreement on how the work and relationship will proceed.
- **Nurturing the president-CEO relationship**—The incoming president must be charged with doing this well.

It is our hope that the following chapters will make these difficult but vital tasks more easily accomplished for the good of each organization, the nonprofit sector, and those it serves.

Endnotes

1 A survey of 2,200 executive directors, commissioned by the Annie E. Casey Foundation, found that 73 percent of the people who now lead charities are members of the baby boom generation—those born from 1946 to 1964. Also, 23 percent of the nonprofit leaders said they would leave their jobs before 2007, and another 42 percent said they expected to leave their positions by 2009.

Part
1

Leadership and the Challenge of Transition

1

What Makes Nonprofit Leadership So Challenging?

Under the best of circumstances, nonprofit leadership is extremely challenging. Those at the helm are generally asked to do more with less than seems humanly possible. Inflated expectations, limited finances, the need for experience across both content and administration, the lack of time and resources for training, and the demands of often contradictory constituencies just begin to describe the difficulties. No wonder so few succeed as much as we would like.

The difficulty of replacing a leader is compounded by the fact that matching talent, one to one, with the job description won't necessarily do the job. Even the most talented leaders succeed in some circumstances and fail in others. Jim Collins urges leaders to create teams of people who fit with the needs of the moment, the right people "on the bus" at the right time and in the right place. This lesson applies first and foremost to the chief executive officer; when preparing for executive search, boards have to consider long and hard what that means.

In general, it means that the incoming leader must be more than skilled. She must fit well enough with the organizational culture to build an informal following to go with her formal power. Her personal values and career goals must fit with the opportunity at hand. Her leadership style—democratic, autocratic, or inclusive, micro-managing or delegating—must be close enough to both the organization's historical style and current needs for him or her to be credible.

The question of fit is complicated by the variety of circumstances that set the scene for each transition—circumstances that affect the balance between welcome and resistance to new leaders. With the departure of a revered leader, new leaders are often presented with a paradox:

We want someone as good as the one who is leaving, someone we can trust and lean on, but we don't want anyone who might really replace her in our hearts. When a reviled leader is booted out, there is a demand for a particularly exemplary person to take her place, but this leader might not necessarily be available in the market. When an incompetent leader departs, the new leader is asked to be not just effective but to compensate for past problems—to be "superhuman."

Comparable challenges apply to the selection of virtually all leaders, whether corporate, public, or nonprofit, but the nonprofit sector presents a few special issues. One such issue derives from the place of nonprofits in our society. From its inception, American society has been ambivalent about government. The belief in limited government is deep in our national psyche. With regularity, however, government services grow to fill social needs such as shelter, medical care, armed defense, and the distribution of food. Alternating with government growth are periodic upheavals aimed at getting government out of our lives. During these upheavals, in particular, the role of civil society grows exponentially to fill the gap created by governmental departures. Nonprofits try to fill the gap. Idealistic young people grow excited by the potential of the third sector. But invariably nonprofits fail to meet all the needs because they have been asked—and ask themselves—to be more than they can be. They cannot provide sufficient housing for the poor and homeless. They cannot provide sufficient medical care and education for everyone.

The crisis of leadership transition heightens our sense of need and our sense of potential. When managing these transitions, however, it is our job to keep the current needs and current possibilities in perspective. Even in the best of times, nonprofit leadership is challenging work. In this chapter, we want to describe the challenge to help boards and search committees to keep the potential of incoming leaders in perspective. Second and more importantly, we want to alert boards to what they have to do in an ongoing way to support the leader they choose.

A Highly Fulfilling Calling

In spite of the difficulties facing nonprofit CEOs, for many people this is the most fulfilling job they can imagine. Every day they go to work for something they believe in—an opportunity not always found by their corporate colleagues. Every day they command the respect of people in many walks of life: staff and board members, the citizens they serve, the funders who support them. Every day they are faced with problems to be solved: practical problems, financial problems, human resource problems. It may not be for everyone, but for those who love to tackle riddles, to face off against "enemies," to work their way through complex balance sheets—for such people, the nonprofit CEO's job is the one to have. Every day, CEOs get to nurture young talent, build programs, and connect with like-minded people throughout their cities, their regions, their nation, and even the world.

By its nature, leadership commands respect. We may put leaders down and fight them, but, by and large, when selecting leaders, we expect to bestow our respect and our support. We must. It is up to us to understand the difficulties they face so that we may eliminate or ameliorate those difficulties. Here, then, is the picture of an astoundingly difficult job with surprisingly little guidance.

What Makes the Job So Hard?

The sheer amount and complexity of demands on nonprofit leaders is stunning and might be enough to discourage almost all but the naïve or the very, very experienced from applying. However, a national shortage of nonprofit CEOs means that many inexperienced leaders end up being selected. Here are some of the difficulties they face.

Multiple and Demanding Constituencies

Nonprofit CEOs are responsible to many, often entitled, constituencies. These include clients, staff, boards of directors, community residents, foundations, government agencies and political office holders, and individual donors. Attending to so many groups is hard enough, but reconciling their often conflicting interests makes the job much harder. When talking about the complexity and difficulties of such reconciliation, many CEOs shake their heads in disbelief and exhaustion; some, in private, offer bitter commentary. It seems almost impossible not to be in trouble with someone. The conflicting constituencies often mirror and exacerbate alliances and schisms within organizations. Not only that, conflicting constituents can reflect the CEO's internal debate—"On the one hand I should do this; on the other hand..." With this kind of convergence of internal and external debates, decision making becomes even harder.

During a strategic planning retreat, a generally cautious CEO was encouraged by a group of board members to "think outside the box." Several weeks later, having overcome his natural caution, he announced to the staff that 20 percent of operational expenses for the next year would be dedicated to incubating innovative projects to serve underserved populations. "I thought I was embracing the vision articulated at the retreat," he later reported, "turning it into an action plan." The innovative mood lasted exactly two weeks when one of those same board members learned that his pet program would be sacrificed to try something new. "He let me know in no uncertain terms that nothing initiated during his tenure could be reduced or eliminated."

Peter Drucker has famously noted that corporate leaders need only pay attention to the customer. If they please the customer and sell the product at a profitable rate, they succeed. But nonprofits have two quite different customers: those they serve and those that pay the way: funders. These include foundations, individual philanthropists (who may have powerful, often idiosyncratic agendas of their own), and local, state, and federal governments. It's not easy to please this group with one, simple set of programs. As one CEO groaned, "...for every approach I try, I lose and gain equal amounts of support."

There are two dangers at work. One is the inclination to be very cautious, to eschew taking stands, to shy away from bold or innovative methods. The other is to chase funding and support wherever it may be. This, in William Butler Yeats' immortal words in his poem "The Second Coming," leads to compromising the mission and values that are the nonprofit CEO's guide star:

> Things fall apart; the centre cannot hold; Mere anarchy is loosed upon the world, the blood-dimmed tide is loosed, and everywhere the ceremony of innocence is drowned

There is, moreover, tremendous pressure these days to join with others through mergers, acquisitions, partnerships, collaborations, and networks to create the scale and power to best serve constituents—and in order to appease funders who want to see their investments "leveraged." These are intriguing approaches that appeal to the adventurer in us, but they are also extremely complex, hard to guide, and slow to act upon. They, too, tend to move leadership toward the middle.

Many talented leaders have learned to affirm this need to "lead from the middle" and have built a set of negotiating skills designed to weave many disparate people and ideas into a coherent vision. But even when they succeed, they succeed with much more effort and patience than they might have thought would be the rule.

Transition teams and boards of directors must take on some of the burden of negotiation and consensus building among stakeholders. At the least, they must introduce new leaders with one voice and maintain a unity of purpose—publically and privately—with the leader during her initial efforts to get her feet on the ground.

Inadequate Preparation

Many nonprofit CEOs have backgrounds in program development and mid-level management but little high-level management experience and even less responsibility for an entire organization, including its relationship to the community. Few new leaders arrive on the scene with expertise in board development, finance, marketing, labor negotiations, and fund-raising. The learning curve is steep for those who try to develop these competencies on the job. The skills that got them the job in the first place—as a great community organizer, program developer, or social worker, for instance—are no longer central, whereas many skills that once seemed peripheral and extraneous are now vital. As a result, many CEOs spend much of each day "out of their sweet spot" or avoiding the tasks that make them uncomfortable by managing specific programs, for example, rather than practicing the CEO's craft.

One CEO confided that he was selected to be the CEO simply because he was the only long-standing staff member after a major disagreement between the board and the former CEO resulted in a hurried resignation. At first, the board asked him to "fill in" while they conducted a formal search. The search soon petered out, and the board claimed that it liked the grassroots informality it had with the "temporary" CEO. He was less sanguine. Almost immediately, he felt out of his depth and so much in debt to the board that he exercised little independent judgment. He rued the day he left the program director position in which he had excelled.

Until recently, there were few formal educational programs to support the development of nonprofit sector leaders, particularly for those who needed to continue working. A relative few people could take a couple of years off to pursue an MBA or a Masters in Public Administration, but even they had to accept programs targeted to young, corporate aspirants that were lacking in key nonprofit topics like governance, fundraising, volunteer management, and consensus building. During the past decade, a flood of new masters-level degree programs focused on the sector has emerged. They are good, but they are also expensive, and many require nonprofit executives to stop working. Few people can do so. The more immediate response has been the emergence of certificate programs—about ten year-long programs in the United States as of 2009, although others are developing—that have been designed for working nonprofit executives.

Transition teams should acknowledge the lack of formal education in their new leaders and, as a matter of course, provide ongoing opportunities for professional development. From the start, this should include an executive coach.

Time and Energy Commitments

The demand on a CEO's time is enormous. It's not at all unusual to find nonprofit CEOs hard at work every evening of the week. After all, they are frequently the organization's primary and best sales representative, its authoritative voice. The CEO's availability makes community groups feel honored and respected. He or she represents a peer-to-peer relationship with foundation and government officials, some of whom will only relate directly to another CEO. The pressure never lets up. CEOs receive hundreds of e-mail and voice messages daily—and many insist on getting back to constituents the same day.

Working 12 to 15 hours a day, CEOs burn out. When they do, they make mistakes, argue with constituents, and grow less passionate in support of their mission. All these developments hurry the path to departure.

It is not unusual for CEOs to have to literally choose between maintaining their marriage and continuing their leadership role in a nonprofit organization. Experienced CEOs find ways to manage the demand. They become masters at dropping in on events and meetings for their specific part of the agenda without being trapped in discussions where they are not needed. Experience also helps them carefully select actions that lead to small achievements, which over time can build on each other. They also seek places where they can serve as the catalyst for other leaders and followers to take up a challenge and carry it forward. Most importantly, they coach team members, staff, and volunteers who can take on leadership tasks so the organization moves forward under a larger and stronger leadership team.

Leadership of nonprofit organizations has to be approached more like running a marathon than a quarter-mile foot race. Just as marathon runners develop a strategy over the course of preparing for the race, nonprofit leaders lead best after they have listened carefully to constituents, developed a vision, and adopted a philosophy for how they will handle challenges and opportunities along the course. This is one reason organizations generally succeed at a quicker pace with tenured leadership.

Board and Constituents Tiring of the Continual Hard Work

Sometimes a CEO comes into an organization that is simply depleted. The board and the previous CEO may have built the organization at such a pace that everyone has what has come to be known as "mission fatigue." One CEO told us about taking leadership of an organization whose mission was to find a cure for a specific birth defect with which children seldom live to adolescence. The organization had been formed five years previously by a group of families who had one or more children born with the defect. The founding board was still in place. Each member was living with the stress of raising a child and family affected by a health crisis. There was a time bomb ticking in the minds of the board members. Although they were successful in raising more than 20 million dollars to assist doctors in their research for a cure, there was no indication that their children would live to benefit from the organization's efforts. The CEO's first job was to help the board reframe their work in a manner that celebrated the daily lives of their own children and develop intermediate organizational measurements of success that could be celebrated while they supported the long, hard process of finding a cure.

Difficulty in Moving from Manager to Leader

The skills required to rise to the CEO position are often far more management focused than the leadership skills that are ultimately required once a nonprofit professional has attained this position. When an employee is moving up within an organization, she is most often developing management skills that require a short-range focus on technical or programmatic actions. She is required to manage budgets, follow rules and procedures, and produce predictable results. However, as she moves into the CEO position, she is expected to focus on the far horizon. Visionary skills, which were of little use in the trenches, become the basis of her entire contribution to the organization. She must develop original agendas and is expected to take risk, seek change, and evolve the systems. This is confusing to a first-time CEO who was previously rewarded for adhering religiously to systems set by the leadership above her.

Many CEOs move up from being the second in command who handled all the details. When faced with uncertainty in the new leadership role, they give into the temptation to "hide" in the area that previously brought them success: making rules and procedures. Sometimes they are not able to find a suitable replacement for themselves. No one else can handle the details because they have held onto this role as a security blanket. CEOs must let go of tightly steering operational details to make room for the visionary role of leading the organization across the horizon to the mission achievement.

The process of moving CEOs' attention from the contained tasks of management and implementation to developing leadership competencies for a long-range perspective is harder in small organizations where they must perform both roles. In small organizations, CEOs must manage the hands-on operations of the agency while carving out sufficient time to lead the strategic thinking process at the end of a long day of making operational decisions.

One CEO who had moved up in a quickly growing youth organization from the program director position lasted only two years as the CEO because he could never let go of his deep involvement in operations. He could not see what he was doing at the time. When he lost his job and moved on to another organization, in retrospect he realized his failure was trying to do too much management and too little strategic thinking. Fortunately, he learned from his experience. His next time as CEO, he was much better at delegating operations.

Inadequate Support and Isolation

Many nonprofit CEOs have minimal administrative help. They are expected to pull their weight in the daily maintenance of the organization while spinning the varied plates assigned to them in fund development, financial oversight, human resource management, program development, and staff and volunteer training and development. In new organizations, some of these tasks are seen to by volunteer staffs, but such help can be inconsistent.

CEOs often lack the support of day-to-day managers like COOs or development directors or even administrative assistants. The smaller the organization, the less support is likely to be available to the CEO. Unfortunately, small organizations usually hire CEOs with the least experience. At the same time they are not likely to have a highly skilled finance director to rely upon for expert advice on budgeting and finance policies and practices or to protect them from the time drain of daily financial oversight. In fact, CEOs in small agencies often have no leadership team. Everyone employed is utilized directly in delivering program services.

One CEO of a small organization finally raised enough funds to hire a development consultant to support her in planning a capital campaign; yet every time they met, the CEO stopped to answer the phone and direct visitors who came to the front door, making poor use of the time she had with the consultant. CEOs who have led increasingly larger organizations observe that they receive higher pay but more importantly are blessed with senior leaders in every area of the work. It may take a budget of $5 million or more for the CEO to be at liberty to actually dedicate her time to vision and strategy, development of governance and policy, and organization-wide evaluation and innovation toward achieving the mission. Until reaching this level of scale, it's easy for the CEO to feel she is "stealing" from operations to focus on leadership objectives.

Finally, CEOs are often isolated. Many of the issues they deal with cannot be appropriately shared with other staff or fully understood by board members. Allegiance to the organization limits the ability to share problems with external community members. And when they get home, they want to separate their family from their organizational life. They have no one who "gets" the difficulty of their days, no one to give advice. Peer interaction, an exceptional board president, or an executive coach can make a huge difference in combating isolation, but sometimes not in a sustained and enduring way. Family pressures increase when a spouse or partner is called on to be the main counselor or listener to day-to-day stresses and frustrations. The lack of mentoring may mean less perspective, which contributes to poorer decision making and increased anxiety. All these conditions tend to encourage a crisis-oriented leadership style.

Methods for developing alternative support include creating a "kitchen cabinet" of advisors who formally agree to nondisclosure and confidentiality. This group of closely held advisors should not be constituents involved in the organization. Rather, they should be selected for objectivity and a willingness to listen to ideas that are not necessarily completely formed and to speak frankly about their impressions and reactions without needing to see change. Peer groups can also reduce the loneliness of leadership. Peer dialogue is most useful when the group is willing to put aside their competitive nature and jointly discuss one member's problematic situation in depth. Again, the group needs to be in agreement that the session is confidential.

A community advisory panel may be utilized as a more formal system for helping the leader both test and expand her perspective. However, the leader needs to possess greater confidence to utilize this group of experts. Also, she may need to take her strategic thinking to a greater level of completion before unveiling it to a community advisory panel.

Increased Professional Leadership's Effect on Volunteer Leadership

As nonprofit organizations have grown more dependent upon professional leadership, boards of directors have often stepped back from their stewardship role. They may think that given the salary and expertise of the CEO, there is no longer a need for them to do any heavy lifting. Board members join grassroots organizations knowing that they collectively will provide the essential energy and commitment to keep the organization going. They accept this role as an avocation, and the grassroots board often meets multiple times each month for extensive sessions of working out both the operational and strategic objectives of the organization. As they are able to employ leadership, they gradually turn over more and more of their work to that leadership.

As an organization's life cycle continues, the board members gradually move from formulating strategy to providing input to simply responding to the CEO's questions, becoming more reactive than proactive. They see the CEO as having it all under control and take advantage of the opportunity to be less involved in the strategic leadership of the organization. It is no wonder then that when an effective CEO announces his departure after a long tenure, the board may be initially ill prepared to step back into the strategic leadership role that their stewardship responsibility demands.

When the new CEO arrives in the organization, the board members are exhausted from providing a level of strategic leadership to which they were unaccustomed, so they welcome the new CEO and step back into their shadow role, hoping to regain their relaxed status immediately. As tired as the board may be due to their increased involvement, the arrival of a new CEO requires a huge commitment from the board for a significant period as they integrate their stewardship and strategic perspective with that of their new leader.

One CEO told of arriving to lead an organization that had not had a CEO for 18 months. She described how articulate the board members had been during the interview and negotiation process. She had been impressed with their ability to describe their vision as well as their knowledge of the organization and commitment to funding and supporting it. She noted that the strength of the board was a salient factor in her decision to take the CEO position. However, she was dismayed upon taking office that the board handed her the reins and informed her that their work was done.

Inexperienced or Ineffectual Boards

Many nonprofit boards are inexperienced. Individual members have had little board experience, and the board as a whole has not coalesced into a smoothly functioning unit with differentiated roles. They lack an ability to guide and hold the CEO accountable and the perspective to consider bumps in the road just bumps. New boards, in particular, are reactive to CEOs. They have overblown expectations, offering exorbitant praise when pleased and exorbitant criticism when displeased. Seldom is there a regularly scheduled performance self-assessment that moves the board to reflect upon its success in carrying out its duties or a meaningful interactive performance review with the CEO.

In general, smaller agencies have less experienced boards, with smaller networks available through the board members and as a result more grassroots fund-raising. If an organization is just starting up, the stress on the individuals who have formed the new entity is particularly heavy. They have had to invent the new organization out of a passion for addressing a cause. There is no previous structure, platform for fund-raising or systems for operations. They have birthed this new entity out of their blood, sweat, and tears. The board may not know how to be a strong organization, but they have amazing strength in their conviction about their cause. As a result the expectations they hold for the new CEO are immense and never ending. Of course, they are unlikely to be able to attract and pay a CEO with an extensive track record.

When a new board is combined with a relatively green CEO, a reactive system is likely to emerge. Each party overreacts to exaggerated behavior in the other, making day-by-day management complicated and responses to genuinely difficult situations, like an absence of funds, even more difficult. Miscommunication and a lack of understanding of each other's perspectives lead to greater isolation of the CEO and less supportive involvement by members of the board. One start-up organization blew through four CEOs in two years before the board members were convinced that they needed to do some training and development themselves to accept the leadership of a professional CEO.

In organizations still led by founders, often the board is made up of the friends and even family who agreed to be the first board. They are the ones the founder felt most comfortable with in the early days, and sometimes as the organization grew, they continued an unspoken agreement not to question the CEO's decisions or directions. They may benefit directly from the CEO's continued role in the community, so they are loathe to suggest a transition or to bring in board members with a more objective perspective. One CEO of a large social service agency who recently retired after 37 years left behind a board president who had once been a student secretary to him while she was in college. They began the organization together, and although she was soon to retire from a prominent position, she still addressed him only as "Mr. Jones."

Less Understanding and Knowledge of Governance Than the Board

CEOs often come into their leadership role with significantly less experience on or with boards of directors than the board members with whom they partner. When their career paths have progressed through operations, they have had only a tangential interface with board task forces and committee meetings. They are unlikely to have extensive practical experience in organizing the work of the board, let alone orienting new board members or containing them within the parameters of their board responsibilities. It is a difficult process for anyone to lead the group that hired you, evaluates your performance, and has the power to end your relationship with the organization.

Board members often have intimate and complex long-term relationships with each other, with funders, and even with staff. They know where the skeletons are buried. They often have made phenomenal contributions to the development of the organization. They may have relatives, if not themselves, who are recipients of the services. It is no wonder that the new CEO wonders how she will lead and manage the board.

One CEO told of taking time to meet individually with each board member early in his tenure. As he researched their credentials and accomplishments in preparation for the meetings, it almost always occurred to him that these people had made contributions to the organization that he could not imagine achieving in the next ten years as the CEO. He went to each meeting with trepidation and significant concern about whether he had the ability to lead such a group. However, he left understanding that it would be an honor and a pleasure to be the servant leader for such an august group of community leaders.

If a CEO leads a local chapter of a national organization, he may receive training in leading his new board or a national support staff member may come in to facilitate the introduction of the CEO and the integration of his leadership with the board's vision and strategy. If not, the CEO can work with the board president to identify an experienced mentor or to build a team of board members who will assist in integrating the new CEO's strengths and needs for complementary support with the skills and talents of board members.

Micromanagement by the Board

It can be said that nonprofit CEOs have a mantra: "If only my board would let me do my work while it raises sufficient funds to operate the organization, life would be good." Over and over, and particularly with new and constituent-dominated boards, CEOs find themselves questioned and overruled on all kinds of issues. No matter how often the CEO reminds the board that "your only operations job is to hire, fire, and evaluate me," boards inevitably express opinions and actively intervene in program matters. One board allowed past presidents to serve without term limits, and it was filled with members who rarely contributed financially and only came to meetings to vote when they disagreed with the CEO. The fractious nature of this board led to a constant tug of war between the CEO and the board, with increasing energy being pulled away from the organization's mission.

Less than 60 percent of nonprofit CEOs report ever having a formal evaluation. They are more likely to receive their performance evaluation, if at all, in a disjointed incidental manner. When the organization has success in a program, receives accolades in the press or receives a major donation, the CEO is heaped with praise, often disproportionate to her involvement in that specific success. When something goes wrong in delivery of service, funding is lost, or the agency receives bad press, the CEO is judged by board members to be performing poorly, again, often disproportionately to her involvement in the event. The lack of specific, measurable performance goals focused upon the work of the CEO and the lack of a disciplined, scheduled review process with and by the board results in little useable feedback for the CEO. Nor are there specific and measurable performance goals for the board so that they can evaluate themselves and their colleagues against the goals of the organization.

Boards often want to direct unevenly, delving into pet projects and events to an unreasonable level of detail. When there is no clear territory established over which the CEO has authority, the board can move the success markers up and down the field, creating confusion and frustration for everyone. Although many nonprofits shy away from developing legal contracts with CEOs, the development of an informal agreement of the expectations, performance goals, and process by which performance will be evaluated is essential. This becomes the working paper by which the board and CEO discipline themselves to action on behalf of their constituents, moving the organization forward to achieve its mission.

Ignorance of the Community

Some CEOs are new to their community. They don't know the local culture, its values, and the networks of influence, power, and money. Yet they are required, almost immediately, to position the organization to make friends, raise money, recruit staff, nurture a volunteer corps, develop programs, and so forth. In addition, some CEOs are not truly extroverted, and both the psychic cost and considerable time invested in community involvement can be wearing. When constantly tired, the CEO's judgment about appropriate relationships and finances, two frequent causes of a leader's downfall, can become issues.

How the board introduces the CEO to the community greatly impacts his effectiveness. If the board does not have the pulse of the community, it is imperative that it find the resource person who can orient a new CEO to the landmarks, culture, and leadership of the community. Through this process, the board is not only refreshing the identity of the agency but laying the groundwork for the CEO to have the necessary standing and connections with funders and community leaders. The board is also giving the CEO an understanding of the community's needs and the opportunities for the agency to serve in a unique manner.

A CEO who had moved halfway across the country to lead a health services organization said that the greatest support her board members provided occurred in the first six months on the job, when they set her up for speaking engagements that highlighted her expertise. Introductions to key leaders increased her credibility and gave her access to the opinion leaders she needed to work with to achieve the organization's mission. Invitations to cultural events helped her build a balanced life in which she could feel at home immediately. She also began to understand quickly that she was a member of an important leadership team dedicated to the agency's mission. She became a partner with the board rather than being subservient to it.

Public Scrutiny and Lack of Forgiveness

The CEO's job is public. Leaders are observed by varied constituencies, each clamoring for fulfillment of its own interests. Constituencies that feel neglected or rejected may fight back in whatever public and private forum they can find. CEOs run considerable risks of unfounded accusations from terminated employees, unhappy volunteers, and even needy clients. The nature of the position may prevent them from responding to allegations, leaving them frustrated and their reputation questioned. Rumor mills are common, and the CEO must develop a thick skin. For those who can't, the job can be painful.

To survive often-unsubstantiated criticism and attacks, the CEO needs the support of senior staff and board members who "have his back." These supporters need to speak out when detractors are premature or acting because of preference for an unsuccessful candidate for the job. When the CEO makes mistakes, staff and board members should help him understand what is happening within the context of the organization and assist with righting the situation. Every CEO needs some leeway for growing into leadership of the organization and a learning process that includes forgiveness for early mistakes.

Self-Doubt

Because the job is so difficult, it is easy for the CEO to doubt her abilities. Such doubts may be minor or short lived for a CEO who has experienced success in the past. The development of detractors and doubters from every level of the constituency reinforces the CEO's personal doubt. As it grows, self-doubt presents a serious obstacle to the decisiveness required. Once self-doubt passes beyond a certain point, it can define the CEO's attitude. It is from this point that performance plunges and recovery is difficult. Escape looks more and more inviting, and the possibility of a new beginning looks as though it would be a relief. Self-doubt and the perceived possibility of a better future all make departure more likely. Harvard Business School professor Rosabeth Moss Kanter recognized how important the CEO's attitude is in her recent book titled *Confidence: How Winning Streaks and Losing Streaks Begin and End*.

Not Understanding the Culture of the Organization

If the CEO is to take leadership of the organization, he needs to create a unified culture. Basically, any culture emanates from the way things are done in that organization. The CEO is likely to need time and assistance in interpreting the signs, the values, and the assumptions that make up the personality of the organization. Whether the organization's current culture is healthy or needs reshaping, the CEO cannot lead until he understands it. If he doesn't see how the organization allows change to happen, he may not be able to get anything done. Once he enters the culture successfully, he will be much more likely to be able to change it, if necessary, to support the new vision of the organization that he holds in partnership with the board.

One of the most difficult organizational culture issues is how conflict is addressed. If the organization does not allow for confrontation or airing of grievances, a CEO may come into a steaming cauldron ready to boil over. Should the new leader's style be to unearth issues and deal with them directly, she may not be sufficiently gentle with the people in this cultural environment to avoid getting burned while beginning the hard work of sorting out differences within it.

Misuse of a Particular Leadership Style and Mismatch of Personality

CEO candidates are noticed because of what they do well as individuals in moving up the nonprofit career ladder. They are used to being praised for being stars, but as they take on a leadership role, their ability to work through others becomes more important. The skills and temperamental inclinations of an individual performer need to change to motivate others to work through and with them. Sometimes it is hard for new leaders to realize, "It's not all about me."

Often a CEO is selected because of her charisma and larger-than-life personality. The person who wins the hearts of a search committee does not always wear well in the trenches. The assuredness that impressed the committee may be seen as arrogance in the field. The ability to quickly solve situations and pronounce solutions gets in the way of working with a team of volunteers and staff to do a full assessment and craft a consensus. If a leader is not cognizant of the organization's culture or is not facile in reading her impact upon a group, initial misunderstandings may get in the way of winning over followers in the organization.

Balancing Territorial Ownership of the Organization

The board often develops preemptive ownership of the organization, and this perspective thrives during the absence of a CEO. Therefore, when new leadership enters the equation, board members sometimes play a kind of "tug of war" with the CEO. They want the CEO to step into leadership, but they also have grown to think of the organization as their firstborn child. They want to inordinately set the house rules. The CEO has to figure out how to move from being a guest in the organization to earning the trust to take on the mantle of leadership.

Limited Resources

Although most people taking leadership of a nonprofit understand there will be limited resources, the extent to which this is true affects the CEO's ability to lead. If all of the agency's funding is short term and fractured into separated funds dedicated to individual programs, the leader may feel his hands are tied. It is difficult to have an impact in any meaningful way if every dollar's use is designated by external funding agents. The leader is likely to get lost in transferring funds to designated uses rather than assigning resources to programs in concert with the organization's strategic plan. Money for capital improvements cannot be assigned to paying for staff to implement a sorely needed program. Personnel are seldom retained when the staff is consistently underpaid while they attempt to add one more program to their overwhelmed plan of work.

One leader talked of receiving a grant for a new HIV prevention program that more than doubled the agency's budget. The organization did not have the infrastructure to design and implement such an ambitious program, but they also did not have the courage to turn the money down. In the end, the organization went broke trying to meet the demands of the grantor and lost the small successful programs upon which its previous success had been based.

The Challenge of Partnership Between Board Presidents and CEOs

According to one nonprofit leader, "there is little focus on the skills required for organizational leadership, either volunteer or professional... People just don't think about it. If you're elected as president of the board, then you're the leader." Board leaders, he continues, "are not chosen because of demonstrated leadership qualities—with the possible exception of fund-raising." The motivation for accepting the board leadership position can range from community recognition to a need for greater power beyond family and work to a passion and commitment to the organization's mission. Often, governance committees (in the past sometimes known as nominating committees) select a candidate for a board presidency based on tenure, service, giving potential, or name recognition. To further complicate matters, candidates are often told that the presidency is a "figure head" position or that they can align the organization's actions to their personal preferences. Furthermore, most people assume the presidency of an organization with the hope, wish, or even unspoken promise that the CEO position will not turn over during their tenure.

The CEO comes in sometimes not even knowing who the board president will be six months down the road. If the president is partway through her term, she is used to a particular kind of partnership with the former CEO, and that arrangement may not be suitable to the new CEO. Having trusted the former CEO to stand by her side and seeing him leave may make the president reluctant to develop a close partnership with the new CEO. If the president's partnership with the previous CEO was a perfect match, the new CEO may despair of ever filling those shoes. One thing is clear: The CEO serves at the pleasure of the board. Therefore, it follows in the CEO's perspective that the inability to partner with the board president is more likely to result in the CEO's early demise than the president's.

The relationship between board president and CEO can change frequently. Both CEOs and presidents come and go. In some organizations, for instance, the bylaws mandate that the presidency turns over every two years. Although this is a salutary precedent, guarding against both burnout and the amassing of power by volunteer leadership, it also means that the CEO-president partnership undergoes constant change. At its best, the partnership is well negotiated, but, even so, there is a period of uncertainty during the negotiations. When organizations do not search carefully for CEOs, CEOs too turn over with regularity, and the partnership is more a wish than a reality.

Conflict between the CEO and board president can prove divisive. Internal achievement and staff support for the CEO, coupled with external difficulties and suspicion on the part of the board, create a volatile mix. The contrast can isolate both CEO and professional staff, who may develop a hostile view of the outside world. At the same time, the board president, feeling responsible for financial and other management affairs, grows increasingly worried and hostile. Without a good working partnership between CEO and president, the two positions feed mutual mistrust and misunderstanding. Often enough, the conflict is broadened and explicit, with the CEO seeking support among constituents and staff, the president from other board members. Now the organization is polarized, and the downhill slide—or leap—toward firing the CEO is virtually guaranteed.

One CEO stated that he felt like it was a bait and switch game. Within three months of taking the CEO position for a trade association, the board president announced that he was leaving the community. As a result, the smooth transition into their partnership was abruptly ended, and the member of the executive team who stepped into the presidency was the only board member who had opposed the selection of the CEO. After six months of hard work and frank conversation about differences in style and ways of work, the new partnership took hold. However, the CEO also observed that the first president's departure gave him a whole patch of gray hair in an already challenging period of his leadership of the organization.

Although there are laws about board responsibilities, the nonprofit CEO-board president partnership is not necessarily clearly defined and supported by law, community and cultural values, or historical precedent. Stable democratic political systems, such as those in the United States, insist upon regular leadership turnover to guard against tyranny, but they also protect the stability of the system through law and precedent. The partnership of volunteer president and nonprofit CEO is, to a large extent, on its own. It must depend on the skills and goodwill of two people dedicated to their organization's well-being. As the founders of the United States knew, dependency on human virtue is unwise; safeguards such as the division of powers must be built into governance. Comparable safeguards have not yet been built into the legal requirements for governance of nonprofit organizations. (See Chapter 5, "Good Governance," for further discussion of the CEO/board president relationship.)

Board President

Some board presidents do not have the desire, personality, confidence, or public persona best suited for leadership. They don't aspire to the role but take the job "because it must be done." They receive the gratitude of friends and colleagues, but that doesn't mean that they are trained as leaders.

At a difficult moment in a search process, in frustration one board president told search committee members who did not agree with him that one of them could just take over if they continued to vote against his wishes. They quickly found a way to agree to avoid this sudden change in leadership! Nonetheless, whoever the new CEO was going to be, he or she was in for a bumpy ride with a board president who believed it was either his way or the highway.

The training and development of the board president is a tricky job for the CEO. In the best case, an outside organization or a local consultant can be utilized in this process. Yet, the CEO must work with the president and governance committee to encourage continual learning on the part of the president and board if the organization desires to create a continual learning culture.

Despite their inexperience, board presidents, particularly of new organizations, may find themselves "doing everything." They may lack the skill, experience, or temperament to rally others to the cause. As a result, others often don't take direction or follow through on tasks, thus increasing the load on the president's shoulders. He may complain, but he picks up the slack. Overwhelmed as he is, he comes to trust only himself. He believes with his whole heart that his job is to guarantee the organization's success. It is an ethical trust, a psychosocial imperative. And, like the CEO, he receives precious little guidance.

Even board presidents who seek mentors and coaches for their CEOs often don't think to do so for themselves. This may exaggerate the difference between the CEO and president, making the former more and the latter less professional. At the same time, the president retains ultimate power both of governance and financial decisions. So, in effect, the leadership team is poorly organized and poorly prepared. There is even less guidance for this partnership than there is for either the presidency or the CEO alone.

On the other side of the experience equation, some board members have served on other boards and insist that each organization should be run the same way. Some significant differences in paid corporate boards and volunteer nonprofit boards may be overlooked. Just as alignment with the organizational culture is essential to a successful CEO, experienced board members soon find that previous experience and ways of work are not necessarily portable to this new board they have joined. Their assumptions about what they were signing up for may be inaccurate and even negate their interest in serving once they understand the organization's dynamics.

The CEO

Unlike board presidents, CEOs often come out of a program background. They may initially impress the board with the articulate passion and hands-on experience they bring to their work—and to job interviews. Confident and self-assured, a CEO is often effective with the board, staff, and volunteers to whom she embodies the spirit of the organization. However, once she demonstrates less-than-adequate managerial and fundraising skills, she may, in the long run, disappoint the board and its president. In the case of a first-time CEO, she may find to her dismay that she has reached her level of incompetence or traded a position where she was passionate and effective for one where she cannot see her way into developing success.

After reviewing this list, one might ask why anyone would want a CEO position in a nonprofit organization. The answer is that, as risky and difficult as the role may be, it is an opportunity to make a difference in the world through the best "skunk works" operation that exists: a committed group of community members acting in dedication to a common mission.

Leadership in the nonprofit sector is not for the faint of heart. There will be obstacles and detractors, people who join the efforts and people who fight them. Leaders seldom have the choice of pouring money into finding a new solution. There is little room for people who prefer individual stardom. It requires the patience of Job to facilitate large consensus decision-making processes. Leaders pour their hearts into a mission knowing that there will be limited resources to achieve mountainous goals. Their ability to lead will be largely controlled by their constituents, an inclusive group of citizens, each with a unique world view. Yet, the opportunity is there to transform civil society in an important way.

Discussion Questions

1. How do the factors that make leadership in nonprofit organizations so hard help or hinder the achievement of an organization's mission?

2. What can be done to align the culture of an organization to support mission achievement?

3. How does a board ensure the inclusion of diverse world views in creating an organization's vision and supporting mission achievement?

2

Why Transitions Fail

If you don't know where you are going, you won't know when you have lost your way.

Wanted: Strategic Process for Leadership Transition

Leadership transition is a defining moment in an organization's life, a time to review what the organization is about—its mission, vision, objectives, strategies, and culture, as well as its strengths, weaknesses, opportunities, and threats—and address these core themes in the selection of a new leader. Simply stated, the lack of a strategic process is usually the core reason for failure in leadership transitions.

A careful and deliberate process is all too rare. Transitions are too often crisis-oriented attempts to replace the departing CEO as quickly possible, even if the choice isn't entirely the best, even if the new person does not fully fit the culture, even if the organization is not entirely clear about long-term goals and how the next CEO might most appropriately lead.

What do we mean by failure? A transition fails when it does not further long-term strategic aims, when it leads to a brief, unproductive tenure, when it does not unite the organization around future development, and when organizational problems that led up to the leader's departure remain more or less intact.

Before exploring how to manage successful transitions, it's important to understand and anticipate the pitfalls.

Bumps and Curves Along the Road to Transition

Leadership transitions, even successful ones, are rarely smooth. A number of difficulties that can be expected during the transition period are not so much due to faulty governance or planning but are natural to any major change effort. These difficulties can be anticipated and managed. In the midst of new anxiety over the future of the organization, people will be asked to do additional work and to create new teams around tasks many have not done before. They will be asked to take leadership in different ways and to play unfamiliar roles.

Unforeseen events inevitably influence the board's deliberations and progress. A transition team member gets sick, for example, and meeting dates have to be revised or a new member needs to be integrated. There may be a shortage of qualified candidates—or so many good ones that the selection process is difficult or more time consuming. The board may grow divided over policy and find it hard to reconcile its differences. The economy may turn up or down, making it easier or harder to raise money and leading to more or less ambitious possibilities for the organization's growth (with repercussions on what kind of CEO to select). A promising candidate may indicate serious interest but later withdraw.

Sometimes key senior staff members resign during a transition process. They may have been anticipating a move before the announcement of the CEO's departure, or they may be approached with an opportunity that's too good to ignore. They may feel anxiety over taking more responsibility during the transition or over new directions the board is considering. The authority to hire new staff may be given to an interim leader by the board, or a decision may be made that temporary staffing is in order so that the next CEO has the hiring responsibility and opportunity. At any rate, this common occurrence shouldn't throw the transition team for a loop.

Preparing the community for bumps and curves may include setting flexible timelines and assuring others that a mission-driven strategic process—not deadlines—will rule the decisions made. Whatever the issues that arise, a commitment to respond to concerns transparently gives the board room to operate and credibility in the face of unanticipated or unwanted events.

Challenges That Threaten Successful Transitions

Pitfalls during the transition process generally can be classified as issues of the following:

- Leadership and governance
- Organizational characteristics
- The external environment
- Planning and execution

Leadership and Governance

The board of directors is charged by the community to fulfill the mission of the organization. Nonetheless, they rely on the CEO to oversee and manage the daily work of the organization. Therefore, the transition of the CEO places significantly more responsibility on the board of directors. Often the CEO has made the governance work of the board easy by their knowledge and expertise as well as their dedication and support of the board. However, the supportive treatment of the board has weakened their muscles for doing some of the hard work of the organization. Board members feel unprepared to take on a strategic transition of the CEO. Members are apt to believe that such comprehensive work is more than what they "signed on for." Board members may have agreed to serve on the board because of their respect and trust of the CEO. Now they are charged with stepping up to some intense work. At the same time, members worry that their liability in their board role has increased significantly. Some may even take this opportunity to step off the board. Those who remain may experience significant shifts in power of certain board members and leaders. Following are some of the challenges that boards facing during their expanded governance and leadership of transitions.

Working Without a Net

Many boards have little experience with leadership transitions. The board president and team/committee members may never have served during a transition at this or any other nonprofit organization. Taking the time to access the organization's vision and create a strategic plan is essential.

The transition process in a nonprofit may vary substantially from recruitment and hiring in a corporate setting. The number of constituencies who desire to have a voice is one difference. Taking time to survey staff, board members who will not serve on the transition team or search committee, funders, volunteers, and community members will pay off in a better understanding of the type of leader needed and in buy-in from these constituents when a finalist has been identified. Regular communication with these "publics" during the transition is essential to allaying fears and rumors and to obtaining their support and participation in outreach as well as preparing the organization's climate for the future leader.

Board members who are familiar with corporate hiring or public hiring situations (such as for school superintendents) may need to consider the differences in the nonprofit community. Maintaining confidentiality of candidate names versus public disclosure and interviews in a "hearing"-style environment are examples. The process may also vary in the amount of participation that team and committee members are asked to contribute. Reaching decisions together as opposed to relying on a hierarchical process is critical.

Board members may resist hiring expert support to guide the transition process. If they do not know what to expect, how to plan, or how to conduct a search, they may over-plan, track false leads, spend too much time with inappropriate candidates, or overreact to community rumors. If they are poor negotiators, they may lose excellent candidates. Having been through one cycle of the search as independent novices, more than one tired search committee has hired an experienced consultant to conduct a second search.

Absence of Decision-Making Clarity

During a transition, it is the board president's responsibility to move the organization down the path to replace the CEO. Even a highly organized president with ample time to devote to the organization will be dismayed by the number of decisions to make. Before engaging in the search process, the board members need to revisit their strategic vision, conduct an assessment of the organization's health, and determine what led to the departure of the previous leader, all to craft the best parameters and characteristics required of their next leader.

The president and board grapple with decisions about how to spread the decision making of the departing CEO among the board president, the board committees, and the full board. They may need to consider engaging an interim CEO. If they want to engage an interim CEO, they need to develop a plan of work for that engagement and determine how to divide responsibility. Often, the decision-making assignments during a successful transition have not been laid out in advance. Few nonprofits have a true succession plan that maps out the process in advance.

When a CEO resigns, a weak board president may be terrified to learn his position requires a shift from partnering with the CEO to leading the organization, or at minimum, to establishing clarity regarding all the players in the strategic decision-making process. During the transition period, the board president must discipline the board to do what it is chartered to do and no more unless other options are unavailable and a conscious and transparent decision is made to temporarily suspend the rules.

It can be difficult to control individuals making promises, overseeing staff without authority to do so, taking on tasks without clear communication, gossiping, and more when the board president is challenged to add many nonroutine functions to his plate.

Engaging in Roles That Are Outside the Norm

After managing the organization during the transition process, boards are reluctant to give up authority and can end up micromanaging the incoming leader. Many boards do not hesitate to take on administrative, programmatic, and other functions that belong with professional management. Such micromanagement is so frequent that it has become part of nonprofit lore. Although micromanagement generally connotes uninvited interference, many new CEOs, feeling at least temporarily insecure, invite inappropriate board participation. Boards, particularly during the early stages of an organization, are accustomed to stepping into the breach—and then staying beyond their welcome.

The board may step in to make a correction not directly related to the new CEO's activities or simply to lend a helping hand—perhaps even upon invitation by the CEO who may get into difficulty trying to turn around a crisis situation. The board may need to assist a new CEO in helping him learn the complexity of the organization. Many new CEOs, after all, have never launched an institution. They are used to working in established organizations or in other roles where they had little need to interact with a board or community members and raise money.

A second scenario has the board stepping in to help but rushing out as soon as the task is done. Board members may be exhausted by launching the organization or hiring a new CEO. They do not, in any case, want to encroach on the CEO's authority. They will, however, step in for a discreet task and then out again as often as the CEO needs help without formalizing that role. They are in and out so often, in fact, that the lines of responsibility and authority blur—not just because of board involvement, but because of ambivalence and inexperience on the part of the board as well as the CEO. The board must act with caution whenever it assumes responsibilities normally designated to the CEO.

The board response to a request to step into the CEO's territory should be: "This is your job. If you need help in fulfilling it, let's figure out together how you can get it done." That kind of clear statement about expectations of the CEO is management, not micromanagement.

The board needs to ensure that there is clarity about the staff's role in the search process. Board members may want to have input from staff about what is needed in the future leadership of the organization. They may want to provide an opportunity for senior staff to interact with the top candidates. However, it should be clear that the decision of whom to hire lies with the board.

Founder or Previous CEO Intervention

Many founders (and founding boards) have difficulty letting go of control. They have grown accustomed to doing everything themselves and have a tremendous stake in the organization. Most boards have good intentions; but many organizations, out of fear of operating without the familiar founder or out of a genuine desire to stay in touch, negotiate a continuing role for the founder.

When a founder stays involved, the moment the new CEO makes a mistake or acts contrary to the founders' vision, she may override her promises and best judgment to step back in and exert control. Naming a founder to the board of directors makes this more likely. Entering into a consulting arrangement with the departing CEO (usually negotiated before the new CEO is hired and is able to express an opinion about how welcome this might be) structurally sets up ongoing conflict.

In one organization, the new CEO's style varied greatly from the founder's, and staff members were concerned about whether the new CEO's priorities were wise. When the board president heard their concerns but asked them to bide their time, they remained anxious and turned to their beloved former mentor. It would have been painful for him to tell them he couldn't help and that they would have to form a new bond of trust with the incoming CEO. He himself was struggling with creating new relationships and a different role, so he took their calls and unintentionally encouraged an insurrection. When the new CEO exerted more stringent measures to get the staff under control, the founder realized he had played a part in a situation that damaged the reputation of the organization he loved.

Unyielding Former Relationships

During the deterioration of a previous CEO's leadership, board members often turn to senior staff for information or support. Out of a need for support during the transition, the board creates a strong alliance with dependable long-time staff. Staff have well-used lines of communication that become less appropriate when the new CEO arrives, and they die slowly or only upon the insistence of the new leader.

The New CEO's Action Tightrope

Thomas Gilmore talks about delicate timing in *Making a Leadership Change*. The unwise or inexperienced new CEO may decide on a course of action before meeting all the players or learning all the nuances of a situation. More communication with the board president rather than less in the early days is necessary to help the new CEO in reaching agreement with the board about strategic decisions. Making moves before making alliances with staff, funders, partners, and the board leaves the new CEO vulnerable to unnecessary mistakes and resentment. Resisting the pent-up demand for action and requests from a line of staff at the door on a variety of issues requires patience. Not acting soon enough has equally negative consequences. At first deemed a good listener, a new CEO without a vision will soon be seen as incapable of leading the organization through challenging times.

Organizational Characteristics

Organizational cultures are defined by the way things are done in that organization; and organizations are by nature resistant to change. Signs of the organization are evidenced in the values and assumptions of the membership. Whether it is the introductory requirements of volunteering for a new organization or rules and regulations of how to operate within an organization, people perceive change as a lessening of control. Perhaps the organization has substantial training requirements for new members that are more reminiscent of earlier times. Long-term members often want to ensure that new members' orientations are as rigorous as their training in a previous era. This ends up in orientation processes that require once sensible training that has evolved to a level of nonsense. For example, a youth leader may be required to be certified in basic first aid and know how to pitch a tent and start a fire without tools in order to lead a computer-based program that is located within fifty feet of a clinic.

Hopefully, the culture changes as an organization grows; but often the time lag is significant. Systems that worked fine in a start-up organization may fail as the membership and complexity of programs expand. Knowledge and expertise needed to deliver the mission may increase, but if longevity is the key requirement to entering leadership roles, members may not have the necessary knowledge to successfully serve the mission. Therefore, redefining organizational signs and ways of work are necessary to successful transitions.

Resistance to Change

Change is hard, and the changes implicit in transition planning will almost invariably bring some degree of resistance. Change can threaten vested interests and make people anxious. It poses a threat even when it means leaving behind painful or dysfunctional ways of operating. Resistance to change takes many forms, from direct opposition to foot dragging to apparent agreement accompanied by inept planning and implementation. It is particularly difficult to deal with indirect resistance. Most people deny inappropriate motivations. In such cases it is difficult to find ways to reassure or motivate them.

Leaving behind a nimble organization that understands change is part of the work of an effective departing CEO. When people know that change is inevitable, they can support it and see a benefit from changing. As a result, a learning organization is created.

Poor Management Processes and Systems

One founder realized that, although his organization had grown exponentially, he was unprepared to lead it to its next level of achievement. His original vision had largely been fulfilled, and his network of funding contacts had been fully tapped. He felt tired rather than excited about the future.

The board members had followed this charismatic dreamer, and they were unaware how little infrastructure existed beneath him. When they formed a search committee and began talking with candidates, they found they couldn't answer questions about the organization's technology, pipeline of potential funders, hiring and benefits practices, staff evaluations, and financial systems. There had been no strategic planning because the founder always had new ideas and directions in mind that excited both funders and the board. In fact, it was difficult to interest candidates because they were less inclined than the founder to trust that it would all work out. They were unable to put the search on hold while they, as volunteers, took the time to develop a strategic plan and institute the systems the organization needed. Eventually, they went back to square one and engaged in a strategic planning process that resulted in the development of the vision for the organization's future they needed to communicate to candidates as well as a clear picture of the requirements for their new leader.

One of the best ways to prepare for transition of the CEO is to be sure that the systems exist for the organization to operate comfortably for a period of time in his or her absence. Budgeting for periodic organizational assessments of systems and regular infrastructure improvement can create a strong organization that will withstand times of change and offer an attractive opportunity to new leadership.

Little Understanding of What Led to the Turnover

It's an old saw, first noted by George Santayana: Those who cannot remember the past are condemned to repeat it. In the case of organizational trauma or crisis, there may be a desire to resolve or even bury things before you understand them properly. Boards and organizations as a whole can be conflict averse. They may have settled into a culture of limited information or busyness that prohibits conversation about stresses or differences. It may have been the style of the departing CEO to prohibit questions about her decisions. Executive committee members may have held onto concern about the CEO's performance without sharing that the issues were serious enough to lead to termination, and they may feel that disclosing the true circumstances would damage the organization's reputation.

When people are confused, hurt, uninformed, or angry, working through the issues may require assistance by an outside professional so that a common sense of the cause of the leadership change is understood. There may be structural or cultural issues that made it hard or impossible for the departing leader to succeed, and if those issues are not addressed before the new leader is hired, that new CEO may step into the same untenable situation. This can lead to continual turnover.

One elder services organization was declining in funding and as a result had to eliminate services in an area it had once served. The long-time CEO had expressed angry opinions to state officials, and both board and staff believed that his combative approach had damaged the organization's reputation with decision makers. The CEO left in frustration, and the board hired a new CEO known for warm relations with state funders in another area. To their dismay, the next budget and the next showed continuing cutbacks. Only when the new CEO also began looking for a new position did the board members see through strategic planning that their peer organizations had been quicker to understand a change in the field's funding models that had left their agency behind.

Lack of Systemic Thinking

Because executive transition may take place infrequently, it may be thought of as a one-off event. Although every CEO eventually leaves, few organizations have created a system for managing the leadership transition so they are ready whenever it occurs.

In the situation of a founder or a CEO who's been in place for many years, the organization does not have a historical memory of the process. Both organizations and CEOs are afraid that raising the question of how long the executive plans to stay is an indication that the partnership may be wearing thin. There is a great deal of magical thinking that if the issue is out of sight, it's out of mind.

Leadership transition is generally seen as the change from one CEO to another, but in fact it involves the introduction of an individual into a system with many processes and series of relationships. This happens when a new CEO arrives, but it keeps happening each time a board president completes his term. When one member of this leadership pair is replaced, in effect there is a new pair and there are *repeated leadership transitions*. The realization that there will be continual transitions should lead the board to put processes in place to make them go smoothly.

Partnerships in Transition

Leaders do not act in isolation. They regularly interact with other key members of the organization, and the interaction between these key people becomes patterned along a continuum from effective to ineffectual. Often the relationship between the CEO and the board president influences organizations more than either of them does individually. When the two are at cross purposes, ineffectuality, crisis, and turnover are likely. When they have a close, supportive relationship, the organization is likely to succeed. A new board president, with different ideas than the previous president, will have to renegotiate relations with the presiding CEO—and vice versa.

Similar partnerships form and dissolve between CEOs and their "number twos." The Chief Operating Officer is often an operationally oriented manager paired with the CEO's externally focused skill set. The partners' equilibrium may become unbalanced and needs to be restored when one departs and another is hired.

It is important to think of leadership transitions not in individual but in partnership terms. Managing the continual shifting of such partnerships can have as important and positive an impact on leadership as selecting a "good" professional leader. Even the best CEO or board president is only as good as the fit and partnership they have with one another.

Leadership is best understood as a partnership between boards of directors and professional leaders—and with senior management. At various times and in various ways, one or the other is primarily in charge. During transitions, the board may be more actively in charge. During stable times, the CEO is primarily in charge. At all times, the board and professionals must work well together according to clear rules of governance and clear strategic directions.

Unrealistic Expectations Versus a Realistic View of Leadership

When describing the CEO job, boards often have unrealistic expectations. When the board (or staff) sees itself in need of rescue, the new CEO may be hoped to be a knight in shining armor who rides in on a white horse. Many new organizations want and expect their CEO to be all things: inspired leader, orderly manager, brilliant strategist, great fund raiser, and community builder.

When the organization discovers that their choice has only some of these qualities, and often many to a lesser degree than they had hoped, they feel let down. Disappointment may turn into anger, with the board criticizing the CEO for not living up to unrealistic and unvoiced expectations. Or, just as often, the board may ignore the CEO's deficiencies, hoping his great qualities emerge with time while failing to give him adequate support. The feeling of betrayal of an ideal persists in boards when, in fact, the responsibility for hiring was theirs. The responsibility of supporting a real-life CEO who falls short of an unrealistic ideal is also theirs.

Rarely can one person "save" an organization. Even those who bill themselves as "turnaround" leaders have often succeeded in large part because of the availability of an effective and committed team of staff, sufficient financial resources, and luck to catch the flow of supportive donors or a rising economy.

It's imperative to establish clear and reasonable expectations of our leaders and of ourselves. Leadership is not a person. It is a collective action in which the "leader" and the "led" meet challenges together. We must measure the results of these reasonable expectations in reasonable ways. This is not to say we should not hold leaders—and ourselves— accountable to high standards. But the standards should be attainable, under real and current circumstances and with board support. If we give people just enough room to fail dismally, they will do so most of the time.

The board's role regarding the CEO is to support and guide in the best of situations. When the CEO demonstrates her limitations, the board's job is to provide a support system to compensate for these drawbacks. Some CEOs, for example, are better at external relationships and fundraising than management and need administrative help. Boards may have to supply support in strategic planning or financial management. Support should be provided, not with great fanfare and resentment on the part of the board, but in a quiet and natural way of the board doing its job. If we give people time and resources to succeed, observe how they do, and regularly adjust our expectations and support according to some measure that balances our idealistic and realistic expectations, we are part of the equation, and our leaders have a chance of consistently coming through over long periods of time.

The External Environment

The economic downturn of the fall of 2008 is a prime example of environmental factors that may create unsuccessful transitions. One CEO announced his departure the day before a dominant financial institution announced that the company was in trouble. He feared a downturn in the organization's funding, but few people could predict what was ahead.

The board moved forward to hire a new CEO without undertaking a strategic process, and over the course of the transition, every month's financial statements brought more dire indicators. During the search, candidates suspected that the staff would be reduced and, to the organization's credit, they were told about significant downsizing that was left to the unfortunate board president and interim CEO. By the time the new CEO took over, it was a smaller and much weaker organization than the departing CEO had left.

Even the best of leaders is forced to operate in the same economy as the surrounding society. Although some industries and sectors are counter-cyclical, nonprofits that depend on state funding are uniformly hit when sales taxes decline and governors amend budgets. Coming into a new position at such an unfortunate time can paint the new leader with an unfair brush just as coming in at the time of an unprecedented rise in the stock market can create a strong endowment balance although the leader had little to do with it.

Planning and Execution

When a board does not see leadership transitions as inevitable—or at least, likely to happen during their tenure—they do not think to put in place the structures and systems to prepare for transition and ready for leadership changes. This is not surprising when you consider the number of CEOs with 30 years of tenure in nonprofit organizations. However, this is largely in the past. Currently, a CEO is likely to serve an organization for 18 months to 5 years. This means that anyone who serves for 6 years on a board is likely to face some leadership change. "Kicking the can forward" to the next group of board members no longer works. Organizations cannot afford to harbor a less than effective leader over numerous years. The competition in communities around mission and funding is just too stiff and the community needs too large. As nonprofit organizations have become more complex, CEOs cannot effectively jump on the "moving train" of an organization without significant support and orientation, so the planning and execution of the transition often determines whether CEOs will be successful during their tenure.

Building Consensus Through Planning

It's important to keep the focus on achieving the mission. Replacing the departing CEO is just one of the ways of doing this and must fit within the larger, complex conversation about the future of the organization. Successful transition requires a consensus about the organization's direction. To write a usable description of the job for the new CEO, for example, the transition team must know the kind of organization into which it is hiring.

When the departing CEO leaves immediately following strategic planning, a road map and community consensus about the future will guide the choices ahead. However, many organizations are in need of strategic planning at the moment transition begins.

In the early 1990s, it was uncommon for nonprofits to have well-developed strategic plans, but in the intervening years, the once primarily corporate process has become the norm in well-run nonprofit organizations. Today, strategic planning consultants for nonprofits abound, and the tradition of an annual board retreat is common yet not universal. Keeping an up-to-date and well-known plan in play enables the board to develop criteria for candidates in line with the needs of the organization for future leadership.

Each organization is unique, but numerous questions that are essential to selecting new leadership stand in the way of careful selection of a new CEO:

- What is the organization's current vision?
- Is there widespread agreement and clarity on the mission?
- Does the organization want to grow? How fast? Under what circumstances?
- Is the current balance of services meeting the objectives for the future?
- Do new board members share the vision of the founders?
- Will the current location of offices and mix of services fit future plans?
- What opportunities and threats exist in the environment?
- How can the organization address its weaknesses and emphasize its strengths?
- How does the culture enhance achievement of the mission? How does it need to change?

These questions are not answerable without conversation and time-consuming debate, which invariably surface differences that must be resolved each in its turn. This may require a new kind of convening, thinking, and decision making in an organization that may be unpracticed after years of relying on the departing CEO. Finding strong facilitation for this strategic planning process is necessary.

A careful strategic planning process is a good antidote for crisis orientation. When reacting to traumatic events or to unfortunate circumstances, it's easy to blame the previous CEO and particular characteristics of her leadership. This may lead to over-reaction. Commitment to planning can give perspective and distance that allows the organization's horizon to shift toward longer-term leadership needs.

Employing an interim CEO may allow the organization time to debate and find agreement on the organization's direction and thus better understand the type of long-term leader who can successfully step in. Without a strategic plan, a wise candidate will see the lack of clarity and wonder if she can lead an organization without an articulated sense of its goals until such a time that she can organize and lead a planning process.

Time and Care Prevent False Starts

Making a bad hiring decision is the number-one fear during a transition. Many people in the organization will have experienced a hire that in hindsight seemed doomed from the start. Avoiding that pain is primary in their minds. Although there is no guarantee regardless of how carefully transition planning and execution are done, less than optimal hires can often be attributed to several common mistakes. Boards are understandably concerned that a CEO's departure can create a loss of momentum and that opportunities may be missed or lost in the transition. That worry can lead to rushing to fill the vacancy by hiring the first apparently qualified candidate.

The emphasis on speed over deliberation can lead to even bigger problems.

It's natural and desirable for board members to network and suggest potential candidates brought to them by colleagues or friends; however, honoring those relationships may lead to an uncritical review of the candidate's experience or assessment of the potential fit. An internal candidate may dazzle the committee by outstanding performance in one division without an investigation into whether the experience is present to guide the organization as a whole. Candidates from afar may paint a romantic picture of their potential.

A careful outreach process to ensure a broad and deep pool of candidates offers the opportunity to compare and contrast the options against the boards' carefully constructed requirements. Meeting the candidates multiple times in different settings and carefully checking sufficient dependable references helps determine if they fit fully into the organization's plans and culture. This takes time.

Time and care continue to be needed after the hire. Exhausted by the greatly increased burden of work created by the transition, the transition team may hand the leadership reigns over to the new leader before he is reasonably integrated or aligned to the organization and the community.

Moving immediately to placing an ad on the job board without tending to a strategic plan inevitably leads to bad decision making. During the time it takes to hire, the staff can become dispirited and lost, worrying that no one is in charge and that the big picture is no one's responsibility. Board members may take on tasks on their own in a desire to help but find themselves working at cross purposes. The chaos or lack of momentum that results makes it harder for a new CEO to take over successfully.

Poor Communication to Stakeholders

The absence of the CEO can create a communication vacuum. This person has frequently been the board's connector to staff, funders, and outside stakeholders such as elected officials. He may have been the one who convened weekly staff meetings about organizational priorities or let local media know of organizational initiatives and events. The board president, while juggling a full-time job, family, and community commitments, may not be able to fulfill this communication role.

In the attempt to hold candidates' names confidential, the search process can be perceived as secretive or closed, leaving those who are not on the search committee in the dark. During a time of normal anxiety, stakeholders at all levels may assume the worst in the absence of information.

New management responsibility and processes may not have been well communicated, and stakeholders may not know where to go when they need something. Chaotic situations can emerge, and in an attempt to calm the waters, promises may be given without proper authority by staff or board members without the knowledge of the executive committee or whole board.

Searches That Seem to Never End

When the work of the transition is slow to start or goes on for many months, anxiety can become a part of the organizational culture. What should have been temporary roles may become embedded. High performers who want to contribute to the organization's progress may despair of that possibility and move on. The community may lose confidence in the board, doubt the organization's viability, or suspect internal strife. The eventual finalist may be seen as a second choice or fallback because a quicker pick has not been made. Candidates who were available when the transition was announced may no longer be on the market, and weary search committee members may have to be replaced with members who need to be brought up to speed with what has happened already.

Setting and holding relatively close to a schedule for the tasks of the transition is vital.

When the organization begins transition in crisis, a period to sort through the issues should precede any announcements of a search process. One organization that needed strategic planning announced that the chief operating officer was named acting CEO during the six-month planning process. The community, staff, and board knew that the organization was in good hands while it underwent a time of exploration and priority-setting.

The Initial Phases of New Leadership

Once a new CEO is named, predictable pitfalls continue to require attention.

Lack of Clear Contracting

After selection, the most predictable way for boards to ensure long-term effective leadership is to form a clear contract with the new leader. This agreement must outline explicitly what is expected of the new leader, a rough timetable for when those expectations should be met, and ways to measure how those expectations are being met—both outcomes *and* movement on the way to outcomes. The contract also should include what the new leader can expect from the board. Tom Adams refers to this process as *social contracting*.

Creating a written document is a way for both parties to see where there is a need to work out difference and find commonality. Returning periodically to this document can provide the opportunity to keep the pact fresh. Revisions can be added where needed and action can be agreed upon. Without this periodic review of the agreement, misunder-standings can occur. This may be the single biggest reason why boards and leaders clash, leading to greater turnover and ever more leadership transition.

Too Much Faith in the CEO

Sometimes board members assume that the CEO will always know what to do. They hired a professional, after all, one that seemed immensely knowledgeable during the interview process. The professional they hired is reluctant to bare his own shortcomings. The new leader is left alone too long, and he doesn't ask for help until problems of staffing, finance, or fund-raising begin to get out of hand.

When cracks show in the armor, the founders or hiring board members rush in and sometimes react too extremely. Feeling let down and even betrayed, they withhold confidence in the CEO's ability to accomplish his tasks and check every detail of his work. This in turn further erodes his confidence. They will now stay too involved in day-to-day operations until the CEO proves himself—or until they fire him.

Inadequate Support

The transition team and search committee members may feel they have given such a significant amount of time during the search that it's time to go back to neglected responsibilities at home or at work. The exhausted board hands the organization to the new leader without orienting him to the strategic plan, the community, the culture, systems that have been in place, or relevant players in the field and the organization. Adequate time for the new CEO to learn the history and operational systems, meet people and create relationships, and develop trust and vision is essential for success.

New CEOs often express surprise at learning information that wasn't obvious (or was even hidden) during the hiring process. Some organizations are afraid that if they provide a full explanation of organizational concerns and worries, they will not be able to attract a sufficient caliber of leadership. Some make every attempt to be open and fully disclose both positive and negative aspects of the operation, but no matter how much is shared, there may be surprises. The new CEO has likely inquired about the circumstances surrounding the departure of his successor, but on arrival he may find that the explanation that the CEO was retiring or "moving on for other opportunities" may cover a multitude of sins.

One search consultant says, "There's always something in the bottom of the bottom drawer in the back that the departing CEO either didn't want to do or didn't know how to fix." The new CEO needs to ask questions and be assured that difficulties he inherits will not be accounted to him but that he will be supported with resources to resolve those issues and be given credit for doing so. That may take time, and having the confidence of the board during that uncertainty is invaluable.

Inadequate Resources

Upon arrival, a new CEO may find that the organization has slipped financially below the viability mark. Although funding was in the bank or promised at the departure of the previous leader, time during the transition can take its toll financially. Without sufficient working capital, staff layoffs in the early days can create tremendous ill will. Cutbacks in essential services may cause the organization to become a target for competition in the community and with funders, and community support may wane if the organization is perceived to be too weak to deliver on its mission. Both the organization and its candidates must analyze whether the resources on hand will fund the strategic plan until there is time for the new leader to get her bearings.

Even the ideal CEO cannot make up for the board's failure to raise sufficient funds to run the organization well, attract volunteers, and bring in excellent staff. Below-market CEO compensation is also a great de-motivator. It is the board's responsibility to know current salaries in peer organizations and to pay a respectful wage that rewards the CEO for hard work and leadership success.

Divided Boards

Board schisms can be crippling to a CEO and to the organization. During the transition process, the transition team should consciously provide opportunities for staff, board, and community members to express their opinions about the organization's strategic plan and the characteristics required of its new leader. Once the strategic planning process has taken place and a search committee has been appointed to find and recommend a new leader, the discussion shifts venues to a confidential setting where various candidates' backgrounds and talents are compared to these needs. Truly delegating this responsibility and putting confidence in the search committee will mean that their recommendation is accepted unless there is reason to believe the committee has acted without full information or diligence.

A divided board regarding the hiring decision gives multiple and often conflicting messages to the CEO. She is wary that judgments have been made before she has had a chance to prove her commitment and capability. When the organization waits to see if the new person is really okay before getting fully behind her, that doubt is likely obvious to the community. This starts a vicious cycle: without a belief that board members are supportive, she worries that she can't succeed. Some board members take her lack of confidence as lack of competence, angering other board members and inflaming board schisms, leading to further conflict.

A unanimous vote for a new CEO starts the new leader on the right foot. Once a new CEO is on board, a quick public vote of confidence by the board makes her success in the community more likely. Coordinating board feedback through the board president can keep the CEO from getting different messages from board members. Regular performance reviews can make it clear where the CEO is excelling and where improvement is required.

No Guarantees

Good people and good organizations aren't necessarily a dependable fit. The lack of a strategic planning process, unclear criteria, or internal politics may bring about a hire that causes one or both parties to worry that they have done the wrong thing. Sometimes unforeseeable circumstances require a change in commitments. The new CEO or a family member may become ill, or the organization may lose a substantial contract.

It may be no one's fault, but terminating the relationship with the new CEO within the first year can be perceived or remembered as a "bad hire." Sometimes that bad hire label is well deserved. The search committee may have misunderstood the needs of the organization, or the new CEO may have misrepresented his skills and experience to get the job. Careful process and reference checking goes a long way but cannot guarantee that a "bad hire" will never happen.

Certainly, there are landmines evident in the transition process. However, adherence to a disciplined process of developing a strategic vision of the future, assessing the organization's strengths and weaknesses, as well as addressing the root cause of the most recent departure sets a sturdy framework for a successful transition process. When a board is fully engaged in governance and the president truly acts in partnership with the CEO, transitions create opportunities to grow exponentially. Staff is invigorated by developmental challenges. Volunteers reconnect to their belief in the mission, and the entire community comes to see the next level the organization can achieve.

Discussion Questions

1. How can an organization turn the risk created in transition into an opportunity for growth?
2. What systems need to be developed in an organization to prepare for successful transitions on the horizon?
3. What ongoing dialogue should be initiated to strengthen leadership partners in preparing for transitions?

Part 2

Fundamentals of Effective Leadership

3

Mission, Vision, and Effective Leadership

When you discover your mission, *you will feel its demand. It will fill you with enthusiasm and a burning desire to get to work on it.*

Beginning with Mission and Vision

The fundamental challenge for all leaders is to align their organizations in the service of their mission and vision, reflected in concrete objectives, realized in strategically developed operations, embedded in culture, and exemplified in their own being.

Leadership, then, begins with mission and vision. These "soft" disciplines steady, orient, and drive the leader. When taken seriously, they provide discipline, inspiration, and guideposts for everything organizations do.

Individual leaders must be clear about their own and their organization's mission and vision. The mission defines what the organization is all about, its reason for being, and what it stands for. The vision is an idealistic and realistic picture of the future, a declaration of where you and others want to be and believe you can be in five or more years. Leaders must articulate their organizational vision in a clear and compelling form so that everyone connected with the organization understands what it is and why it is important. What's more, the leader champions the mission and vision so that it provides guidance for all organizational decisions and permeates the organization's culture, structure, and processes.

Everything a leader does becomes an expression and an extension of the organizational vision. He embodies it and it embodies him, or at least his dreams. It is the fuel that keeps him in motion from early morning to late at night, and it is the fuel he provides for others who often extend themselves well beyond the requirements of a job.

Although mission and vision look outward, defining how leaders measure their and the organization's success and failure, they also have a powerful impact on leaders. They are the vehicle by which leaders transcend themselves. Dedication to mission and vision ennobles leaders, lifts them out of the mundane, adds a luster to the most common activities, and provides a rationale for even the most difficult and disheartening decisions.

Definitions from Sector Leaders

Most books on nonprofits begin with mission, but most books on corporations do not. Many corporate missions are, in Peter Drucker's words, "pious platitudes." But he goes on to say, "Starting with the mission and its requirements may be the first lesson business can learn from successful nonprofits,"[1] and an important lesson at that.

Mission

A well-wrought mission statement announces the organization's reason for being, its essence. "Mission is the guiding star," says Frances Hesselbein, former CEO of The Girl Scouts, which Drucker called the best-run organization in the country, corporate or nonprofit. It is "why we do what we do. Our values hold, permeate, bring certainty in uncertain times...Leaders are the embodiment of the mission, values, beliefs, and principles that are the soul of the organization. Mission can mobilize the people of an organization around why they do what they do, and it gives purpose to what they do and how they do it..."[2]

According to Drucker, a sincere mission statement, if it is kept vividly in mind and invoked with great frequency, provides coherence and discipline for organizations. "It focuses the organization on action. It defines the specific strategies needed to attain the crucial goals. It creates a disciplined organization. It alone can prevent the most common degenerative disease of organizations, especially large ones: fragmenting their always limited resources on things that are 'interesting' or 'look profitable' rather than concentrating them on a very small number of productive efforts."

Missions communicate the basic philosophy upon which an organization is built. A great mission effectively communicates the direction that the organization is headed to all constituencies. It informs the core values of the organization, and it begins to frame the culture and ethics of an organization. The goals are developed from the mission, and performance criteria are designed to move the organization toward realization of the mission. The mission should provide a touchtone for decision making at all levels of governance and operations. This is why it is essential that the mission statement be revisited at the beginning of transition. It brings everyone together to move forward through the change process.

Vision

The organizational vision is just that: a picture and a story. It is more evocative than analytic. In a good vision, you can see and feel the organization, what it is like to enter its doors, what people are doing, when, with whom, and for what reason. It expresses aspirations and a confident feel for the future. Because it is evocative, everyone can relate to it, can see themselves in it, feel themselves into their future roles, and do the same for peers and managers, employees, customers, and the communities and markets they serve.

Here is how three major organizational and leadership theorists define vision:

Burt Nanus—"...a vision is a realistic, credible, attractive, and inspiring future for the organization."[3]

John Bryson—"...a clear and succinct description of what [an] organization or community should look like after it successfully implements its strategies and achieves its full potential."[4]

John Kotter—"A sensible and appealing picture of the future."[5]

Visions are the constant reminder of what we are reaching for, according to Sister Margaret Leonard, revered leader of Project Hope in Boston. In a personal interview with the author, she stated, "Visions are in us as constant companions and we move toward their realization inch by inch and sometimes leap by leap. At rare and special times, our efforts reach a tipping point, which catapults us into entirely new ways of thinking and acting. In this way, visions call us into a future yet to unfold."

Visions, Change, and Paradigm Shifts

The underlying purpose of visions is to imagine and name the fundamental change required of organizations to realize their missions. The changes are twofold. First, there are concrete changes: We will grow from 50 to 300 students; revenue will grow from 10 to 100 million; our decision making will be based on factual information and research.

Second, everything we do will be infused with the values and spirit of the mission. Therefore, we will not teach youth that they have the power over their own lives but maintain autocratic controls within our organization. Instead, organizational processes will mirror, teach, and amplify the power of these values through ongoing experience with them. We will not measure our progress simply by numbers and concrete goals but also by the path by which we achieved them. In other words, organizations motivated by missions and visions aim to transform the organizational culture, and by changing the culture they change the way people think and feel about themselves and the world around them.

This change in the basic assumptions about what is important, how things work, and how things change is called a *paradigm shift*. And a paradigm shift is the ultimate aim of organizational missions and visions.

Components of Organizational Visions

Warren Bennis, in *On Becoming a Leader*, says that people want three things from their leader: direction, trust, and hope. Good mission and vision statements from credible leaders provide or elicit all three.

In other words, the vision statement is comprehensive. It permits people to see the whole and to see the relationships among the parts. It shows how the mission is derived from philosophical premises and core values and how it informs and infuses everything else. It breaks the more abstract vision into concrete, realizable objectives, and it demonstrates what kind of strategies will bring the objectives to realization. It indicates how people will know they are moving toward its objectives and when they have reached them. And it articulates the rules of governance and decision making that define how authority and responsibility are shared.

Effective Missions and Visions

Although there are common elements to effective missions and visions, each organization must shape these elements to their own values, goals, and circumstances. "The right vision," says Burt Nanus, "will reflect the distinctive character and culture of the organization and will leverage its history and network of connections. This vision will incorporate high ideals, pointing to how the organization can achieve greatness or excellence in its field. It will be ambitious, setting challenging expectations and stretching everyone associated with the organization. It will be easily understood and capable of being expressed in a few short sentences."[6]

Too many mission and vision statements are plain vanilla, motherhood, and apple pie. They are so general or grandiose that people within the organization don't relate to them and customers don't notice. Like strategic plans that mostly gather dust on bookshelves, most mission and vision statements remain ornamental, perhaps framed and hanging in executive offices, but not really speaking to the organization in an authentic voice.

One reason these statements are easy to ignore is that they are carelessly done. Another is that they have no bite. They don't compel choices, priorities, or sacrifice. "The best nonprofits devote a great deal of thought to defining their organization's mission," writes Peter Drucker. "They avoid sweeping statements full of good intentions and focus, instead, on objectives that have clear-cut implications for the work their members—staff and volunteers—perform. The Salvation Army's goal, for example, is to turn society's rejects—alcoholics, criminals, derelicts—into citizens. Girl Scouting builds girls of courage, confidence, and character, who make the world a better place. The Nature Conservancy preserves the diversity of nature's fauna and flora."[7]

A third reason that mission and vision statements fail is that they are often inward looking and—in an anticipatory way—self-congratulatory. Instead, the point of focus must be outward, on what the organization produces for its customers. Again, let us listen to Peter Drucker. "A well-defined mission serves as a constant reminder of the need to look outside the organization not only for 'customers' but also for measures of success. The temptation to content oneself with the 'goodness of our cause'—and thus substitute good intentions for results—always exists in nonprofit organizations. It is precisely because of this that the successful nonprofits have learned to define clearly what changes *outside* the organization constitute 'results' and to focus on them."

John Kotter has outlined the practical characteristics of an effective vision. His criteria are primarily directed at effective implementation. They are process criteria and largely deal with psychological impact. He says that an "effective vision must be:

- **Imaginable**—Conveys a picture of what the future will look like
- **Desirable**—Appeals to the long-term interests of employees, customers, stockholders, and others who have a stake in the enterprise
- **Feasible**—Comprises realistic, attainable goals
- **Focused**—Is clear enough to provide guidance in decision making
- **Flexible**—Is general enough to allow individual initiative and alternative responses in light of changing conditions
- **Communicable**—Is easy to communicate; can be successfully explained within five minutes"[8]

We would strongly add three more qualities of an effective vision:

- **Authentic**—It must sincerely express the leadership's own aspirations and values. The vision should be in keeping with the organization's identity, values, objectives, and capacity. If not, those who hear it will receive it cynically. The statements will alienate rather than motivate.
- **Broadly owned**—It must be broadly affirmed if it is to be successfully and wholeheartedly implemented.
- **Leads from strength**—It must begin with core competencies, values, strengths, or spirit and portray the future as an extension of what is best about the current organization. While openly admitting difficulties and weaknesses, the vision should point to the path to overcoming them.

Conceiving Missions and Vision

There are so many ways to work toward mission and vision statements. Drucker suggests that there are only three questions that need to be answered in formulating a mission:[9]

- What is our business/mission?
- Who is our customer?
- What does the customer value?

During strategic planning, consider the following mission and vision guidelines.

Mission Statement

Purpose—What is our organization's purpose?

This question addresses the question of why the organization exists, not what it does. It asks for a succinct statement describing the ultimate result you hope to achieve.

The emphasis is on outcomes. For example, our aim is to build a community of like-minded people, to eliminate homelessness, cure AIDS, or educate civic-minded youngsters.

Method—What is our primary service or activity?

The emphasis is on what we do. For example, education, disease prevention, new housing construction, shelter, research.

Values—What values guide our work and our interaction with one another and with the community in which we live?

The emphasis is on what we believe is right. For example, we may believe in compassion, generosity, or equality among people, in empowering all constituents, or in being good neighbors.

Vision

Tell a story that envisions how your organization will look in three to five years. The story should blend hope and idealism with a sense of realistic possibilities.

Guidelines—When writing the story, consider the following questions:

- What distinguishes yours from other comparable organizations?
- What makes it special?
- What kind of changes do you want to make, for example, in values, services, leadership, and community relations?
- How could the organization be more effective?
- What do our "stakeholders" want from us?

Stakeholders include clients, families, staff, members of the larger community, funders, regulatory agencies, and so forth.

Story Components—As you tell your story, make sure to cover the following themes.

Values and Philosophy

For example, what does it mean to be a youth development organization, or a community development organization? A pluralistic community? A focused community?

Programs

- How should they be focused on the average client?
- Should they be focused on the exceptional client or equally on all potential clients?
- What kind of balance should you strike between inclusive and selective?

Services

- What are the core services provided and to whom?

Staff

- How should the organization be staffed?
- How many staff should there be?

- What qualifications are needed by staff?
- What kinds of attitudes and values should staff hold?
- How should the physical plant and location be designed?
- What kind of building(s) should house the organization, and where should it be located?

Size

- How many clients should the organization reach?
- How large a community should the organization embrace?
- What kind of revenue goals should it set?

Stability and Growth

- Should it reach a certain size and sustain it, or should the organization consider ongoing growth as part of its nature and mission?

Leadership

- What kind of professional and volunteer leadership should the organization have?
- What characteristics, skills, and experience should the CEO have?
- What characteristics, skills, and experience should staff have?
- What characteristics, skills, and experience should the board president and the board of directors have?

Resources

- How should the organization be funded?
- For example, what balance of public and private funding; how much generated by fee-for-service activities?

Community Relations

- How should the organization relate to local institutions, such as local governments, schools, and police departments?

Communicating Vision

As Peter Block points out, visions must be owned by those who rally behind them and carry them out. Robert Rosen concurs: "The best leaders know that a vision with a single voice never amounts to much. So they share the vision across the organization, enlisting input and participation of all constituents. By letting everyone shape the vision, the leader inspires people and builds commitment."[10] There are many ways for people to be involved: at the initial creation of a vision, after a rough draft is formed, or before those who draft it begin to talk and write.

John Kotter has provided a tidy listing of the "Key Elements in the Effective Communication of Vision:"[11]

> **Simplicity**—All jargon and "techno-babble" must be eliminated.
>
> **Metaphor, analogy, and example**—A verbal picture is worth a thousand words.
>
> **Multiple forums**—Big meetings and small, memos and newspapers, formal and informal interaction—all are effective for spreading the word.
>
> **Repetition**—Ideas sink in deeply only after they have been heard many times.
>
> **Leadership by example**—Behavior from important people that is inconsistent with the vision overwhelms other forms of communication.
>
> **Explanation of seeming inconsistencies**—Unaddressed inconsistencies undermine the credibility of all communication.
>
> **Give and take**—Two-way communication is always more powerful than one-way communication.

In a mission-driven organization, if you follow an effective leader, you will see her stopping here and there, praising workers and telling stories that link their efforts to the organizational vision. It is personal. It also links the leader, staff, and volunteers in a common purpose. You will hear the conviction and passion in her voice. You will note that during hard times, especially during crisis, the centrality of mission and vision becomes even greater. And you will notice that, more often than others, great leaders live their mission and vision.

Embodying Vision

The greatest leaders—including those Jim Collins calls *Level Five Leaders*—embody the vision of their organizations and movements in their own character.[12] Their action is or appears to be today what the organization aspires to be tomorrow. In this sense they are living models of the organizational vision, and, in their movement through the world, they teach the meaning of the vision.

Gandhi, for example, represented a free India, with all its hopes and contradictions. He was humble—wearing tattered clothing and weaving yarn like a peasant—and proud of his heritage and people. He was an ardent Hindu and a modern man, educated, knowledgeable, and versed in secular ways. He seemed natural, and he was highly strategic. He was forceful and nonviolent. He was, as many saw it, Mother India itself.

In an entirely different arena, Bill Gates embodies Microsoft. A brilliant "techie" from his youth, he represented and attracted a brain trust of young, ambitious, restless people to his company. But Microsoft did not succeed because it created the best software platform; rather, it grew on the back of its marketing genius and its sense of a limitless world in which Microsoft and modern society would travel together. Gates blew life every day into the Microsoft image—it was him—with a vast and communicable optimism and pleasure in creation and growth.

We needn't only turn to great public figures. For instance, Sister Margaret Leonard, with her fierce desire for social justice and her even fiercer capacity for compassion and generosity, embodies Project Hope, a Dorchester, Massachusetts organization that provides shelter, education, housing, leadership training, and emotional support to homeless women.

Revisioning

Whereas mission statements often hold for lengths of time, vision statements do not. They must be adapted to new circumstances.

Let's briefly sketch some circumstances that commonly require or call forth the revision of the organizational vision.

Leadership Transitions

Sometimes when organizations write job descriptions, they make them congruent with their vision. They rethink their vision to determine what kind of leader they need and then match leader and vision. But this kind of foresight and rigor is unusual. More often, leaders take the job, get to know the new organization, and then announce or initiate the development of a new vision. To some extent, all leaders must reshape vision statements to fit their own goals, character, style of working, and values, but the change can range from small to radical, from necessary to narcissistic, that is, required by organizational concerns or simply personal ego concerns.

Lack of Alignment

When current or new leaders realize that resources, culture, structure, and strategy are not aligned with one another and with the organization's mission, they must construct a new vision. Signs that the organization is out of alignment include moving without purpose, being out of sync with community needs and technological trends, and a sense that the right people aren't in the right jobs.

Changes in the Social, Political, or Economic Climate

In the United States (in 2010), there is considerably less money for public and nonprofit social service agencies than in years past, and that situation looks like it will continue for some years. Organizations dependent on such money have to re-envision their future, and their leaders must be the ones to raise these possibilities. Demographic changes make some organizations unsustainable and cause others to thrive, with all manner of adaptation in between. Leaders should be the catalysts for envisioning anew the realistic possibilities of the future.

Troubled Situations

Sometimes, when a leader enters a bad situation, a new vision is particularly needed. Nanus elaborates: "When a leader finds confusion about priorities, lethargy, a lack of pride, or a tendency to play it safe, she knows a new vision is called for."[13]

Mergers, Acquisitions, and Strategic Alliances

Mergers, acquisitions, and major strategic alliances generally create major organizational change: financially, culturally, and operationally. Many fail when business-as-usual is assumed. Many falter when the organization is run in an ad-hoc way for too long. A new vision is generally required for newly configured organizations.

Board Leadership Transitions

As we have noted, organizations rest on an effective partnership between board presidents and professional directors. One is charged primarily with policy and strategy, the other with strategy and operations. When board presidents change, it can dramatically change the partnership. With each change, these relationships need to be carefully negotiated, and with the negotiation may come a new conception of organization direction that in turn calls for a new or renewed organizational vision.

Aligning to Vision

In other chapters, we will take up the question of what happens to mission and vision after the statements are written and put into play. For now, we want to foreshadow their relationship to the other primary activities of leadership.

Internal Clarity and Coherence of Leadership

Leader, vision, and mission are inextricably connected; defining one shapes another. Without internal clarity and coherence, leaders are not credible enough to serve and champion the vision to optimal effect. Only by being the voice, the embodiment of the vision, can the leader hope to transcend his ordinary capabilities and motivate others to do the same.

Bridges

Leaders communicate vision most effectively when they are already deeply connected with others. Deep connections are built through bridges. When roles are well negotiated, for example, leaders are designated champions of visions. Their own stories about themselves, their identities, are in sync with the visions. Remember Gandhi in India,

Gates with Microsoft, and Margaret Leonard with Project Hope. The third bridge is a covenant—part agreement, part sacred trust—that joins leader and followers in pursuit of their cause. The fierce effort to close the gap between espoused and lived values represents the primary way that leaders try to infuse the whole organization with its core mission and vision.

Strategic Thinking

Strategic thinking means identifying the significant ways that organizational activities and resources can be focused on the realization of its mission and vision.

Leveraging

Leveraging represents the way that leaders prioritize their own activities and focus their impact to develop and implement strategies that move organizations toward the realization of their mission and vision.

Managing to Strategy

Managing to strategy is the practical partner of strategic thinking. It means mobilizing all the organization's resources in the service of its mission and vision.

Opportunism

With a clear vision in mind, leaders can take decisive action on opportunities that further the organizational mission and dismiss opportunities, however tempting, that do not.

Resilience: Riding the Cycles and Stages of Organization Development

It is hard, if not impossible, to continue functioning at a high level during downturns and other organizational and personal crises. But such functioning is often made immeasurably easier when leaders believe deeply in missions and visions that transcend their personal concerns.

Patience While the Vision Permeates the Organization

It takes a long time for vision to permeate the organization, for all to be infused with it. It is like cultural change. Although some practitioners approach cultural change early in organizational change efforts, we believe such effort almost always fails. Culture anchors everything else: structure, processes and procedures, and planning. A leader can change a structure—the hierarchical organization, compensation, and promotional ladders, for example—by fiat. He can introduce new processes—consensual decision making, project planning forms—with effort and persistence, but without a long developmental period. Culture includes the implicit assumptions about everything, from what kind of person is effective, how change takes place, to human nature. Are people fundamentally good and independent and only need to be freed from constraints to work at an optimal level? Or are people fundamentally lazy or greedy and need to be carefully watched and probably controlled in what they do?

Visions and missions eventually enter the culture. They form its backbone. They become the almost unconscious basis for setting priorities, making decisions, structuring work, and management practice.

Many if not most organizations and their leaders give up too quickly on the veracity and the power of missions and visions. When they notice people acting according to other visions, values, or rules, they are likely to do one of three things: give up and just stay "practical"; push harder and shout louder about the implementation; or change the vision, adapting it prematurely to the current "reality," without giving it time to work its way into the organizational DNA. When there is a downturn in the business—a loan is called or customers decline—there is an inclination to denigrate and dispose of the vision.

Once a vision is crafted, however, and seems to be backed by a good percentage of the people—at least the key decision makers and opinion leaders—it needs to be talked up and supported by creating structures and processes in keeping with its message. This takes persistence but not stubbornness. Approaches to instilling the mission and vision can vary. They can be adapted to new circumstances. They can benefit from an analysis of the experience of trying to implement them and infuse the organization with their story. And they can be changed a little. But give it a good, long try before giving up!

Leaders Transcend Themselves Through Visions

In creating, championing, and managing to mission and vision, the leader is proactive. But, paradoxically, leaders are also acted upon, even by their own creations. With time, missions and visions take on a life of their own. Leaders live continuously with their missions and visions. They invent and repeat stories that illustrate the key points. They give speeches that urge people on in the name of the vision and mission. They judge project design and financial developments by their contribution to vision and mission.

The more leaders live with their mission and vision, the more they become the agent of the mission. The more they are the agent, the more they are ennobled. The speeches, stories, and plans are lifted from their literal and mundane meaning into something that is beyond themselves. A project is no longer just a project; it is part of the road to realizing a dream. A new hire is not just a person but a new member of the crusade. Common financial reports come alive with significance.

Operating at the center of this metaphorical universe, the leader's every act and utterance takes on greater significance. Employees make the best of it, see what it means for them, and try harder to fulfill its explicit and implicit call. As momentum builds, the leader feels this energy around him and senses that his moves are in some ways more than his own. He is speaking for something greater and, by so doing, has become something greater than himself.

Discussion Questions

1. What does an organization's mission and vision say about the type of leader who can best serve the organization?
2. How has your organization "lived" your mission and current vision?
3. What is the organization's vision for the next leadership team?
4. How is the mission reflected in an organization's strategic plan and operational efforts?

Endnotes

1 Drucker, Peter F., *The Essential Drucker*, Harper Business, 2001, p. 21

2 Bennis, Warren, *On Becoming a Leader*, Addison-Wesley Publishing Company, Reading, MA, 1989.

3 Nanus, Burt & Dobbs, Stephen M., *Leaders Who Make a Difference*, Jossey-Bass, San Francisco, 1999.

4 Bryson, John M., *Strategic Planning for Public and Nonprofit Organizations*, Jossey-Bass, San Francisco. p. 35.

5 Kotter, John P., *Leading Change*, Harvard Business School Press, Boston, MA., p. 71.

6 Nanus, Burt, & Dobbs, Stephen M., *Leaders Who Make a Difference*, Jossey-Bass, San Francisco, 1999. p. 83.

7 *The Five Most Important Questions You Will Ever Ask About Your Nonprofit Organization*, The Drucker Foundation Self-Assessment Tool for Nonprofit Organizations, Jossey-Bass, San Francisco, 1993.

8 Kotter, John P., *Leading Change*, Harvard Business Press, Boston, MA p. 71.

9 *The Five Most Important Questions You Will Ever Ask About Your Nonprofit Organizations*, The Drucker Foundation Self-Assessment Tool For Nonprofit Organizations, Jossey-Bass, San Francisco, 1993.

10 Rosen, Robert H., *Leading People*, Penguin Books, New York, 1996. p. 34.

11 Kotter, John P., *Leading Change*, Harvard Business School Press, Boston, MA.

12 Collins, Jim, *Good to Great: Why Some Companies Make the Leap and Others Don't*, HarperCollins Publishers, New York, 2001.

13 Nanus, Burt & Dobbs, Stephen M., *Leaders Who Make a Difference*, Jossey-Bass, San Francisco, 1999.

4

Leadership and Strategy

Leaders without a strategic plan have nowhere to lead.

Good leadership is strategic leadership. The fundamental challenge of leadership is to align all resources—human, technical, and capital—in the service of the organization's mission. But missions are broad statements of purposes. They don't speak specifically about what is needed to succeed. Strategies do. They specify. They prescribe how to focus energies and resources. A good leader, then, must have an effective strategic plan and must manage that plan with great discipline.

In the introduction, we proposed that leadership transition represents a crisis, a moment of both danger and opportunity. Consider a board president leading the organization during a transition. The apparent dangers are many, among them that the organization becomes chaotic, lethargic, panicky, or short-sighted. There is another important danger to consider: The board might hire someone who is not qualified or aligned with the fundamental strategy and objectives of the organization. This often occurs because the board members are in a rush, they are afraid to fully understand what went wrong with prior leadership, or they didn't take time to understand the strategic plan well enough to find someone who could lead according to it. The opportunity, then, is to seek and hire a strategic leader: one who can be focused, prioritized, leveraged, and competitive, all based on an organization's fundamental purpose and direction.

How can an organization take advantage of that opportunity? To begin, the board must revisit their current strategy:

1. They must clarify the core strategic idea. This means reviewing how they have been translating the mission into action. We say

95

"translating" because many organizations do not have a succinct statement of their strategic direction. Many boards cannot say how they have turned their mission into a set of achievable goals.

2. They must bring the strategy up to date. Transitions are not leisurely periods, and it may not be time for the revision to be exhaustive and complex, just updated.

3. The board has to communicate the revised strategy, at least to the search committee and transition team, but likely to the entire organization and to the greater community.

4. The board must identify a person who wants to and can lead based on the strategic idea. Hiring the leader follows clarifying the core strategic direction. The board must hire a person who can turn strategy into concrete accomplishments. This means that the new hire must be in full sympathy with the strategy and possess the practical skills to realize it.

5. This might seem like the end of the transition, but it is not. The fifth major task is to charge the new person to lead based on the strategic plan—that is, to take the strategy as his banner and organizing principal. Agreement between the transition team and the new leader then becomes the fundamental "contract" that binds the board and the CEO.

6. The board must hold each other accountable for following the strategic plan and achieving the organizational objectives. Movement toward these objectives becomes the basis of performance review, when the board reviews the CEO and itself. The board must ask, for example, whether it is providing the support and the resources to enable the CEO to carry out the strategic plan. This kind of reciprocal accountability is what keeps the organization aligned in the service of its mission. It is not a one-time process. All of these acts—clarification and review of the strategy based on evidence; review of the leader based on strategy implementation; and providing resources for implementation—must be conducted repeatedly.

Introducing Strategy to Nonprofits

In our experience, nonprofit organizations are not essentially strategic. Although many strive to manage strategy and objectives, they are really only rallying the troops behind vague banners of mission and vision. The addition of strategy to mission represents a commitment to perform specific, measurable activities to achieve mission and vision. Commitment to specific activities to achieve measurable goals is the key. If we are to insist that new leaders are hired to implement strategy, we have to understand what strategy is.

Let's say, for example, that an organization's mission is to end homelessness. This means that the strategic focus on shelters has to decrease because shelters provide only a short-term solution. A core strategic plan emerges to replace shelters and to create empowered, self-reliant lives for women who have found themselves homeless. Concretely, this might mean a focus on job creation and training, the development of affordable housing, and child care resources. The creation of jobs, housing, and child care is measurable. All emanate from a core strategic plan: empowerment and self-reliance. A board can hold a CEO accountable for realizing these objectives. Likewise, a CEO can hold a board accountable for providing adequate resources.

The application of explicitly strategic thinking in many nonprofits is relatively new. It is more highly developed in the corporate world. The difference between these worlds has many roots. One difference may be simply financial. Fewer nonprofits have had the resources to carry out extensive and exacting strategic planning. But the assumption that all for-profit corporations are more strategic than all nonprofits is false. One major difference grows out of the imagery associated with strategy. Strategy, with its insistence that organizations differentiate themselves to create a competitive advantage over others, can be seen as aggressive and noncollaborative, two qualities that nonprofits may balk at. To put the matter bluntly, nonprofits have been squeamish about the martial flavor of some corporate strategic thinking.

But there is little wrong and a great deal right about consciously and intelligently thinking through how to accomplish goals—maybe even figuring out how to do that better than anyone else. And that is the tone taken by many of the new breed of nonprofit consulting firms as well as books and journals that explain and expand on the application of strategic thinking to the third sector. Many of the most prominent and, by some standards, most successful nonprofits have clearly brought the strategic mind-set front and center within their organizations.

In the following sections, we sketch the nature of strategy, strategic planning, and strategic management.

Definitions

There are innumerable ways that practitioners and theorists think about strategy development. Among them, there are Weisboard's future search, Hamel and Prahalad's strategic intent, Mintzberg's strategic thinking, and Senge's scenario planning. Each of these consultants would define strategy differently, although each is part of the movement to change strategic planning from a rigid plan for a knowable future to more flexible ideas, images, plans, and ways to mobilize around relatively unpredictable futures. Still, all planners would agree with the need to find a coherent set of ideas to reach our goals.

Simply put, strategy is a plan to move from here to there, from your current state to the achievement of your objectives. When elaborated, strategy should include specific tactical or project plans. For example, if an organization decides it will thrive by building the best staff possible, that is its strategy. Plans for how to build that quality staff—how to pay, recruit, and train them—are tactical plans. Tactical plans tell us how we will implement our strategy. But as Michael Porter (Harvard Business School and father of the modern strategy field), would say, strategy itself is a broad formula, not a detailed plan.

The broad formula tells a story of cause and effect. If you do this, it will lead to that result. The clarity of such stories focuses resources and energy. It identifies how we will spend money, deploy people, and communicate to customers. The strategic story sets priorities: We will choose this path and not another. No matter how alluring the other approaches seem, we are committed to playing out particular means to achieve particular ends. There is no way to underplay the importance of commitment.

The commitment is not to just any set of activities, however. It is to a set of activities that leverage our resources to achieve higher levels of performance. For an idea to be strategic, it must bring all areas of an organization into concert, so that each improves the others: the budgeting process supports program development which, in turn, supports marketing. Organizations are systems, and all the parts are related. If strategy works, it moves an organization into a virtuous cycle, where one activity supports and improves another, which improves another.

Strategy has its origins in military culture as a way to overcome an enemy. Porter and other corporate theorists continue the competitive emphasis, as does David La Piana, a nonprofit strategy theorist. The goal is to be the best, or at least be perceived as the best, thus attracting funders, clients, and partners.

Robert Sheehan translates the corporate competitive style by emphasizing achieving high performance rather than "overcoming enemies." "Nonprofit strategy," Sheehan says, "is a coherent set of general ideas which explain how the organization is going to pursue its vision and carry out its mission during the years ahead. The strategy explains how the key functional areas of revenue generation, staffing (paid and unpaid, i.e., volunteers), and mission impact will operate and interrelate. The strategy is generated by the organization's commitment to accomplish its mission and attain its vision."

Current State Analysis

Strategy development and transition management share a keen interest in the analysis of an organization's current state. Its current state includes operational effectiveness, positioning in the market, and fiscal circumstances. If strategy takes you from here to there, we need to know the current state upon which we build a bridge to "there." If we are to select and position a new leader, we need to know how well the old leader's efforts were supported by the organization and how effectively the current organization is likely to support a new leader.

Defining the Transition Period

Earlier it was noted that the failure of many leadership transitions begins with an overly narrow frame for the transition period. It should include both the period leading up to the departure of the old leader and the period immediately following the hiring of the new leader. It is more likely to be an 18-month than a 6-month process. Calling for both stamina and a great deal of perspective, it's a bird's-eye and not a worm's-eye view.

Search committees want to know, for example, what worked for the previous CEO and what did not. Given the current state of the organization and of the economy, what special challenges will the new leader encounter? What particular organizational resources can the new leader depend on? If possible, the board should know the regular course of leadership in a particular organization. In some, for example, leaders encounter hard times proving themselves worthy of the last leader's legacy but, once beyond that challenge, the new leader tends to last a long time. This knowledge might lead the board to focus its efforts on helping the new leader through the inevitable early challenge. Other organizations may have repeatedly welcomed new leaders with great, perhaps exaggerated anticipation. Then, let down by the first signs of the newcomer's mortality and obsessed about each flaw, the organization hounds the new leader to leave. Knowing and preparing for these regular patterns substantially increases the possibility of future success.

During periods of leadership transition, there is usually little time or appetite for full-fledged current state analyses to go with full-fledged strategic plans. Modified, briefer analysis, however, is possible and important.

A Brief, Effective SWOT Analysis

SWOT is an acronym for strengths, weaknesses, opportunities, and threats. Strengths and weaknesses are internal matters: How effective is the leadership team, the programs, resource allocation? Opportunities and threats come from the outside: What revenue streams have not yet been exploited; what partnerships have not yet been tried; what will be the impact of foundations having less to give? New leadership plays in all four of these categories. How much, for example, could a new leader motivate employees (currently a strength) and volunteers (an underutilized opportunity) during times of economic hardship (threat), and how much can he change the crisis orientation (weakness) to a deliberate and strategic culture (potential strength)?

Ordinarily, SWOT analyses take months to complete and include many interviews, focus groups, financial analyses, and organizational assessments. Even when there is a strategic plan in place that guides current operations and tactics, the announcement of a leadership transition suggests the need to revisit this plan. Many organizations decide to wait until the new leadership is on board to review or address strategic planning; and, in fact, within six months of having new leaders take the helm of an organization, an in-depth strategic planning process should occur. During the leadership transition period, a much more compact process is needed, a process that focuses on the organization's relationship to leadership.

Facilitation

Although it is possible for an organization to conduct a current state analysis internally, it helps immensely to hire a professional facilitator-planner who is not personally invested in particular outcomes, who knows how to bring conflicting positions to compromise, and who will move the process along. An experienced transition consultant may begin her consultation with the organization in this manner.

Begin with a Coordinating Group

One way of approaching an analysis is to put together a coordinating group of eight to ten members, drawing from all the major organizational stakeholders: board members, members of the ongoing management team, perhaps a funder, and, if possible, one or two concerned outsiders who understand how the organization is perceived by the outside world.

A Contract

At the beginning, the group needs to reach an agreement, a "contract," on how decisions will be made (consensually, by majority, or by leaving it to the board's executive committee).

An Analysis

Boards that are candid and as forward-looking as possible will further the analysis of how effective the organization is and can be. This is called a gap analysis, and it speaks to the gap between what the organization could be and what it currently is. The new leader will be hired primarily to close that gap.

The coordinating group is asked to bring relevant information to the table: budget and balance sheet, strength assessments of senior managers, cultural analysis, organization chart, program evaluations, and so on. A member of the group should meet with the entire senior management team or key staff to determine that truth telling has been part of the organization's culture and to make sure that the board has been receiving both the good news and the bad news about performance metrics. It's essential to analyze the strengths, weaknesses, and learning opportunities afforded to the staff. Is the organization growing leadership internally? Although it is not always healthy to promote from within an organization, nonprofits have an obligation to the sector to collectively grow strong leaders for the entire community.

Brief reports are made and analysis of the whole is conducted. The emphasis here is on what will enable or disable the effectiveness of the soon-to-be-hired leader. The reporting can take place in a day's work.

Recommendations

There are two main objectives for the SWOT analysis: to understand the organization and to develop a set of concrete recommendations about improvements that need to be made. Along with the strategic initiatives themselves, these operational recommendations form the basis for the new leader's job description. If, for example, organizational growth has outpaced the introduction of personnel, information, evaluation, and other systems, you will want a new leader with skill and experience in putting systems into place. If, on the other hand, the organization has become slowed and dulled by too many rules, too much hierarchy, and too little creativity and inspiration, you will look for more of an entrepreneurial and inspirational leader.

Objectives

If strategies take the organization from here to there and current state analyses describe what is here, they also have to know where they are going. In other words, what are the organization's objectives? An *objective* is a specific, concrete, measureable achievement. For example, "the work of the organization will change from 40 to 75 percent of students graduating high school; 100 new affordable housing units will be created in a neighborhood; the organization will increase the confidence of low-achieving youth as measured by their ability to get jobs and thereby help them to achieve more."

Sometimes it is easiest to understand things by what they are not. Objectives are not missions. Missions invoke big-pictures goals. For example, an organization might want all the children in its neighborhood to live productive lives. How will the organization know that children's lives are productive or that the children are on the way to being productive? Greater graduation rates, fewer teenage pregnancies, and increased engagement in civic activities or other indicators of mission achievement may become the objectives.

In other words, objectives stand between mission and strategy. Once the mission is known, it can be broken down into concrete, measurable, and achievable objectives. Then strategies are developed to reach the objectives.

Like strategies, objectives must be prioritized. For example, the organization to end homelessness could aim to improve the education of all young women so that they are rarely out of a job. It could develop workforce development programs, housing programs, neighborhood consciousness programs, day care, after school, or maternity education programs. But few nonprofits are likely to succeed at all of these programs. Instead, the organization may do well to focus on one or two primary objectives around which it can center its resources.

Ultimately, leaders are judged by their ability to move organizations in the direction of their objectives. By clarifying objectives during the transition period, the board clarifies what they are asking leaders to do and how their accomplishments will be measured.

Effective Strategy

Earlier, *strategy* was defined as a cause and effect story. It is a broad-based plan to achieve objectives, a bridge between the current state of the organization and where it wants to go, a way to focus and leverage resources. When selecting new leaders, describing the strategic direction helps people understand what the organization really is and what kind of leadership is required. How potential leaders respond to this strategic direction will give the search committee as good an indication of fit as it can find.

Not surprisingly, there are many different approaches to strategy development or strategic planning, as it is commonly called.

Peter Drucker's Key Questions

To develop an effective plan, Drucker poses five questions.[1] They are deceptively simple:

1. What is our business (mission)?
   - What are we trying to achieve?
   - What specific results are we seeking?

2. Who is our customer: primary and supporting?

3. What does the customer consider value?
   - How well are we providing value?
   - How can we use what our customers consider value to become more effective?

4. What have been our results?
   - How well are we using our resources?

5. What is our plan?
   - Where should we focus our efforts?
   - What, if anything, should we do differently?

Notice, above all, Drucker's focus on the customer. For him, strategic planning is not primarily about operations but what you want to achieve, how you are going to do it, how you are going to measure it, how you are going to make adjustments to improve the quality of your work, and how you are going to hold yourself accountable to keep this process going.

Bridgespan's Key Questions

The Bridgespan Group emphasizes a balance between accountability to a plan and flexibility in adjusting the plan to its changing environment with these questions:[2]

1. "What are the organizational strengths that have made the organization successful in its work to date?

2. Given those strengths and their knowledge of how change occurs in their mission arena, what specific goals does the organization want to hold itself accountable for, over what time period?

3. What activities should the organization focus on to move furthest toward its goals?

4. Given the ever-changing nature of its work, how can the organization balance the desire to hold itself accountable for definite goals with the need to ensure that it has the necessary flexibility to respond quickly and appropriately to changing circumstances?"

La Piana's Approach

During the past few years, David La Piana[3] has popularized a business-like approach to nonprofit strategy planning. La Piana has long and deep experience in the nonprofit world but integrates corporate ideas, insisting that organizations determine their business model. To do so, they must answer these questions:

1. Who are you?

2. What do you do?

3. How do you do it?

4. How do you finance it?

La Piana wants nonprofits to create a strategic focus that gives them competitive advantage. This is where he departs from previous nonprofit norms. Most organizations do compete. When they go to funders or conferences, they trumpet their organization's strengths. But they compete quietly, and usually not by comparing themselves to others. That kind of "aggressive" competitiveness brings out discomfort in nonprofits and violates unwritten rules or values.

La Piana defines *competitive advantage* as the "ability to sustainably produce social value using a unique asset, outstanding execution, or both." The themes he identifies provide an excellent place for transitioning organizations to assess themselves.

Additional Qualities of Effective Strategy

There are some important, additional qualities of effective strategy that are not elaborated in the three schemes we have noted.

Flexibility

Most of the best strategies are flexibly applicable—over and again—to opportunities that arise. In other words, they have a large opportunistic component. This is the opposite of plans that assume a fixed future or are rigidly applied no matter what the context. Rather, they assume constant changes in the social and economic climate and changes wrought by technological advances. Strategies, themselves, can and must be flexible to fit a variable environment.

Suppose, for example, an organization believed that it needed to grow, that the benefits of scale would help it in innumerable ways, and that it could best scale up by acquiring other smaller organizations. To do so, it might develop certain criteria for good acquisitions, build a team to vet potential acquisitions, and then integrate them into the larger organizational structure and culture. But, as has often enough been the case, a large organization with many assets might be out of alignment and available to acquisition. In this case, the acquiring organization might flex its purchasing criteria and add its most senior team to the vetting process.

Let's go back to the organization dedicated to eliminate homelessness through job creation, inexpensive housing, and child care. Suppose an education program with teachers, curricula, and facilities becomes available. Might the organization flex and acquire the program? Might it argue that empowerment is the core strategy and that it can be augmented by education without there being either mission drift or too much of a departure from its core strategic focus? We think so.

What may be most important for purposes of leadership transition is that the search committee can articulate flexible strategic initiatives and interview candidates at least partly on their agility in applying them to future scenarios.

Affordability

There is no point in developing strategies that can't be implemented. This does not mean it must be obvious how to implement the strategy.

Sometimes strategic implementation is expensive but still affordable if other initiatives are dropped. For example, the Trustees of Reservations decided to stop buying and maintaining so much land—a strategic centerpiece for decades—and, instead turned more attention to education to increase its influence in the conservation movement.

Focus

The nature of good strategic planning is to force organizations to make choices. Strategic planning processes set priorities and insist that the organization focus resources on the areas most important to their mission. This will result in eliminating other activities that do not sufficiently move the mission forward. As we know, this kind of priority setting and focus is difficult to accomplish. Organizations tend to keep doing what they do even when it no longer makes strategic sense. There are people within each organization with vested interests in one approach, one project, or one department who will not easily let their preferred activities be eliminated. This is a matter of values, ego, habit, and fear of change. To be effective, however, the board of directors is charged with steering staff and volunteers toward the most strategic actions.

Leverage

In physics, *leverage* is defined as using a lever to increase force or power. In organizations, leverage has come to mean investing or intervening in a relatively small or focused way to create a big impact. In this sense, a strategic initiative should give the biggest bang for the buck. The objective might be to create a school that all local students want to attend. Perhaps it is decided that the best way to create the attraction is by bringing in highly qualified teachers and by advertizing their hires as though the organization were acquiring celebrities. These are two related strategies: to hire and to brand. The leverage may go this way: Better teachers attract more good teachers, which attract better students, which, in turn, make the school even more attractive for teachers, which makes the branding effort easier. Eventually, the organization may not even have to pay the teachers much more than other schools because the culture is so attractive. A virtuous cycle has been created in which an initial investment leads to positive effects, which lead to other positive effects. That is leverage.

These qualities—flexibility, affordability, focus, and leverage—provide a blueprint for interviewing leadership candidates, for checking their ability to reason in a strategic way. Here are the kinds of questions that emerge:

- How would a particular strategic approach proposed by the candidate be affordable?
- How would the candidate apply that new, affordable approach to changing circumstances?
- How, exactly, would the new initiative focus the organization's resources?
- How would the candidate overcome resistance to changes inevitably required by focus and priority setting?
- How would the candidate leverage the resources of this organization to increase its effectiveness?

In summary, no matter how urgent the need to bring in new leadership, bringing the strategic plan up to date is essential to a successful leadership search. Not all leaders will fit the organization's strategic plan to achieve its mission. Strategic fit with leaders trumps charisma, stature, credentials, and availability. First the organization needs to figure out where it's going. Only then can it know who it needs to lead it.

Discussion Questions

1. How does your strategic plan form the framework for the organization's unique objectives?
2. Having updated your strategic plan, what type of leadership will you need over the next few years?
3. What can you do during the leadership transition to bring constituents into supporting the strategic plan?

Endnotes

1 Drucker, Peter. *The Five Most Important Things That You Will Ever Ask About Your Organization*, Jossey-Bass, 1993.

2 Salls, Manda. "It's Back to Business Basics for Nonprofits," HBS Working Knowledge Newsletter, 2004.

3 LaPiana, David. *Nonprofit Strategy Revolution: Real-Time Strategic Planning in a Rapid-Response World*. Fieldstone Alliance, 2008.

5 ——————————————————————

Good Governance

In times of transition, manage carefully but think ambitiously. This is your opportunity to embolden your organization's passionate vision.

Ensuring Excellence in Governance

Governance in nonprofit organizations refers to the processes and structures used to ensure the accomplishment of the organization's mission. However, the concept of "good governance" expands to include the achievement of the mission while operating in a consistent and moral manner within the organization's culture.

What Makes for "Good Governance" During All Parts of an Organization's Life Cycle?

As we have discussed, everything that a nonprofit organization achieves is based on its mission and vision, and it is the board's responsibility to ensure that everyone involved in the organization and the communities it serves are aligned in their understanding and devotion. To keep so many constituents on track, the board leads the strategic planning process and becomes aware of the characteristics, traits, and skills that a CEO needs to best serve the organization. These are the framework around which the CEO search is designed.

The CEO is selected to be in concert with the mission and strategic plan, and the board supports and evaluates the CEO's leadership to ensure that it is in alignment with the organization. It also partners with the CEO in planning the process by which they will monitor the agency's progress toward the mission and develop the communication plan that is also aligned with the strategic plan. Board members enhance the organization's image in the community by working closely with the CEO to seek opportunities to give voice to the mission and illustrate how it is being achieved.

Finally, the board members do their own self-evaluation of how well board actions support the CEO in alignment with the mission and strategy; and they give continual attention to developing greater board competencies.

Shaping the Board and Future CEO Partnership

Board Source identifies 12 principles of governance that empower good governance.

1. Constructive Partnership

Boards that recognize their interdependent nature and that work at maintaining a constructive partnership with their CEO through effective communication build strategic and tactical forward movement toward their organization's mission.

One of the first tasks a board must do during leadership transition is to look at itself and ask the following:

- How can we organize ourselves to provide optimum support to the next CEO?
- What strengths have we brought to the partnership? What strengths must we continue to bring?
- What are our problems? What problems have we created for the former CEO?

It serves a board well to assess its partnership with a departing CEO to address any needed changes that will serve to build a healthy partnership with the next CEO.

When a departure follows a board-CEO conflict, the board must also ask itself:

- What have we done to bring about—or fail to resolve—the conflict?
- What have we failed to do to facilitate the CEO's success?

Until these questions are satisfactorily answered, there is no point in finding a new CEO. The planning and search processes will be flawed and the new hire doomed to failure.

2. Mission Driven

Boards that test their decisions and actions against their mission and strategic vision align their entire organization to achieve the mission through deliberate strategic priorities. A leadership departure creates an opportunity to revisit the organization's strategic plan and engage in evaluating how the board is supporting this plan as it welcomes new leadership.

3. Strategic Thinking

Boards spend time thinking and discussing what they are doing in relation to how their actions are leading the organization in the strategic direction that will best achieve their mission. As much as boards just want to start a search and fill the void left by a CEO, it is important to take the time to conduct a dialogue with the full board about how this leadership transition can be used in an optimal manner to move the organization forward. It is never useful to act before you have fully assessed the opportunity inherent in a leadership transition.

4. Culture of Inquiry

As a board embarks on a leadership transition, it is important to seek input from all members as well as other constituents. It is truly a time to seek more information to inform the board's planning, to question previous assumptions upon which the organization has acted; and to analyze all their options moving forward.

5. Independent

Each board member must seriously examine all the information available and come to a reasonable understanding of the options before entering into a group dialogue. In this manner, members can be assured that they have not been unduly influenced by another or lost an opportunity to look at an issue from a differing perspective.

6. Ethos of Transparency

During leadership transitions, it is essential that the board maintain transparency in their actions. Some grassroots boards, founders and inexperienced CEOs tend to keep plans and financial information close to the vest, trusting only their inner circle and sometimes their families with such vital matters. This situation leaves staff, and often the board, out in the cold, not feeling trusted and too ignorant to help plan and execute projects. These feelings rankle and limit commitment, cooperation, and collaboration, eroding administrative and even programmatic excellence.

The information that the board gathers and the resulting plans should be shared broadly with stakeholders. Internal staff and volunteers will most likely be feeling anxious during the transition; and the open sharing of the board's process and decisions will help to alleviate any unease. Although secrets poison, information sweetens the well and opens the organization to the thinking processes of many more stakeholders who are committed to the mission.

7. Compliance with Integrity

Boards that practice disciplined oversight of an organization are well served as they enter a transition period. They are aware of the budgetary implications of their strategic plan. They know what can be realistically financed with current financial resources, and they are aware of the priority strengths needed in their incoming leaders. With this knowledge in hand, they can revisit their vision, balance their current strategic plan for the interim, and begin an effective search process.

8. Sustaining Resources

Boards that are intimately involved in creating and sustaining resources are prepared to reach out to foundations and long-term partners and invite them to participate and contribute to the search process. Long-term funders are invested in the mission of an organization. These funders look for ways to have a catalytic impact on their achievement. Therefore, in addition to communicating with funders about the leadership transition, good governance boards look for opportunities to invite participation.

9. Results-Oriented

Boards that measure their organization's success by measureable outcomes know how to assess the current performance of services. They can more easily evaluate potential new opportunities, and they can communicate to potential leaders about their expectations for the future. This leads to an effective filtering of a pool of great candidates to select the candidate who is the best fit.

10. Intentional Board Practices

When a board is structured to provide all the governance duties that support organizational health, it is easy to realign members' strengths to support any necessary change. By being intentional in their provision of support, the board has an ongoing dialogue that enables it to refocus on the future of the organization rather than lamenting the departure of current leadership. It also has practiced thoughtfully addressing leadership needs directly in alignment with the strategic plan. Good governance dictates that the board plan for its succession in a manner that achieves representation of stakeholder and reflects the diversity of its community. The succession plan should make sure that on-board directors bring the needed experiences and expertise to fill out the profile of the board.

11. Continuous Learning

A board that has a practice of self-evaluation can easily utilize those skills to determine what positive or negative messages the leadership departure brings to the board's governance practices. The board more readily embraces the learning opportunities in a leader's departure as an event that will ultimately strengthen the organization, and they appreciate the opportunistic nature of what many boards initially interpret as a crisis.

12. Revitalization

Good governance demands that boards anticipate and plan for leadership changes. After all, if you accept little or no change, the organization becomes stagnant at best and potentially begins to recede in its effectiveness. There are even schools of thought that believe professional leadership should have term limits in much the same manner as volunteer board leadership. In this complex society, an argument can be made that maintaining the same CEO for 30 years actually stunts the organization's ability to benefit from new perspectives and differing leadership styles. At any rate, when leadership transition occurs, an organization gains the benefit of revitalization from the leadership of new people with fewer assumptions about what works in the best interest of the organization and how new opportunities might be addressed.

The Board's Legal and Ethical Duties

In addition to the 12 Principles of Governance, 5 basic duties ensure the legal and ethical conduct of the board.

1. Loyalty in the Best Interest of the Organization

Simply stated, board members must put the best interest of the organization above any personal gain. Examples of loyalty that come into play during leadership transition include the duty to select the best volunteer leadership for the board regardless of personal interests or connections. During a transition of the CEO position, should any board member choose to apply for the CEO position, loyalty to the best interest of the organization would require that he step out of his board position. The duty of loyalty also demands that board members put personal connections aside to allow for a carefully structured search process. That eliminates short circuiting the search or trying to position friends or colleagues to gain advantages outside of the stated search process.

A board member who served on the board of a Senior Citizens Center told how that board utilized the advice of a nonprofit capacity building agency in setting up its search process for a new CEO. The process was clear and transparent and based on a thorough assessment of the Center's needs. The search committee had selected the pool of candidates and conducted interviews to determine the final three candidates. Then the search committee chair announced that he had come to realize that none of the candidates could fulfill the CEO position as well as he and proceeded to put himself into the final pool. Although some members were uncomfortable, they knew and liked the search chair. None of the other candidates was as familiar with the Center, and no one else would consider taking the position for the salary he professed willingness to accept.

In fairly short order, the search was corrupted and the search chair/board member was hired in the CEO position. Within six months, it became evident to the board that this new CEO was not the leader they needed. However, reluctance to approach their friend resulted in three years of chaos and a significant reduction of funding and services before they fired him.

2. Disclosure of Any Potential Conflict of Interest

During a leadership transition, it is important that the staff, the operations volunteers, and the public be assured that board members are acting in the best interest of the organization. They need to operate with transparency in developing and implementing an objective search process and separate personal business interests from their board roles. This becomes particularly difficult when a nonprofit is endeavoring to save money by using discounted or free services. It is difficult to hold a fellow board member to professional performance when he is donating his services.

An example of good intentions gone awry was shared by a search committee member for a youth orchestra. One of the members of the board owned a firm that specialized in placing administrative staff. He volunteered to provide the CEO search out of his firm as his personal contribution to the organization. The organization had limited reserves and did not want to deplete them with a fee to an independent search firm. So, the board agreed to use the contributed service in conjunction with a volunteer search committee that would act as the experts on what was needed specifically for this organization's leadership.

The process got underway, and everything seemed to be proceeding smoothly until the chair of the search committee became ill and had to resign. The board member who owned the human resources firm stepped into the leadership vacuum. His perceptions about the skills and talents needed for the CEO position differed from the volunteers on the search committee. He agreed to find candidates who met the committee's requirements; however, the pool of candidates was insufficient, and eventually the search had to be restarted with another firm. As a result, the board lost six months of effort, and one of its valued members resigned in embarrassment.

3. Duty of Care

Directors are charged to perform their board duties with the care that an ordinarily prudent person in a like position would exercise in similar circumstances. Directors need to develop and maintain their knowledge and understanding of the organization and the field of work in which it engages. During a leadership transition, the board's ability to represent its organization throughout the community is put to the test. Board members should be actively engaged in constituent meetings, helping to shape the organization's readiness for new leadership. They should embrace opportunities to engage with their communities in sharing the organization's vision, and they may be called upon to meet with funders, legislators, and other constituents to maintain the organization's position within the community.

4. Managing the Organization's Funds in a Manner That Serves the Mission of the Organization

The board is responsible for ensuring that there are sufficient resources for the organization to fund its strategic plan and to take significant action in alignment with the mission. Within this responsibility is the need to provide financial oversight to the organization. The board is responsible for protecting the organization's assets and for ensuring that sufficient financial controls are in place.

The community expects the board to serve as its overseers in using contributions for its charitable purposes. In a small organization, the absence of the CEO often requires active participation by members of the finance committee to ensure that it is possible to continue proper checks and balances. In addition, broader budgetary oversight is necessary if there is not sufficient expert staff to engage in operational processes. There may be a need for meetings with finance staff on a regular basis.

5. Set Policies for Employment Practices, and Oversee Implementation of Personnel Policies for Both Volunteers and Staff

The board assures that the framework is in place for the organization to function legally and ethically as an employer. Boards need to review the human resource policies to ensure that they are up to date and reflective of the board's philosophy before engaging in a CEO search. Some boards choose to develop a separate agreement with the CEO; however, any agreement should be developed in concert with the personnel policies.

The board works in partnership with the CEO to ensure that the levels of authority and responsibility between the board of directors and staff members are clear and that the organization chart depicts these levels clearly. Any necessary interim reporting relationships during the transition should be communicated with the staff.

When board members accept these responsibilities and duties at an active level, they set the foundation for continually being prepared for leadership transitions in both volunteer and staff positions. When the entire board is active in fulfilling these five duties, there is always a pool of people with resources and knowledge ready to lead the organization successfully through transition.

Governance Challenges During CEO Transitions

Few presidents of nonprofit boards take their positions thinking that they would like to lead a CEO transition. In fact, it's not unusual to exact a promise from the CEO that she will stay through the current board president's term when accepting the nomination as a volunteer leader. However, the stewardship of a nonprofit organization cannot be handed over to the CEO by the board without maintaining an active partnership, no matter how much a board respects the CEO's skills, talent, and integrity. Concurrently, even if the president is seen as "walking on water" by the community, she alone cannot steer the ship of a nonprofit organization.

In a world that is increasingly polarized in every area, nonprofit boards must hold organizations in trust for the community through the dedication, skills, and talent of the entire board membership. The governance committee leads the board in developing its members to think and act strategically during a time of transition. Effective practices dictate that the governance committee works year round to strengthen the capacity of the board to ensure success in an organization. If the board is constituted with active members who are educated about the organization they serve and engaged in its strategic plan, a transition in leadership can be accommodated without the board losing its direction.

However, boards are made up of real people, with full lives, personal agendas, and an affinity to resisting change. As a result, the announcement of a resignation from the CEO or from the president is bound to be met with a level of consternation and some amount of chaos. Often when the board has operated for many years with the same CEO, there is complacency about the governance work of the board. Of course, board members are aware of their stewardship responsibilities, but they've become accustomed to their "fit" with this CEO and have grown to expect that the CEO will handle most of the "heavy lifting" for the organization. The long-term partnership has been built upon trust, experience, and negotiated ways of work, all of which need to be rebuilt after what looms in the "too near" distance following a search process involving a lot of work.

It's no wonder that boards sometimes hold onto their CEOs long past their strategic fit with the organization. They know this CEO's skills and capabilities. They've seen what the CEO can deliver for the organization, and they've gotten used to accommodating her weaknesses. It is just easier to stay with the status quo. Most likely, the CEO has been the primary representative of the organization within the community. The community places trust in the organization by what it knows about the CEO. The board may not see the timing of the CEO's departure as optimal for the organization, with each member secretly wishing that the CEO transition could be deferred to the year after they complete their tenure on the board.

Of course, there are also circumstances in which the CEO's announced departure is met with relief, or even jubilation. The partnership of a CEO and a board does not always fulfill initial expectations. The CEO may find the demands of the job to be more than anticipated. He may not learn to love the culture of the organization. The board may become doubtful of the CEO's operational decisions, or the CEO may not agree with the strategic vision of the board. The CEO may simply not be able to meet performance expectations. Whatever the reason, it is the board's job to govern the organization and continue to hold it in stewardship for the community while seeking new leadership.

Once the strategic planning process is in place and performance metrics have been established, it is time to conduct an assessment of the capacity of the board of directors.

There are many checklists available for board self-evaluation, which includes assessment of the board's understanding of the mission, goals, programs, finances, and fund development. Two are included in Appendix C, "Sample CEO Job Descriptions." They are meant to be illustrative, not definitive. In addition, board evaluations are available through *Board Source* and through *The Drucker Foundation Self-Assessment Tool.*

Sample Board Self-Assessment Checklist

1. Do all board members understand the organization's mission?

2. Is the board's diversity and expertise sufficient to represent the organization throughout the community? Are the right people with the right competencies in place to steer this strategic plan? What new competencies are needed? Are there board members who need to step down because they do not currently have the time, skills, experience, or passion that is required?

3. Do board members effectively communicate and champion the organization's key message throughout the community?

4. Can board members describe the programs provided by the organization? Can they explain the outcomes that result from those programs?

5. Do board members receive regular and sufficient periodic reports on finances, fund development, programs, performance outcomes, and achievement of strategic goals to provide effective oversight? Does the cost/service ratio make sense?

    Boards often have unrealistic expectations of how much it costs to run the organization they govern. Perhaps they believe that their voluntary contributions of time and expertise are sufficient; however, volunteering on a board does not pay the utility bills. The board may need to ask the finance department for an orientation to the true costs connected to each hour of service to the community. Although many board members are initially surprised at how high the cost is, they come to understand the cost of not providing the organization's programs to the community, and this empowers them with the reality necessary to really sell their mission.

6. Do board members have a clear understanding of their roles and responsibilities? Do they hold themselves accountable to focus on the most important strategic issues? Are the board structure, committees, and evaluation process effective? Can you identify significant contributions that board members have made in the past year?

7. Does the board participate in setting fund development strategy, and are they actively involved in fund-raising?

8. Does the board regularly evaluate the CEO (at least annually formally), provide effective feedback, and offer the opportunity for continued professional development?

   Has the board developed a process to transfer the intellectual capital of the current CEO to the organization's collective knowledge base?

9. Does the board make policy decisions in a manner that effectively guides the operational work of staff? What kind of bench strength exists on your staff? Does interim leadership need to be engaged during this transition? Does the board designate a percentage of the annual budget for staff development? Do staff members receive cross training on essential tasks?

10. Do board members declare any conflict of interest they encounter, and do they maintain confidentiality about board matters?

Although reviewing the achievement of the basic board functions is helpful, the most important self-evaluation process is for the board to participate in a guided discussion through which the full board assesses its leadership. The board should examine its strategic successes and areas in which it needs to change direction. It should weigh the fiscal stability of the organization and the board's role in raising significant funds to sustain and grow the mission. Finally, the board should assess each member's personal strengths and resources, experience, and expertise contributed.

The board needs to ask the following questions:

1. Do we have the fund development capability to support the strategic plan?

   All too often, CEOs have departed out of frustration with a board that refuses to face reality in developing a strategic plan that the organization can actually fund. Now, with the CEO departure, the board thinks that all that needs to happen is to find a new CEO who is a money-raising machine. Although there are CEOs who have significant fund development skills, this is not an issue that is solved simply by finding a new leader. The board members may need to add donor tracking software, prepare to build an experienced fund development department (a significant investment in itself), and most importantly, step up to the plate themselves.

2. Do members make an annual donation to the organization that is in the range of their top three charitable gifts and is truly a stretch given their funding ability? Do board members mine their social networks for funding connections, assist with preparing donors to be solicited by communicating their passion for the mission, and find the right person to accompany the staff on a donor visit to ask for significant contributions? Does the board recognize the need for a portion of the organization's funds to support capacity building rather than earmarking all monies directly to program?

The officers of the board should anticipate planned and sudden transition of volunteer and staff leadership. An annual assessment of the volunteer leadership transition plan might include discussing how each board member has worked to develop the expertise needed to lead the next phase required in the strategic plan. Discussion should also center on the development of staff leadership. One of the keys to maintaining a tenured CEO is to provide the opportunity for continual renewal through professional learning experiences.

When volunteer leaders transition off a board, a process should be put in place for the exiting leaders to orient the new leaders to the organization's ways of work, governance strategy, and oversight instruments. Much as sailors sign off from their watch by updating their successors,

exiting leaders should provide incoming leadership with a clear understanding of the organization's position in the community in relationship
to their mission. They should discuss any upcoming potential issues, disclose the financial health of the organization, and thoroughly discuss the
funding plan. They should conduct a review of the most recent audit and
discuss any needed action with the audit committee and incoming and
outgoing leadership.

Boards should consider certain key questions on a periodic basis, but
particularly at the point of leadership transition. Are the board and staff
in agreement about the strategic priorities of the organization? Is the
strategic plan implemented effectively throughout operations? All too
often, strategic planning is seen as an exercise to placate the board. In
reality, each department may continue its traditional ways of work with
the majority of available resources and allocate little of the work effort to
the organization's strategic plan.

One CEO who had recently been hired to lead a family services
agency talked about how clearly the search committee and board leadership had described their strategic plan to expand services to developing
immigrant populations that had moved into their service area. However,
when she started meeting with staff, she encountered significant resistance to this goal. One staff member told her that these targeted populations "did not value family." Another staff person stated that the
organization's primary clients would not feel safe if immigrants were to
take over the agency. A third staff member agreed that indeed this strategic priority made sense. However, three years after targeting these new
populations, there was no one on staff who spoke the immigrants' lan-
guages, understood their cultures, or had made any inroads into becoming knowledgeable of the targeted communities. The new CEO had to
begin her work on the strategic plan by doing a realistic assessment of
operations. She brought the board and staff together to work out a true
partnership about the strategic priorities. The board was astounded
because reports had only shown good news about a small number of families who were comfortable in the majority culture and had been served
successfully.

A second core area that the board needs to keep apprised of is the
public's perception of the organization. The board should participate in
developing the key message that the organization communicates to
stakeholders. It is important that board members take every opportunity

in their communities to actively communicate key messages, endorse the agency's work, and market the mission. An incoming CEO observed that, during the search process, she Googled key board members and researched them on Facebook. She was pleasantly surprised by how many of them used their Internet presence to endorse the organization and raise its visibility.

Although branding an organization is a continual process, it is essential that the board pay close attention to the organization's image during a leadership transition. Stakeholders are looking for assurance that the organization will remain stable throughout transition. Ne'er-do-wells are looking for signs of trouble and will overinterpret any missteps on the part of the organization as sure signs of doom. An active and positive board shows staff and clients that business will continue. Also, members of the community who are considering becoming engaged in the organization will assess the quality of leadership throughout the transition as major indicators of how they will succeed.

Often during transitions, there is new board-level information about things that have gone wrong. It is often strategic to keep this information within the domain of the board except in special circumstances. If the transition is occurring on a less-than-positive basis, it may be within the board's discretion to hold personal information not required legally to be disclosed in confidence. Although American society loves drama and gossip, sharing war stories from the boardroom can create significant liability and serve to lessen respect for the board member as well as the organization.

Preferably, any new volunteer leaders, such as the president and executive committee members, will have already served as members of the board. Nonetheless, taking over the leadership reins of a nonprofit organization as the president of the board requires a complete orientation to fiscal and legal responsibilities as well as understanding the full position description. Often, organizations associated with a national movement will receive training for the board president from the national affiliate. In addition, many community organizations dedicated to increasing capacity within the nonprofit sector offer board president training as well as training for other officers and board members at large. In addition to any other available training, the governance committee serves as the team that orients new board members.

In a time of leadership transition, it is important that board recruitment and development continue. When new volunteer leadership is recruited, the governance committee helps them understand the roles and responsibilities as well as the current board structure and bylaws. The board orientation helps the new leadership understand the history of the organization, the current strategic plan, the financial position, and the programs and services that are delivered through the organization.

Professionalizing the Employed Leadership Transition Process as a Responsibility of the Board

Leadership transitions at the CEO level provide the opportunity for the board to improve the organization on a professional basis. This is particularly true for organizations seeking to move beyond their grassroots origins and style, but it also holds true for established institutions where leadership transition is the culmination of a long, painful process that divided the community or where a founder or long-time leader with a particular style or skill set has created an organization with complementary characteristics. Before we consider the transition itself, it is worth outlining some of the goals to which the board might aspire.

Key Organizational Processes

The processes that distinguish the transition to professional management are well known and easily distilled.

1. Delegation of Responsibility and Authority

As organizations grow in size and complexity, boards must hire effective professional leaders and trust them to do their job. Often enough, professionals are hired but not trusted. Subsequent micromanagement leads to a high rate of turnover. Alternatively, less qualified candidates may be hired. They do an inadequate job, confirming the board's belief that it is responsible for everything and must make all key decisions. The lack of trust on the part of the board creates a self-fulfilling prophecy.

Without trust, the new CEO is hampered from moving into the leadership role for which the board has hired him. The board must take the leap of faith in its candidate to extend the necessary trust. Otherwise, the passage of the mantle of leadership is stopped in midair. In addition, when CEOs have been granted sufficient autonomy to do their job, they often have to learn and apply the same lessons about delegation and collaboration with both staff and volunteer leaders. The board should encourage and reinforce the expansion of this leadership base so that the organization can continue to grow.

2. Consistency

Sometimes grassroots, founding CEOs, and new CEOs with less experience are impulsive—perhaps that is the flip side of their previous entrepreneurial experience that called for daring and creativity. Staff and board members want and need some degree of consistency. They need to know what to expect, what tasks they are responsible for, and how their performance will be evaluated. There's nothing new here: The American Revolution was fought to replace the whimsical power of even benevolent kings with a written constitution whose rules were known and applied to all. In this sense, the transition to professional management is revolutionary. Both the board and the CEO, in partnership, must demonstrate consistency.

3. Planning and Prioritizing

Typically, founders and grassroots boards don't have the luxury of planning far into the future. There is simply too much start-up work that takes precedence, or they are wearing too many hats in the organization. They are absorbed in the struggle to survive, trusting that they will "feel" their way through even the most complex decisions. What plans they do make, they often keep to themselves. Secrets and factions may abound on founding boards and between the board and the first CEO. To succeed, managers (as well as others) need to consider their present actions in the context of plans and goals. Otherwise, it is hard to prioritize—to know what, of all that needs doing, is important and what is trivial. To marshal organizational resources, CEOs, boards, and staff—and probably constituent groups—must share the same information and the same basic goals.

4. Control

During their initial phases, organizations rarely exercise sufficient controls over key processes like budgets, member recruitment, fund-raising, and staff performance. As the organization grows in size and complexity, these controls become essential to maintaining financial viability and educational quality. There's an irony here. Founders and grassroots boards are often known as micromanaging "control freaks," and this very nature limits the existence of formal controls managed by others. This, in turn, decreases their control. As organizations grow, boards must learn to trust CEOs and management processes precisely to maintain control.

Board Self-Evaluation

As discussed previously, those who select and manage the employed head of the organization need to evaluate not only the new CEO but also themselves and the processes that they have put in place. Board self-evaluation is part of the overall cycle of leadership and is critical to bringing a professional perspective to the process. It also leads to the successful alignment of the CEO, the organization, and the community.

Changing the Board's Composition

During the transition, board members may be assuming more day-to-day responsibilities as well as search responsibilities. For this reason, the board may need to reorganize. This process also provides the opportunity to address board issues and confront disruptive board members. Often individual board behavior that has been benignly irritating can create a schism within the board. Therefore, it is wise for the board to take the time to reorient itself to the mission, board responsibilities, ways of work, and ethical communications within the board and to be sure all members are playing constructive roles.

A board member should not become the interim CEO. Such appointments break down important distinctions between board and staff responsibilities. A board member cannot serve both the board and as interim CEO without at least the question of motives and priorities. The stress such crossing of boundaries places upon the entire board and the staff is untenable and is unlikely to result in a positive transition to the new CEO. Furthermore, after the new CEO is in place, the only way to re-create the balance between the board, staff, and CEO is for the organization to remove that valuable board member or for the board member to make a difficult transition back to the prior role. Finally, it is a rare board member who has the time, expertise, or relevant experience to be a better candidate than a professional nonprofit interim director.

Examining the Partnership of the President and CEO

Although the CEO serves at the pleasure of the entire board, the quality of the president and CEO relationship can make or break an organization. (See the Introduction and Chapter 1, "What Makes Nonprofit Leadership So Challenging?") This partnership going awry often becomes the basis of an unexpected leadership transition. These two partners must work together to lead the strategic development of the organization. They monitor communication of the vision, mission, and values as well as setting direction for programs. Each has a specific role. The CEO is hired to carry out the strategic direction of the organization with the support of the board. The president is charged with guiding the governance process. Together, they are responsible to stakeholders for the success of the organization in achieving its mission.

It is important that the president and CEO set agreed-upon expectations of each other so that they can perform in a unified manner. The dynamic of their leadership must be based on respect and strong continual communication. In successful partnerships, the two devote time and effort to open discussions about what each can expect from the other as well as agreeing to the logistics of how they will work together. They should develop a "no surprises" policy and be committed to communication that is open to discussing differences and working out conflicts beyond their own egos. Trust is developed or lost over time, and the erosion of trust by dishonesty is hard to rebuild. The president trusts that the CEO is carrying out the strategic direction of the board, whereas the CEO trusts that the president will lead the board in making sound decisions in carrying out its governance responsibilities.

Nonetheless, there are some inherent problems between these two roles. First, the partners seldom start at the same time, and they rarely share the same length of tenure. One is almost always in place, with the advantage of tenure, when the other arrives in her leadership position. Second, the CEO is much closer to the day-to-day activities of the organization and has greater knowledge of the other board members. The president leads the board of directors, and the CEO is accountable to it. The president leads the board in evaluating the CEO and the board's own performance. These realities require a high level of maturity and objectivity on the part of both partners.

There are practices and procedures that can minimize the conflict potential in this partnership:

- There should be written procedures for the board's annual evaluation of the CEO. The evaluation process should allow for significant input from the CEO about his own performance.
- When a new partnership is created, the two leaders should take time to discuss and determine how they will work together as a team. The CEO's as well as the president's accountabilities should be mutually developed and put in writing to be reviewed by the entire board.
- The president should ask for input from the CEO when appointing committee chairs and members.
- There should be clear written directions to staff supporting board committees so that the CEO's authority for direction to staff is not truncated.
- Boards should have full discussions on policy issues rather than allowing the president to presuppose policy solutions.
- The organization should conduct regular orientations to ensure that all members understand the role of the board and its current committees.
- The organization should ensure that the president possesses basic meeting management skills by providing training if necessary.
- The president and CEO should completely share all information with the full board. Every board member has the right and inherent responsibilities of knowing the status of the organization.

When It Is Time to Make a Transition Happen

Sometimes the CEO initiates a change. Other times the board does this. The annual evaluation of the CEO offers a regular opportunity to evaluate continuing and comparative effectiveness. It also sets the stage for frank discussions of unmet expectations on either side. One of the best questions to be asked each year is, "Do you feel continuing excitement about your role, and do you feel that you are still uniquely qualified to lead the organization in achieving its mission?" If either side waivers in answering that question affirmatively, it's time to discuss a plan for renewal or eventual succession. In the case of founders and long-term CEOs, it should not be an insult—rather a recognition of the organization's and the leaders developmental needs—to have this annual conversation.

It is a significant task of governance to ensure that appropriate leadership stands at the helm of the organization. Far too often, boards let minimal leadership continue for a lack of will to address this difficult issue. The development of an annual process that creates the necessary dialogue for both the CEO and board leadership takes the personal stress out of the issue and emphasizes the organization's vision and strategy where it belongs.

In considering whether it is time to initiate the transition, the board members consider what plans and obligations need to be deferred, delayed, or transferred to staff or board during the leadership transition. The board should pay particularly close attention to funder obligations as well as ongoing fund development, service delivery, and staff maintenance and development. Wherever the transition has impact on constituents and stakeholders, the board must create a communication plan to let them know what will be done when and why this timeline is necessary at the appropriate moment in the transition.

How the board performs during transition will speak to the community about the efficacy of the organization. Communities place a high level of trust and expectation of performance on the boards of nonprofit organizations because they are charged with investing the community's resources of time, talent, and money to enhance the ability of the community to care for its members. Effective stewardship under the community spotlight is possible only if the board has a disciplined practice of good governance.

In summary, a leadership transition demands of a board that it step up its governance and organizational oversight. It is a time of high demand upon board members in exchange for incredible opportunities to create a seismic change in the organization's ability to achieve its mission. This is the fulfillment of years of board service. Board members can collectively serve the community with a level of stewardship that will enhance, if not redefine, the organization's vision for its future in the community.

Discussion Questions

1. What are the key areas in which a board needs to step up its performance in governing well?
2. What opportunities exist in this leadership transition to catapult an organization toward mission achievement?
3. What is the ideal partnership a board should establish with the new leadership?

6

Alignment

"Leaders establish the vision for the future and set the strategy for getting there; they cause change. They motivate and inspire others to go in the right direction and they, along with everyone else, sacrifice to get there."
—*John Kotter*

Guiding Principle

The fundamental challenge of leadership is to align organizations in the service of their missions, as articulated in strategies. This is a complex statement that we need to unpack before laying out its full meaning.

First, boards need to be concerned with leadership, not just leaders, and leadership transitions, not just the change of leaders. Leadership is concerned with organizational objectives, not just and not primarily the character of the leader. New leaders should not be chosen because they are charismatic, smart, experienced, charming, or any other such quality, although these characteristics are often important in their success. New leaders should be selected for their ability to implement the organization's strategic plan, to realize its objectives, to bring its mission closer to the practical world: in short, to get things done.

Leadership is enacted through a web of relationships—staff, board of directors, funders, community members—that enables the organization to accomplish its goals. The finest leader or the best-looking leader may or may not be able to form and sustain these relationships. Or he may have been able to form relationships in one setting but not in others. So it is not the individual but the relationship that is the most important thing.

131

Strategy

Nonprofits are mission-driven organizations. But missions can be a little broad and idealistic in their definition:

> "Ending homelessness"

> "Affordable housing for everyone who needs it"

> "Leveling the playing field for all children through equal educational opportunity"

Strategy is more limited. It first tells how an organization is going to realize its mission and what practical steps will be taken to achieve it. It also, implicitly, uncovers the compromises an organization needs to make. For instance, a practical goal might be to reduce homelessness by 50 percent within the next 10 years, and the strategic plan will address that 50 percent reduction—not 100 percent. This is what is meant by "mission, as articulated by strategy."

Alignment

The next challenge is resource alignment. Nonprofits always have limited resources to work with: less money, fewer people, fewer people who are highly trained, fewer buildings, and less political capital than they would like. So they have to make the most of what they have. To succeed, they not only have to focus and prioritize their resources on clear objectives and strategic approaches, but they have to make sure that each resource supports and amplifies the others. Nonprofits depend on synergies and must align people, finance, and reputation to create those synergies.

Finally, organizational alignment is not something leaders can simply conceive of as "out there." They must look at themselves and ask if they are aligned with the organization that they are charged to lead. They must be aligned with the organizational strategy. They must believe in it, believe in the capacity to make it happen, and believe that they know how to bring others on board with it. They must inspire others to experience their leadership as aligned with them. What is more, the leader's skills, values, personal goals, and styles of leadership must mesh with the resources, culture, objectives, and mission of the organization she leads.

Leadership as Alignment

In his iconic book, *From Good to Great,* Jim Collins focuses like a laser on a single proposition: the importance of having "the right people on the bus" in the right seats and at the right time. It's a compelling and deceptively simple picture of alignment. If you get people on board, doing things that they both believe in and are capable of doing, and if you coordinate their efforts, you should succeed. Collins, however, insists that the "who" is more important than the "what." In other words, really talented people will succeed no matter what is asked of them, and they will even figure out what is the most important thing to do. This may be true in the corporate world, where profits are such a clear objective. It doesn't work quite as well for the nonprofit sector.

When it comes to nonprofits, the "what" comes first. It is essential that boards know what their organization's mission is and understand what strategy articulates that mission. Only then can they find people (the who) who best address the work (the what) with vigor and commitment. Gathering brilliant people is not alone the touchstone of organizational strategy. David Halberstam's *The Best and the Brightest*, the story of John Kennedy's brilliant administrative team, shows the fallacy of just finding the most talented people. They may be enamored of their own brilliance and caught up in their own need for recognition and their own personal goals. As a result, they can lose sight of the collective goals. In general, all-star teams, made up of the best individual players, typically lose to well-coordinated, close-knit teams of less talented players who like playing with one another—and want to win for the team.

The belief that fit, alignment, and relationship are at least as important as individual leadership talent is paramount in selecting the CEO candidate that will best serve an organization. Here's the basic concept.

If you assume that leaders have skill and motivation, and the majority of leaders have this in abundance, the fit between leaders and their circumstance turns out to be a better predictor of effectiveness than any particular set of personal characteristics. Winston Churchill may have been a magnificent wartime leader, but he was often inept during times of peace. The Civil Rights Movement was attributed to the leadership of Martin Luther King, Ralph Abernathy, Stokely Carmichael, and others with considerable oratorical flair. Yet much of the grassroots leadership came from virtually unsung black women whose years of church and community participation had positioned them and honed their skills perfectly for organizing local political campaigns. They were the right people at the right time and in the right place to lead one of the most crucial phases of the movement. It is doubtful that anyone else could have done their job.

In *Leadership in Nonprofit Organizations,* a pluralistic idiom is adopted that describes how many kinds of leaders fit in distinctive ways with different kinds of organizations: entrepreneurs during the start-up phase of organizations; managers for more mature times; and local people, deeply immersed in community for community-based organizations. Even a venture capitalist might be good to lead a rapidly built organization that "scales up" exciting pilot projects. Community organizers like Barack Obama, with their own disparate backgrounds, are naturals to bring together disparate elements of the communities they work in, like the Chicago South Side, to win legislative and economic victories.

Fit

What exactly is meant by the word *fit*? It is a word, like *rhythm* or *timing,* that is often bandied about but rarely defined or understood. Of rhythm and timing, people say "you've got it or you don't." But it can be defined, taught, and learned. Boards can time organizational interventions to the moment when people can use them. A process can describe how managers can most effectively introduce innovative programs and manage substantial change projects by paying attention to the readiness of their followers.

In a similar vein, *Leadership in Nonprofit Organizations* demystifies the idea of fit. When it is unpacked, this apparently simple idea, upon examination of its various parts, comes out looking like alignment. We described the powerful impact of a leader's character, skills, values, and personal objectives being aligned with the character of her organization, its defining structures and processes, resources, culture, and objectives. We discussed how that internal organization is made more powerful when aligned with the communities and markets it serves. The leader's primary charge is to align the organization in the service of its objectives. When this happens, all the parts amplify the effectiveness of all the others. The organization's alignment drives productivity, and individuals exceed expectations.

The following table describes the basic dimensions of alignment.

	Leader	**Organization**	**Community/Market**
Basic Nature	Character and style	Character: structure, processes, organization type	Structure of class, race, gender, and power
Underlying Principles	Personal values	Organizational culture	Community and s ocietal culture
Means Available	Individual skills	Organizational resources	Economy, government policy, organization sector
Purpose and Direction	Personal objectives	Mission, vision, and strategy	Community needs and market demands

For example, consider that leaders range from democratic and facilitative to autocratic. A particularly facilitative leader would be a poor fit for an organization that is highly structured and hierarchical and where its staff, never having participated in making decisions, just wants its "marching orders." Similarly autocratic leaders would prove poor fits with organizations accustomed to building consensus after long conversation, in which making everyone comfortable was as important as making the "right" decision.

The skills appropriate to small, grassroots organizations tend to be inappropriate to large, bureaucratic ones or to social venture organizations, looking to "scale up" at a rapid pace. Those who thrive in the helter-skelter organizational culture of start-up organizations often do poorly in more orderly, more "mature" organizations. Stable organizations that are attached to things as they are may prove a poor fit to ambitious, young leaders, who want to quickly make a name for themselves.

Certain organizations tolerate a narrow range of values. Some are so passionate about their mission that they would be hostile to even the best technical manager if he wasn't that interested in the mission. Organizations like art museums hire those who circulate easily in moneyed worlds where they find most of their donors. Organizations in African American, Latino, or Jewish organizations often hire members of their "club."

The point is that leadership style needs to line up with the organization's culture, structure, resources, mission, and strategy. So does the leader's values, skills, and personal objectives. You can just as easily begin with the organization's culture and, during search, say that it needs to line up with qualities in the leadership and characteristics of both the immediate community and the larger market of clients and funders, economic conditions, and perhaps technical possibilities.

Alignment is achieved in a variety of ways. During strategic planning processes, organizations consciously and intentionally try to align their structure, processes, resources, and culture to accomplish their objectives. New programs are screened according to their alignment with mission and strategy, hopefully before funding is sought. And when the programs are constructed, they are not only aligned to the organization's capabilities, but the general organizational resources are realigned to facilitate program growth.

The selection and introduction of new leadership may be the preeminent opportunity for organizational alignment. The board must ask itself if it is clear about its mission and strategy, if it can select a leader who is well enough aligned to implement the strategy, and if it can manage the organization during the transition period so that the transfer of leadership to the new CEO is as seamless and powerful as possible.

Cycles of Alignment and Misalignment

No matter how well you align an organization, it will regularly go off kilter. Important people may leave. New technologies may make current strategies obsolete. Board presidents come and go, requiring the CEO to make regular adjustments. Economic recessions and rises deplete and augment resources, which, in turn, require program cuts or permit program expansion. New ideas influence alignment. When, for example, shelters represented the best thinking about helping the homeless, a whole set of strategies naturally followed. When shelters seemed only to mitigate the status quo—while education, housing, and job creation pointed a more permanent way out of homelessness and poverty—then new strategies, programs, and financial objectives came into play.

In other words, the loss of alignment is natural as organizations respond to internal and external changes. At first, organizations may try to maintain their current alignment, may force new people, ideas, and programs to fit with the old. But the refusal to adapt to changes more often than not leads to ineffectuality. With time, the disciplined effort to maintain alignment turns into rigid adherence to plans that may no longer be appropriate. These efforts turn against alignment. When we fail to notice the movement away from alignment, rigid attachment to old ways becomes the norm, and it becomes harder and harder to let them go.

Fortunately, there are "natural" moments when we can assess alignment of a leader to the organization and to the community and markets and make true adjustments.

Opportunities for Alignment

The most obvious moment for realignment is during the strategic planning process, when organizations generally affirm and possibly tweak the mission. They adapt current strategies and create new ones. They determine how to configure programs, people, and finance to implement the strategies. All of these are ideal opportunities to address organizational alignment; however, other opportunities abound.

During the Introduction of New Programs and Cross-Departmental Projects

Major new projects and programs, many of which cut across organizational boundaries and involve top leadership, finance and marketing personnel, and perhaps IT people or consultants, demand an assessment and adjustment of the organization's alignment. Major projects cry out to be aligned with all other functional and programmatic elements in organizations. How will this new after-school program, for instance, intersect with the current weekend services you perform? What kind of fund-raising will it require? What kind of marketing to build clientele and community support will be needed? What kind of data and information systems will be required to track the program's progress?

How will the organization sequence everything so that it is ready on time? Take, for instance, an affordable housing organization. Its investors are ready, and the lawyers have prepared a draft of the arrangement with the city. One has to ask, "Is our finance team ready to take on their part?" If they are not, there may be delays, creating doubt in the mind of investors and city officials and amplifying ill will between the housing and finance departments in your organization. As an organization prepares for such a project, its plan must consider the alignment of internal departments within time.

During Performance Review

Each time a leader reviews the performance of a manager, it is not just the quality of the actual work that is at stake but also how it contributes to the work of others and how it aligns to collective goals. Individual and collective interests may sometimes seem to diverge. It is well known in commercial sales departments, for example, that if the majority of pay is determined by individual sales commissions and almost none to collective interests, there will be no attention to collective interest. However, if a significant percent of salary is pegged to collaboration and collective goals, the salespeople are easier to manage and more aligned with organizational objectives.

During performance review in a nonprofit, the same principles exist. When supervisors make it clear that collaboration with others and the alignment with organizational plans are essential ingredients of effective performance, alignment is more likely. Of course, leaders must be disciplined, repetitive, and rewarding when their supervisees actually put effort into keeping their work aligned to organizational purposes.

During the Annual Review for the Board of Directors

As discussed in Chapter 5, "Good Governance," boards must regularly review themselves. One key criterion in the review is whether the board's financial, human, and marketing resources are best suited to assist in the organization's success. Are the board's processes in keeping with staff processes and the organizational mission? Take, for instance, an organization built to encourage civic engagement and democratic process. The staff tries to stay true to this spirit, not only in its work but in its internal dealings. An autocratic board with few participants would be misaligned to that organization.

Regularly occurring events provide opportunities for organizations to exercise a disciplined review and realignment of their efforts.

During the Transition

New leaders don't usually walk into systems that are perfectly aligned. The opposite is usually true. Some leaders depart because they have too few resources to succeed or because they have drained the coffers. Human resources may also be in turmoil. Conflict and turf wars may have built up, making it impossible to mobilize people in coordinated efforts. Leaders may leave because they no longer believe in the mission or the board has grown tepid in its commitment. There are so many ways that alignment can be askew. This is generally the situation during contentious departures but often enough also during friendly departures, where established leaders have simply failed to keep up and are no longer aligned with communities, markets, or their own staff.

When a transition occurs, if the organization immediately began its search (a fairly widespread occurrence), the departing leader would be replaced with the most talented person available. The board would assume, no matter the fit of values, culture, and objectives, that the new person would find a way to align his new organization. That's what leaders do, isn't it? Unfortunately, leaders may not really understand issues of alignment.

Often CEOs enter with a powerful agenda of their own or with the need to rapidly prove their effectiveness. They often don't take the time to assess their new organization, to learn about its culture, its people, and its deeper strengths and weaknesses. Rarely do these leaders strike a sustainable balance between fitting in and leading change, but this is not entirely their fault. More often than not, a board selects a new leader it believes will improve or rescue its organization, a leader who is different from the old leader and who will be more accountable to the board, which will hold the employees more accountable. In other words, a leader is generally selected to change an organization, to "take it to the next level" without sufficient board and cross-organizational involvement.

New leaders are often not brought into an organization with a clear idea of what the next strategic step is, with a sense of clear direction that the board will support, or with a clear idea of how to align themselves with the new organization to be entrusted with the leadership of major change.

There is a far greater chance that new leaders will succeed if the organization is moved toward alignment during, not after, the transition period. That is the subject of Part 3, "Professionalizing the Transition Process." It is briefly foreshadowed here to show the emphasis upon leadership alignment.

Transition Planning

A transition plan has several well-known components: how decisions will be made and by whom, who will manage the organization during the interim period, and how leadership will be transferred to the incoming leader. The planning process determines how the search for and selection of the new leader will occur. The plan will be communicated to the organization's chief stakeholders, such as community groups and funders, and should prescribe how the board will articulate its strategic direction to the search committee. The search committee needs to be clearly aligned to the plan's direction. In other words, a key to transition planning is the development of a transitional statement of the organization's strategic plan.

Transition management means that a leader is selected with the skill to carry out the organization's plan as well as the character to embody its mission and vision. The combination of these two qualities is of critical importance. Some people are highly successful in one, two, or even three organizations yet fail abysmally in another. There are also leaders who have come to embody their organizations—often founders with long tenure, but whose skills and adaptability are no longer matched to the challenges presented by a growing organization or an organization caught in hard economic times.

Interim Leadership and the Quest for Alignment

When organizations are badly aligned or when there is uncertainty about alignment or a need to "decompress," it is best not to bring a new leader immediately into the situation. Rather, it is best to have an interim leader move the organization into greater alignment, including making hard changes with budgets, human resources, structural rearrangements, and so forth, so that the new leader can enter in the most positive and aligned manner.

Creating Alignment Through the Proper Introduction of the Leader

The CEO has to be publically charged with the implementation of the organization's mission, vision, and strategy. Her skills, values, and personal objectives have to be shown to align with those of the organization. And the new leader has to be connected with the right people and well positioned in a way that enhances her capacity to align the organization to its strategic plan.

Selecting Leaders with the Skill to Align an Organization

Fit and alignment mean more than cultural affinity. They also point to the skills necessary to lead the organization toward the achievement of its goals.

The ability to describe an organization's mission in a coherent and compelling story is important. So much depends on it: developing good relationships with funding sources; motivating and organizing employees; and relating the big picture as embodied in mission, vision, and strategy to the everyday grind. Leaders need to develop a story that assures their listeners that the organization's strategy is likely to bring about the objectives the organization seeks.

Articulating and Living the Mission and Vision

Like giant magnets, leaders focused upon the mission pull all other elements of organizational life to them. Mission and vision statements provide the organizing principles. The new leader must believe in these organizing principles if he is to communicate them with the personal conviction required when attracting people and money to the nonprofit. It is also important that the leader embody this illustration of the mission in how he lives his life, in accordance with the organization's values. This is what we mean by fit and alignment in leadership.

Articulating and Implementing Strategy

In most nonprofit organizations, mission statements are value statements; they're a little broad, which lends a dream-like quality to them. If a leader believes in the mission, he must lead people on a practical path to its realization. Strategy provides that pathway. Organizations must identify leaders who are practical visionaries, who can articulate the steps to achieving the organization's objectives. Leaders must have the discipline to prioritize only those activities that drive the organization toward those objectives.

Coordinating Resources

Nonprofits can call on many resources: employees, funders and other revenue streams, reputation, volunteers (board members and others), partners, and networks, to name the key players. They are often deployed in disparate and unconnected ways. The authors hear story after story of one department not supporting another, of plans being made before financial resources are attained or solidified, of programs being started not because they supported strategic objectives but because the funding was available. These programs then divert resources from the organization's main business.

The questions you need to ask of prospective leaders are these:

- What is an example of how you have gotten all the organizational resources to work together?
- How is funding sought that can support the mission and connect organizational energies?
- How do you reward collaboration as highly as the achievement of individual goals?
- How can an organization leverage a good reputation in the community for larger projects?
- How does the marketing story of an organization, the "brand," fit with its mission, vision, and strategy?
- How does a leader sustain an effective relationship with the board of directors?

Logic Model

It is rare that organizations think deeply about their logic model, why what they do should lead to what they want to achieve. The relationship between means and ends tends to be loose and intuitive and rarely checked against evidence. Program and organizational evaluation are the formal means by which the accuracy of the logic model is checked. This kind of evaluation must be built into the strategic plan at the beginning rather than the end of a process. If an organization has plans, it must ask how to realize them. It must know the plans will be achieved. In seeking new leadership, boards and search committees must look for people with this frame of mind and with commitment to measurable achievements.

Illustrating the Organizational Story

The mission of the Institute for Nonprofit Management and Leadership at Boston University (the Institute) is to educate, support, and connect the next generation of nonprofit leaders, with a particular emphasis on young people of color because such a large percentage of nonprofit clients are, themselves, people of color. To fulfill that mission, it envisions well over 300 executive directors and senior managers taking the year-long program over the next 5 years.

The skill-focused part of the program takes place in the management seminar. Students learn about managing individuals, building and managing teams, managing projects, planning budgets and financials, marketing, using information technology strategically, and so forth. They learn from core instructors and from guest instructors with whom they often stay connected once the program is completed. Education at the Institute includes course work combined with a connection to powerful and informative people in the larger nonprofit sector. Through pre- and post-program surveys with the students and their supervisors, the Institute learns whether, in fact, the students' skills have increased. The Institute also enhances the dialogue between the students and their supervisors (often board presidents), which tends to cut down on costly leadership turnover. Regular feedback creates information-rich decisions and informed connectivity.

A key part of the program is the practice seminar, which consists of seven students and a faculty member who has been both a nonprofit executive and a teacher or consultant. These senior fellows draw from a range of organizational experiences and approaches. The seminars help students integrate skill-based learning such as finance, marketing, IT, and program evaluation into their personal skills and within their own leadership style. Intimate groupings help students navigate the difficult transition from individual performer to manager, from doing things themselves to doing things through others, from a tenuous belief in themselves as leaders to a confident sense of leadership identity.

People keep these groups alive after the formal program is over. That is one way the Institute's sustained influence is evaluated. How much the students continue to support one another's work, sit on each other's boards, and collaborate on projects is also measured. The Institute's idea about "connection" means that the students create a more collaborate ethos in the nonprofit sector as a whole.

A third key element of the Institute is its mentor program. Each student is assigned to a senior nonprofit executive. The explicit goal is twofold: to better articulate the student's developmental course, and to determine the next steps in their career and the connection with major figures within the nonprofit community. Mentors connect them to others, and mentors substantially enhance the Institute's network. They continue to connect with the Institute's students and with its programs long after their formal affiliation ends.

Through its Internet portal, the Institute makes all kinds of resources available to its students. They can write in with a specific problem: What legal considerations should I be concerned with when I fire such and such a person? A position is opening in my organization—do you have a good candidate? Between the 300 students, 200 mentors, and 30 or 40 faculty members to date, the person writing in is likely to find good sources of information and advice.

The Institute is a lean program: an executive director, a faculty director, many part-time faculty members, a part-time alumni director, a student support to generate foundation grant proposals, and both administrative and marketing support from the School of Management. The diminutive core staff size makes alignment easier. All efforts focus first on the educational program. Reading materials and effective practice research are provided that support current and past students. Some programs are created to supplement others: For instance, the Institute is in the process of creating a network-based educational program for "high potential" young people who will become a pipeline to the executive program.

The strategic focus is twofold:

- To create an outstanding educational program utilizing community-based faculty that both educates and builds loyal connections

- To connect students with one another and with community resources (such as foundations and legal services) through the program structure, Internet connectivity, outreach, mentoring, and the development of an alumni association

According to the Institute's logic model, these strategies will have a direct effect on students and their specific connections. Perhaps more importantly, there will be a tipping point, a point at which the Institute-centered network begins to shift the whole city's third sector in the direction of blending practical experience with formal education, and in the direction of partnerships, collaborations, and the leveraged impact of networks. This is what we mean by aligning strategy in every aspect of service delivery.

Putting Alignment into Time

Aligning organizations is not a one-time thing, like fixing a machine that then runs in the same orderly manner it did at the beginning. Organizations live in changing worlds. They struggle to remain stable and true to their character, and they struggle to adapt to changes in their environment. Poor economies require program cuts; rising economies create growth opportunities. New technologies, new ideas, and new government policies require adaptation.

Each time organizations adapt, they tend to go out of alignment. The loss of a program, for example, may require the deployment of personnel differently, which may change the culture of other departments, which...you get the picture. Adaptation and change in one area of an organization is almost always an occasion for realignment.

Alignment and Transition

Loss of a previous leader and the entry of a new leader is also an occasion for realignment. (The professionalization of this transition is described in Part 3.) However, a brief description of the relevance of alignment to that the transition process is provided here.

The first shock to the organizational system comes with the announcement that the old leader is leaving. If this signals the departure of a revered leader with a lengthy tenure, the whole fabric of the organization has most likely been built around the leader's character and philosophy, his strengths and his weaknesses. For example, charismatic leaders who have lacked the ability or interest in day-to-day management may have depended on powerful operational managers. These managers may not relish the challenge or thrive when asked to change roles and represent the organization to funders, volunteers, press, or communities.

With the departure of the CEO, the current organization is thrown off balance. When a leader is dismissed for wrongdoing or incompetence, the entire organization may be thrown into doubt and confusion. Programs may falter. Financial positions may weaken. Realignment around a new, more optimistic future is essential.

If, during such times, the focus is almost exclusively on the search for a new leader, there is a good chance the organization will grow more and more unaligned. Too often in transitions, managers just try to hold things together until they find a new leader. That is a natural impulse. The organization may feel like a boat without a rudder. Even if the ship sails reasonably, it may be moving without a defined direction or commitment to that direction.

As quickly as possible, then, the board of directors, in partnership with current senior executives, must take the leadership mantle. For the transition period, the board, in the form of a transition team, takes on a much more direct and directive leadership role. If there is an effective management team in place, the transition team needs only to provide closer supervision. If no effective executive management team is in place, the board-led transition team will have to take on day-to-day operational leadership until a new leader is found or an interim leader is securely in place.

This is a difficult task, and not one that most board members signed up for. It is time consuming and filled with uncertainty. But, if the board takes hold strongly, there is opportunity as well. The desire for guidance may be high.

There are three main challenges for the transition team as it prepares to select a new leader. The first is to create a sense of solidity: "We will be all right." This declaration should be public and in a realistic tone.

It must include and own up to the problems to be solved. Otherwise, the declaration will not seem believable.

Second, the team must clarify the organization's mission, vision, and strategic direction. How else can you search for a new leader unless you know the direction you want her to lead?

The third task is that the transition team must do its best to align the current organization in the service of its mission, to make sure that all programs contribute directly to the strategy and support one another in contributing to strategic success. In this effort, make sure financial, human resources, and marketing support to programs match their strategic importance. If the transition team takes these steps toward alignment, the team will have served its organization well and paved the way for the incoming leader to succeed.

Some organizations hire interim directors to secure day-to-day operations. The interim leader may be called on to make the hard choices necessary for aligning the organization: he may reduce or cut programs that do not contribute significantly to the strategic plan. He may release poorly performing staff and staff that have not bought into the strategic plan. He may reconfigure the organization so that it can best pursue its organizational direction. The relative freedom of interim leaders to make such changes is one of the best arguments to utilize them. Interim leaders also free the transition team to focus on the review of its mission and strategy and the search for new leadership. (Chapter 10, "Using Interim CEOs During Transition," describes the benefits and challenges of interim leadership and its capacity to enhance organizational alignment.)

Even as interim directors and transition teams align the organization, the search process may be in full swing. Here, too, the theme of alignment is paramount. The search cannot focus on qualities of leadership independent of context. It must seek the best possible leader for a particular situation. In other words, the committee must search for a person whose skills, values, personal goals, and leadership style are aligned to the resources, culture, objectives, and organizational style that he will lead. That kind of alignment provides the best opportunity for new leadership to move the organization toward its goals.

The quest for alignment does not stop here. The introduction of the new leader goes a long way toward his success or failure. If, for example, a leader is introduced in a tepid way, the likelihood that she will be able to mobilize organizational resources in the service of the mission is decreased. At the same time, there is little advantage to introducing the new leader as a savior. That very characterization tends to demean current employees and suggests that organizational resources are barely up to the task. But, if the new person is introduced as fitting well with the organization and its aims and promised the support she will need for her initial efforts, she has a far better shot at succeeding.

The introduction, all by itself, is a way for the transition team to announce what the aligned organization's strategy is. The team can describe the resources that will be dedicated to its fulfillment. It can show how these resources will be organized and deployed. Also, the team can explain why this approach will work and how the new leader will manage that effort. This kind of introduction is both an endorsement of the new leader and a challenge to the leader and the staff as a collective unit. It signals the receding influence of the transition team and the board.

The alignment effort does not stop with the introduction of new leadership. During the first year, it is important to charge the new leader with the assessment of the organization. In particular, the new leader will determine how well the organizational resources, structure, process, and operating systems are aligned to the strategy. This assessment should culminate in a formal report, along with a plan to improve organizational alignment.

Finally, within a few months of the beginning of the new leader's tenure, she and the board should join in building a new strategic plan, in which all organizational resources will be aligned to the newly framed organizational objectives.

Discussion Questions

1. What changes are needed to bring the strategic plan into alignment with achieving the mission of the organization?
2. What changes are needed to bring operations into alignment with the organization's strategic plan?
3. What experience, skills, and characteristics are needed by leadership to implement the organization's strategic plan successfully?

Part 3

Professionalizing the Transition Process

7

Creating a Transition Management Plan

Leadership transitions are ripe with opportunity. When they can avoid the inclination to rush and to move into reactive activity and crisis mode, organizations can take the time to review and renew the vision and strategies that have guided their actions. To do so, they must mark off this transition period, affirm it, and reconceive it as a special time—and manage it with the rigor of a major project.

All organizations operate through projects: building new programs, putting in information or financial systems, conducting year-end performance reviews, and the like. In some ways, project planning and execution form the most basic building blocks of organizations. When projects are well planned and executed, organizations thrive; otherwise, they become sloppy and uncoordinated. One of the great opportunities provided by the transition is to reestablish the value of project planning and management and to model it for future organizational efforts. It is this skill—the skill to plan and execute projects—that we will discuss in this chapter and Chapter 8, "Transition Management."

What Is a Project Plan?

At the core, project plans consist of the following elements:

- A set of objectives.
- The background that sets the stage for the project and provides the context in which it will succeed or fail.
- The type of leadership and decision making that will be most effective.

- The scope of the project: what needs to be done and what concrete "deliverables" will be required.
- How the organization will approach the project. What management style will be most effective? What are the cultural concerns?
- A timeline, sometimes called a Gantt chart, that details what needs to be done, by when, and by whom.
- A communication strategy to orient and reassure all the stakeholders.
- A budget: roughly what the project will cost and how the organization came to those figures.
- A method of evaluation: how the organization will know it's moving toward its objectives and when it has reached them.
- An assessment of the risks, obstacles, and general challenges that the project faces, because all change efforts face resistance and challenge.

This seems simple enough, but in meeting after meeting with CEOs and other senior nonprofit managers, the authors find that organizations rarely go through all these steps of project planning. It is unlikely, for instance, for project planners to identify all the objectives sought by the project. They might name the primary objective—say introduce an organization-wide IT system—and base their planning on that, but they may not say that they also want to use the project to bring better collaboration among departments, a secondary objective. Then, neglecting to name the secondary objective, they fail to plan and manage for it. They may or may not budget for the project or discuss past efforts to achieve similar objectives that may provide clues to the success or failure of its execution.

Few organizations take enough time for thorough transition management. More typically, boards—or rather two or three central board members—put together a "game plan" almost entirely focused on hiring a new leader and perhaps naming a staff person to look over daily operations. But, as the preceding list suggests, the transition period is a complex time, requiring the execution and coordination of many critical subprojects. Taking the time to gather all those who will be part of the plan's execution and building a strong plan with broad buy-in pays great dividends.

Like almost all management skills, project planning requires knowledge (how to do something) and discipline (the will to put that skill to use with your full, focused attention). The plan is not for one person. It is meant to scope out an agreement and a commitment among a group of people who will share an important project.

More Than Executive Search

Transition management consists of a wide range of activities of which the search for a new leader is but a part. Organizations must form interim leadership, with designated authority and responsibilities, ways of monitoring effectiveness, financial prudence, program excellence, and the like. How will the organization be managed during the transition period that can last from six months to two years? The organization's everyday business cannot be neglected. Who will manage it? Who will hold the managers accountable? The organization's primary stakeholders will have to be tended to. Clients must be served. Funders will have to be reassured, and grant proposals and foundation reports will have to be written. Regular financial statements will have to be created and reports given: by whom and to whom? Staff performance reviews will need to be continued.

What is more, the general purpose of the organization—its mission, vision, objectives, and strategy—should be reviewed. The purpose of new leadership is to further these ideas and values, and new leaders are best chosen with them clearly and crisply in mind.

The project of interim or transition management is a daunting one, particularly when assigned by and in part to volunteers (which is what board members are) who, in their own minds, did not volunteer to be responsible for everyday organizational leadership.

One of the reasons transition management often devolves into only executive search activities is that board members are unprepared to take on this responsibility yet also unwilling to hand over the reins to the departing leader's subordinates. Resolving this internal conflict and committing to be responsible that management happens (generally through hiring an Interim Director or delegation to incumbent professional staff) during the transition period is the first order of business for the board. Then the organization can attend to planning the work to come.

A Project Planning Chart

Following is a chart for general project planning that works perfectly well for transition planning. Answer the following questions:

- What are the objectives?

- What is the relevant background—for instance, what has enabled and interfered with the success of other people in this position?

- How will the hiring decision be made? By one person? By a manager in consultation with his boss (or the full board)? With others on the management team or committee?

- What are all the steps needed to ensure a "good fit"? These might include framing the job, checking the frame with others and revising it, finding an appropriate consultant, deciding who will narrow the choices, and so forth.

- What will be said (to whom, how much, when) to others about the process?

- What is a reasonable timeline based on other work in the organization and available personnel?

- What is the budget, and how much should be allocated for search, salary, and so on? Just checking the budget assumptions will illuminate how the position is valued and conceived as well as the new job and the person who will fill it.

- How will progress toward the objectives be measured?

- What obstacles are likely to occur? The old saying that "whatever can go wrong will go wrong" is helpful to develop some contingency plans to take those detours into account.

Project Planning Chart

1. Project Name

2. Project Objectives

3. Project Background
Background
Case for proceeding

4. Leadership and Decision Making	
Sponsor	Project Manager
Decision-Making Rules	

5. Project Scope
Project Scope Statement

6. Project Approach (Process Considerations)		
Management Style	Cultural Fit	Search Style

7. Timeline		
What	*When*	*Who*

8. Communication Strategy

9. Project Cost
Estimated Cost Range
Cost Assumptions

10. Evaluation		
Objective	*Indicator of Progress*	*Outcome Reached*

11. Risks, Obstacles, and Challenges

A Chart Sketching a Leadership Transition

This is a general idea about project planning. The following chart illustrates a transition management plan and how it works.

Transition Management Planning Chart

1. Project Name
Leadership transition at the Longmeadow Youth Center (LYC), Springfield, Massachusetts, December 6, 2009

2. Project Objectives
Create a road map for the LYC transition period: from now through the introduction of CEO.
Review and revise the mission, vision, and strategy of LYC to clarify the organizational spirit and objectives for new leadership.
Conduct a SWOT (strength, weakness, opportunity, threat) analysis of the LYC to guard against problems and take advantage of opportunities.
Develop leadership and processes for the transition management period.
Develop a process to identify, select, hire, and introduce a new CEO for the LYC.

3. Project Background
Background
The Longmeadow Youth Center is 15 years old. Since its inception, its mission has been to even the playing field for youth in the Latino neighborhoods of Springfield, resulting concretely in access to educational resources, the political process, and workforce opportunity. Its strategic focus is youth empowerment—that is, to engage teenagers in the leadership of projects that address these opportunities. For instance, youth-led teams have made schools more hospitable by creating experiential civics courses that involve the youth in political campaigns and history courses that include the cultures of Latin American nations. The LYC and its approach won kudos throughout the state, and its funding increased dramatically over the years.
The long-time CEO, once a charismatic figure for youth, community, and Springfield political forces, began to ignore his board members—they had always sided with him. With his help, the board added members who had not been "raised" on his benevolent rule, and for the past three years the board has increasingly asserted its independence and its wish to exert a strong influence, first over policy but soon over the hiring and supervision of senior managers. The struggle between the board and the CEO eventually grew acrimonious and polarized the LYC community. The board began to circumscribe the CEO's autonomy, requiring increasing numbers of reports on programs, finance, and personnel, and eventually the CEO grew angry and alienated. At this point, with the organization frustrated but unprepared, the CEO took a new job with a larger, more prestigious organization.
In keeping with the goals of youth empowerment, the LYC culture has long been explicitly democratic, participatory, and inclusive. Young people, neighborhood people, and staff, for example, join in the strategic planning process. The conflict between the CEO and the board reflects an implicit, more autocratic side to the LYC, one that had not previously required much attention. The leadership transition process will have to address the issue.
Case for Proceeding
In this situation, there is no choice but to proceed. No cost-benefit analysis can avoid the need for new leadership.
There is a choice, however, about how to proceed: directly to new leadership or through the appointment of an interim leader whose tenure will "buy" us time to figure out what kind of long-term leader would really fit our needs, objectives, culture, and strategic directions. This is a case we'll make midway. If we are proceeding well, getting clear about what got us in trouble, getting clear about where we want to go—within a reasonable time, say 2 months—then we will make the case to proceed to a full leadership transition. If we are not clear, we will add an interim leader into the mix.

4. Leadership and Decision Making	
Sponsor	*Project Manager*
The board of directors (15 members) is officially charged with hiring the new CEO and must hand off the day-to-day management of the transition process to a more manageable and knowledgeable (about day-to-day operations) team. If the team experiences trouble with the stakeholders, the board must provide support, explanation, and protection.	We will create a transition team consisting of three board members (president, treasurer, head of governance committee) and two staff members (director of programs, CFO). One member of that team, the head of the governance committee, will chair the team.
Decision-Making Rules	
Because decision making has become such a bone of contention, we want to make the process clear and to strike a practical balance between the transition team's need to move efficiently and its need to endorse and model the LYC's values of inclusiveness and democratic participation. As a consequence, the team will at least consult all stakeholders on major decisions. For example, when detailing the objectives of the transition and the project approach, there would be an early meeting in which all stakeholders—board, staff, youth, community representatives, and, perhaps participants in major projects, like a public school superintendent and a small business owner—will meet to pass on the team's initial formulation.	

5. Project Scope

Project Scope Statement

In this section, we want to articulate our plan for all phases of the transition process. For each phase of the planning, we want to be mindful of the previously unresolved disagreement about how the LYC is to be led: how much power in the hands of the few and the many.

Identify and commit to objectives for the transition process (not for the organization). The team will take an initial position, run it by the full board, rewrite the objectives, and communicate them to the full LYC community.

Name and charter a transition team, team leadership, and decision-making process.

Announce the team, team leadership, and decision making to the larger LYC community.

Announce a budget, including elements needed for the transition period, such as a search consultant; a consultant to facilitate team effectiveness (possibly the search consultant); a contingency budget if the process takes 6 months to a year longer than expected or if the decision to hire an interim director is made.

A timetable:
- When the team will be formed
- When the search will begin (and end)
- When the SWOT analysis will take place

Assignments: for example,
- Who will lead the search process?
- Who will conduct the SWOT analysis?

Assessment—Identify and commit to a process of assessing the organization and its leadership, volunteer and professional, including an understanding of how and why the current and past leaders departed. What organizational changes would enhance the new leader's potential for success?

Construct a communication strategy—Who will be the point person to staff, board, and other stakeholders? How transparent will we be about transition management, the search process, and recommended changes?

Interim or not—Decide whether to install an interim director as soon as possible and for what period of time, or whether there will be a checkpoint during the transition management and search process to make a decision to select an interim director.

Plan to manage the departure of the current CEO—How much will you depend on his knowledge, how long a period will there be between announcement and actual departure, should the CEO be part of orienting the incoming CEO, and so forth.

(There are, no doubt, more items that can be included in the scope of the leadership transition process and will need planning, but this gives an idea of what would be included.)

6. Project Approach (Process Considerations)

Management Style	*Cultural Fit*	*Search Style*
We want to strike a better and less conflicted balance between leadership (Team) and stakeholders who will be honored consultants in all matters.	Our culture, at its best, is highly ethical. We try to live our values, which include an affirmation of diversity: race, nationality, gender, age. Our transition management should embody that value so much that the new leader, chosen to fit with it, will have an easy time joining.	We will avoid the temptation to draw inward. Even at the risk of lengthening the process and making it more complex, we will be as transparent and consultative as possible.

7. Timeline		
What	*When*	*Who*
Objectives defined	2/6/10	First by team, then by board of directors
Project plan published	2/20/10	First team, then broad circulation, then voted by board
Team named	2/20/10	Same as above
Budget	2/20/10; then monthly	Team reports to board
Plan to manage departing CEO or the "image" of the departed leader	3/20/10	Team
Organizational SWOT analysis	From 3/30/10 to 6/30/10	Joint board-staff committee, with external consultant
Plan to introduce new CEO and phase out team	2/20/10; reconsidered after organizational assessment	Team plus senior management team

(The timeline would be considerably more detailed. Alternatively, a Gantt chart can be used. Gantt charts are readily available on the Internet and provide excellent graphic representations of a project's movement.)

8. Communication Strategy

In peaceful times, when trust is high, the team can communicate its plan, announce the rough timeline, perhaps indicate a rough budget estimate, and then wait to communicate again when the project is pretty far along. But in this situation, with conflict rising, and the key piece in the organizational puzzle—a charismatic leader—leaving, it is best to communicate regularly and fully. As a consequence, the team will assign one of its members to write a monthly newsletter, covering all major events, decisions, achievements, and challenges faced by the LYC.

9. Project Cost

Estimated Cost Range

Direct costs: $35,000 (search and assessment consultants)

Potential total cost: $110,000 (includes interim director for one year) paid with money freed up by the departure of the CEO

Cost Assumptions

The organization is particularly busy with newly funded programs and can't afford to spend too much time with the SWOT analysis.

Replacing the charismatic founder will be hard, at best. We will want to draw from a large pool of talent, not all local. There is also factional fighting on the board catalyzed by struggles with the departing CEO. The discovery and initial sorting will require objectivity and much time. Because the board is already more than usually occupied by taking on some of the operational management, it and the team will need professional support.

10. Evaluation

Objective	Indicator of progress	Outcome reached
Create a roadmap for the LYC transition period: from now through introduction of CEO	Planning committee formed	Transition plan written and approved by the Board
	Questions framed	
	First report on roadmap submitted	
Review and revise the mission, vision, strategy of LYC to clarify the organizational spirit and objectives for new leadership	Committee formed	Revised mission and vision approved by board
	Consultant hired and oriented	
	Background material read, analyzed, interviews complete	
	Report on review	
	Plans for organizational change developed and approved by Team	
Conduct a SWOT (strength, weakness, opportunity, threat) analysis of LYC in order to guard against problems and take advantage of opportunities	Same steps as above with same consultant	
Develop leadership and processes for the transition management period		Organizational change plan approved by TMT, Board
Develop a process to identify, select, hire, and introduce a new CEO for the LYC	Team proposes	
	Board selects search firm	Board approves
	Search consultant does assessment and initial report	
	Candidates sorted and field narrowed	Search is underway, with clear timeline, costs, and methods delineated

11. Risks, Obstacles, and Challenges

The obstacles begin with getting our divided board to reach a consensus on all the preceding issues: objectives, communication strategy, CEO selection, and the like.

The fundamental challenge is threefold: 1) for the board to agree to a common direction, leadership style, and organizational design for the future, so that the new CEO can hit the ground with support and momentum; 2) to protect against the impulse to reject anyone trying to replace the current CEO; 3) to withdraw gradually and completely from operations management after spending so much, often satisfying, time taking it on. We will be exhausted and want to hand the "baby" over to the new caretaker without supporting and monitoring it carefully. And we will be tempted to control and mute his every move after feeling so controlled by the former CEO.

As a consequence, we will have to trust our stamina and meet more often than we want toward the end to complete the project well.

Key Elements of Transition Planning

A few of the key planning activities bear further explanation.

Beginning with the "Right" People Sitting at the Table

Project planning begins with the issue of who we should bring to the table. Who has information, skills, and authority to help frame the project and, later, to carry it out? For example, who has an idea about what the organization wants to achieve and to avoid during the transition period? Who will later be essential to carrying out the transition plan and should be included in the planning as a way to empower and bind them to the organizational objectives? Who, if they opposed the plan or even just tepidly endorsed it, might get in the way? They, too, might be good to include in the planning process.

In short, the "right" people include the following:

- **Project sponsor**—The sponsor is the person who lends his authority—his imprimatur—to a project and who guides it through the organization. In large organizations, this might be a vice president who finds the resources to implement a project, who speaks for it at organization-wide meetings, and who helps to resolve difficulties encountered between the project manager and the larger organization. During leadership transition projects, the sponsor is likely to be the board president. He may not head up the search process, the communication committee, or any everyday duties, but he holds everyone else accountable.

- **Project leader**—Project leaders manage project activity from conception to completion. This includes the management of those with specific tasks, such as the head of the search committee. The transition process is a complex and often lengthy process, much in need of someone who keeps track of all the details; holds people accountable for completed tasks; makes sure that necessary resources are provided, on time; and coordinates the various activities with one another. For example, the organization may determine that the search process cannot officially begin until the board authorizes money to pay a search consultant, completes a review and revision of the strategic plan, and communicates the transition process to key stakeholders. Coordinating the timing of these activities is an essential part of the project leader's job.

- **Skilled people**—The need for skilled people is obvious if the project is building a bridge or creating a financial statement, but it's just as important for planning and executing a transition management plan. Where possible, the organization will need people who can manage projects, who can communicate with a variety of stakeholders, and who can frame a job description. It helps to include people who have helped organizations move through major transition processes—ideally leadership transitions, but other transitions as well. Often the board decides it does not have sufficient skill and perspective within its own ranks and hires a search consultant. (In Chapter 9, "Managing the Search Process," we discuss the search process and the pros and cons of hiring a search consultant.) As we have suggested, though, executive search is only part of the leadership transition. The organization may want, instead or in addition, to find someone to guide it through the whole process.

- **Potential opponents**—Change and resistance go hand in glove. All serious organizational change—in leadership, programming, or strategy, for instance—tends to threaten some, confuse others, and bring to the fore competing interests. Including potential skeptics and opponents in the planning process tends to defuse or at least diffuse their opposition. In a more positive light, their ideas, although not necessarily those of the majority, may enhance the planning. At the very least, the organization wants to establish the habit of respectful dialogue with them so that they do not obstruct the realization of the project.

Often enough, there are deeply etched schisms in organizations, among or between board and staff members. These conflicts may have played a major role in the departure of the CEO who could not operate effectively with such divided loyalties, authority, or resources. If the conflicts are not resolved or at least mollified, or if compromises cannot be worked out, the fighting will simply reemerge during the transition process or after the new leader is selected, creating a repetition of the problems that led to the failed leadership of the last CEO. Therefore, opponents with the capacity to derail or weaken transition management and the new leadership are the "right" people to include, and an attempt to resolve long-standing differences should precede the planning process.

Decision-Making Process

Before going further, it is vital for the board to decide how decisions will be made and by whom: the transition team leader, team consensus, or team majority decision? Which decisions are the leader or the team empowered to make? Which must they bring to the full board? Clearly defining both process and roles at the outset will eliminate considerable confusion and conflict later on. People will know when they can expect to be included, or at least consulted, and won't feel insulted when they are not. Nor will they feel that they have been entrusted with too big a responsibility. This dialogue in advance will facilitate the acceptance of actions taken by the transition team and the search team by the entire board.

Problem Definition: What Led to the Departure?

What is the transition from, and what is it a transition to?

A transition plan must take into consideration the issues that led to the CEO's departure and the results of the board self-evaluation (Chapter 5, "Good Governance"). If the CEO's departure was accompanied by considerable divisiveness, the plan must address the causes of division and emphasize ways to heal it. An acrimonious departure should raise alarm bells—something other than the CEO may be flawed. It may be the board or the board-CEO relationship. It may be unrealistic expectations against which the CEO was measured. It may be that the organization exists in a community that won't readily support it: not enough constituents, donors, staff, or volunteers.

If the departure followed a period of either hands-off management or micromanagement by the board, an overhaul of the board's role needs to be built into the transition process. Even with a perfectly amicable departure, the organization should be asking whether it is moving in the right direction and what improvements it can make.

Leadership transitions present opportunities for self-reflection and growth at the very least. Organizations should ask what kind of leader fits with their hopes and plans for the future. They must be able to say, with clarity and succinctness, who they are and where they are going. The answer to this question will permit the organization to interview candidates with a clear set of goals and parameters in mind.

Objectives

Once the right people are at the table, the organization can ask what it wants to achieve during the transition period. Without defining the objectives, it is hard to align and prioritize activity. As the LYC case suggests, there are multiple objectives for transition management.

Obviously, the organization wants to do a good job of hiring a new leader, but this can be divided into several separate tasks: for instance, selecting and empowering a team to carry out the project; writing a job description; performing the search; interviewing and selecting the "right" person; developing a strong contract to align the new leader with the organization.

But there are other objectives, almost as important, including these.

Stability and Productivity

The search, itself, can take from six months to a year, sometimes longer. The organization needs a plan to keep the organization productive, to retain key managers, to assure stakeholders that the organization is more than the departing leader and won't decline precipitously.

Clarify Mission, Vision, and Strategies

If the fundamental challenge of leadership is to align organizations in the service of mission, vision, and strategy, transition management has to review and refine just what they are—before hiring the new leader.

Determining What Kind of Leadership Is Required

As suggested in Chapter 6, "Alignment," the fit between leaders and organizations is as or more important than the skills of leadership. The organization will want to determine who has the right skills and temperament. For instance, does it need a more managerial or a more entrepreneurial person? Must the person be an exact professional fit—for example, a doctor in a hospital, a teacher in a school—or will universal managerial skills be credible enough or more credible in a moment of disorganization?

Modeling the "Right" Leadership Style

Before hiring a leader aligned to the organization's proposed organizational style—open and inclusive; passionate and dedicated; clear and authoritative—it is extremely helpful to set the example you want the organization to achieve. If, for example, the transition is from a founding leader who has managed through charisma and close attachments to key people but without adequate accountability or effective information and financial systems, and the organization wants to make the transition to a more closely managed organization, transition management must model the new, sought-after behavior. The modeling makes clearer than words what is sought and makes the transition to the new leader far smoother.

Introducing New Leadership in an Empowering Way

Many organizations work hard at the selection process and then introduce the new leader in a casual and haphazard manner. We have seen boards, exhausted and frustrated by the transition period, hand off the new leader without providing sufficient support. And we have seen new leaders introduced as though they were heroic knights come to rescue an organization in distress, thus overrating their capacity and setting up failure. The manner of introduction is of critical importance. It should blend optimism and realism, momentousness and the commonplace. It should provide an opportunity for the transition team to set the long-term agenda and to make expectations of the new leader explicit. There should be introductions to all the major stakeholders.

A Plan for the Transition Team to Withdraw

Should the team simply dissolve after introducing the new leader? Hold her tightly accountable for several months or a year, or until she has proven her metal? Are there markers for the new leader to hit that automatically call on the team to diminish or end its role? Right from the start, it is important to determine how the transition team will hand off power, both to the new CEO and back to the board. When the hand-off is done at the last minute, control struggles frequently arise. Transition teams can be like founding boards: They work so hard—developing such dedication to their work and to the organization—that it can be hard for them to let go of the reins. Supporting the new CEO in establishing new roots in the organization is a vital part of the transition team's work.

Creating or Reviewing/Renewing the Strategic Plan

As a Neighborhood Reinvestment Corporation report (1998) put it, "an executive transition provides a unique opportunity for introspection, beginning with the question of why it is faced with this event. This analysis often leads the organization to reevaluate its mission, goals, and operations."

As discussed in Chapter 4, the relationship between the selection of a new CEO and the creation and review/renewal of a strategic plan is straightforward. The strategic plan defines the organization's aspirations, its identity, its practical resources, and its values. In doing so, it clarifies what kind of organization the CEO is being recruited to lead. Because the fit between the CEO and the organization is paramount, the plan must be absolutely clear about the kind of organization to which the new CEO must align.

For example, an organization with rapid growth plans should look for an aggressive, entrepreneurial CEO and reject even the most compelling candidate if he is most at home in a stable environment. If the organization plans to emphasize innovation, a CEO with little personal experience in change management is not a good match. For an organization located in a contentious community that plans to improve integration within the larger network of nonprofit institutions, community-building and negotiation skills are most important. An organization that is already mature in its provision of services and financial capability located in a stable neighborhood may want to sustain its current ways with minimal change. It can recruit from other stable organizations without worrying about the entrepreneurial and fundraising capabilities of the new CEO.

If the organization does not have a strategic plan, the transition team sets about helping define the organization's *mission*; its *vision* of how the organization would look, feel, and act like once that mission is actualized; and its *objectives*. Objectives are specific ways to accomplish the mission. If, for example, the mission is to transform a neighborhood from disorganized and disengaged to engaged and coherent, one objective might be the creation of ways for people to meet both formally and informally. Another objective might be to create a sense of pride and pleasure in the neighborhood. In other words, concrete goals are aligned with the more impressionistic mission and vision statements.

There are a variety of ways to elicit stakeholder ideas about missions, visions, and objectives:

- One or several small group meetings can be organized with various constituencies whose input is later synthesized.
- Several smaller meetings can be conducted, culminating in a meeting of major stakeholders.
- All stakeholders can meet in a single large group.
- Input can be derived from ongoing organizational meetings.
- Constituents can be encouraged to respond online to the evolving process of defining the mission and vision.
- "Open space" meetings can be held to encourage interaction between disparate stakeholders about this important topic.

Each of these styles reflects the preference of a different organizational culture. Each is also more or less powerful in its emphasis on alignment. For example, conducting all work in large groups is designed to maximize buy-in and alignment.

If an organization has recently undergone strategic planning, calling to attention the direction set by that plan will inform the transition team's future steps. If the strategic plan is out of date, stopping to review and renew it with the organization's key constituencies will be time well spent.

Customize the Plan to Fit the Organization's Character, Culture, and Practical Realities

When formulating a transition plan, the team must consider the organization's needs, character, and culture and then tailor a plan with these realities in mind. Teams whose members are accustomed to planning may come up with elaborate, even obsessive plans. Others will formulate more basic guidelines for action, which may prove insufficient.

Current State Analysis

As in a strategic planning process, it is essential for the team to determine the state of the current organization, to develop a realistic picture of the gap between that state and where the organization wants to go. It is this gap that determines the objectives that the organization hands off to the new leadership. It is essential that the team takes this step before selecting the new leader.

Advice and Consultation

The board should realistically assess their ability to plan and manage the transition process. First they should ask themselves whether they have the requisite experience. For example, have they gone through comparable experiences at work or in other nonprofit organizations? More importantly, have they been in leadership positions during important leadership and organizational transitions? Is there a volunteer to manage both the tasks and the interpersonal dynamics of a staff management team or of a search process that may stretch over six or more months? The search process alone is particularly time and labor intensive and can take as much as 200 hours of administrative time. Does the board have the contacts needed to recruit a variety of capable candidates?

One of the principal challenges of transitions, particularly those accompanied by haste or acrimony, is to gain and maintain perspective. Board and staff close to the action often have too many hurt, angry, and frustrated feelings to make clear judgments and may respond reactively. Transition periods can be chaotic. Inexperienced boards may rush to hire the first reasonable candidate who comes their way instead of patiently assessing applicants until the best possible one is found, or they may delay working with the best candidate available, believing someone else may be just around the corner.

Current administrators are sometimes elevated to positions of interim authority that later they are reluctant to relinquish. Out of misplaced sympathy, boards sometimes select a friend, board member, or volunteer in search of a job as CEO. Interim CEOs, reluctant to let go of their authority, can also create conflict with an incoming CEO. Because giving way may feel like being demoted, the internal interim when replaced may depart. As a result, instead of the new CEO having an experienced guide to support her orientation to the organization, the CEO and board are left without that valued employee.

In many situations, it is helpful to call upon an outsider. She can be a trusted community member whose perspective, skills, experience, and ability to be calm in the midst of crises make her a good person to offer perspective and advice. She can be a sympathetic former CEO or a board president from another organization. Or she can be a professional consultant, for whom crisis resolution, candidate recruitment, and organizational planning are her daily work. Increasingly, there are professional executive transition consultants who specialize in nonprofit organization support and can bring the experience gained through many transition processes.

Leadership and Management Style

The transition team will have to determine how to manage the staff. Who will be charged with what? What kind of goals will be set? How frequently will the team meet with staff? How much authority, responsibility, and autonomy will be granted? And how, in what style, will the team members operate? Will they basically defer to staff? Hold them tightly accountable? Require constant or infrequent reporting? The transition plan needs to ensure that the organization will carry on well during the transition period, and the staff needs to know what is expected of them. The answers should sustain and improve the organization's alignment and cultural coherence.

Timetable and Coordination

As with any project plan, a timetable is required for the team to hold itself accountable and to coordinate activities. For instance, until the current state analysis is completed and the strategic plan is reviewed, you can't or shouldn't select your leader. Until your decision-making process is set, it can be destructive and wasteful to try making key decisions.

Once a plan is constructed for one of the subtasks, you can build a somewhat flexible timetable. In the previous example, the timetable should specify when to complete a plan for finding a search consultant and when to hire this individual.

Hard deadlines can be controlled: writing a job description or profile for the new CEO, conducting an organizational assessment and writing an organizational description, preparing an information packet, and placing advertisements. *Soft deadlines*, which are out of your control, include receiving good responses to ads, scheduling interviews, and making decisions about the best candidate. Soft deadlines may be renegotiated throughout the process to keep quality, rather than compliance to the calendar, as the ultimate goal.

Make both hard and soft deadlines public, and keep the board, staff, and community up to date on progress. If it's not a *written* timeline, it's not really a timeline.

Graphics

It helps to have a graphic depiction of both master and task plans. Think of the big graph outside a hospital that charts the progress of its capital campaign or the thermometer showing progress in the United Way campaign. A graphic project plan makes it easier to orient stakeholders and inform them of milestones reached and tasks remaining to be done. Making this information available to the community generally cuts down on uncertainty and anxiety. It also makes it easier to hold those charged with each of the tasks accountable for their work.

Communications Plan

There is a difference between an action and how that action is interpreted. Although you can never fully control how people understand your activity, you can influence it. This is the purpose of a communications plan. During crises and transitions, the need to reassure staff, clients, communities, funders, and other stakeholders that things are under control and moving in a productive direction is critically important. Funders have to believe in this kind of stability to keep investing. Staff needs to believe to keep working with purpose and energy. Clients need to believe to continue to seek services.

Minimally, communication strategies begin by identifying stakeholders and determining what kind of information each will find reassuring. For example, funders might wish for frequent financial reports and an indication that the search will promote the kind of leadership they invest in. Staff may want assurance about their jobs. The style of communications may differ. For instance, a transition newsletter can be created to provide general information updates to all stakeholders. Specific and private reports and meetings may be planned with funders. The team may decide to meet regularly with a senior management group to keep them informed.

Not only do regular communications provide the opportunity for positive "spin," they can guard against negativity, rumors, and the development of secretive opposition.

Although you should conduct some of the search process, such as candidate evaluation, strictly in private, most of the transition process is best made public. Names of applicants generally should not be known outside the search committee; yet the process itself can be transparent. Communication can and should take several forms: announcements and articles in newsletters; personal conversations; updates in staff, board, and community meetings; and the graphs we just discussed, to name a few. In general, the more communication, the better—particularly if it is thoughtful, regular, and based on the transition team's commitment to keeping all concerned in the loop through accurate progress reports rather than rumors. The entire community can follow the process and feel part of it.

To be systematic and personal, make a list of all major constituencies. They will include, at the very least, board, volunteers, staff, funders, potential donors, program partners, colleagues and constituents, and possibly the media. Then assign to a specific team member the responsibility of keeping each group—or all groups—informed. At each meeting, a clarification of the message at this stage for these groups can prepare the communicator to deliver a clear and consistent message.

Because communication is a two-way street, the team member who provides the communication should also be responsible for reporting feedback—positive and negative responses, concerns and relieved anxieties, new information, and ideas—but must be careful to maintain confidentiality as appropriate.

Last but not least, regular communication to stakeholders is a good way for the team to hold itself accountable. The commitment to a degree of transparency—to share information about the style and progress of the search and about the day-to-day management—guards against a strong tendency, almost an undertow, to be secretive and exclusive during times of change or crisis, a tendency that often erodes the trust of stakeholders.

Budget

A transition management budget does not have to be elaborate, but it is important as an indication of fiduciary responsibility. Minimally, it should estimate the cost of a search consultant, if that is the choice. If an interim CEO is being considered, the team has to consider how and how much to pay him. It should also anticipate indirect costs, such as extra management or consultants to fill in for work ordinarily conducted by the CEO.

Establish a separate budget for the transition process that anticipates the cost of stakeholder meetings, interim management, information packets, advertisements and online postings, candidate travel, consultant fees and expenses, relocation expenses, and the like. As much as anything else, an explicit budget sets a professional tone and adds to the transparency of communications within the organization. Arranging for invoices for these expenses to be paid promptly maintains a positive image of the organization's fiscal stability during the transition.

Risks, Obstacles, Challenges

Although risk analysis is common to corporate planning, it is sometimes absent in nonprofits. People want to skip this part, assume that things will go according to plan or assume that they will make adjustments on the fly. Unless you plan for risks and build in contingencies, problems are likely to catch you off guard and unprepared.

There are, for example, predictable risks in transition management. Here are a few:

- The search will take longer than anticipated and longer than you would choose. This in turn is likely to exhaust and frustrate board members on the team. It is also likely to increase expenses, particularly when an interim CEO is in place. So it helps to think ahead about the team's workload, where increased funds will come from, and so forth.

- The search may not come up with the "right" person. There are nonprofit subsectors that have a dearth of good or experienced leadership. There are organizations that have specialized leadership needs—professional standing, cultural specificity, and so on. What happens if a new leader is not found who at least approximates the job description the board has written?

- The search committee finds that it will have to spend considerably more than anticipated on the new CEO's salary—either that or it will have to accept a person of considerably less skill or standing.

- Funders get cold or, at least, nervous feet and either limit funding or make it contingent on finding a leader that fits their profile more than the organization's profile.

- The search consultant who is hired turns out not to be effective, and the board will have to decide to spend more money on a new consultant or take over the time-consuming work itself.

There are more risks, but these examples should be suggestive enough for the organization to think about contingency planning.

There are also obstacles and challenges that should be expected, among them:

- Minority stakeholders—Those who believed that their values and interests were not well represented by the departing leader may be obstructive or may see the transition period and new leadership as the opportunity to push their own agenda. It is common enough that boards are close to evenly split about strategic differences, preferred management style, and even values. The time and effort to reconcile differences must be planned for and included in the transition project plan.

- Board members who serve on the Search Team are often overwhelmed by the process. They are often inexperienced in nonprofit searches. They don't always foresee the delays caused by scheduling candidates; and they may be tempted to risk shortcuts that will sabotage their search. Finding the additional time, energy, and money required during the transition period often proves challenging and requires planning.

- Day-to-day management—Programs, finance, fund-raising, and human resources—are all likely to be more erratic during the transition period. Who is responsible and how these "normal" challenges will be dealt with requires forethought.

In general, whatever fault lines and weaknesses there are in organizations stand a good likelihood to emerge during the transition period. This is why a "current state" or SWOT analysis should be part of transition planning. It will help you anticipate problems and then manage them rather than have them become crises. Even so, crises are also likely during transition periods, and it helps to imagine ahead of time how the team and staff will handle them.

Alternatively, in conflict adverse organizational cultures, the important discussions will be avoided for fear of fighting. When differences are glossed over, decisions are made with inadequate information, and simmering splits persist in underground currents that can be corrosive over time. There are two arenas where superficial, too-easily compromised decisions can especially hurt. The first is organizational direction as laid out in vision and strategy. As we've already insisted, leaders are hired to execute on strategy; without a clear idea of strategic direction, the choice of leader is almost inevitably a guessing game. The second is a superficial discussion about the choice of the leader can lead to compromises that satisfy no one and limit the organization's ability to pursue its ends.

Evaluation

It is important to build evaluation into the transition management process: evaluation of the planning, itself, of the management, of the board's effectiveness, and of staff capability. The best organizations create ongoing feedback systems through program evaluation and individual performance review. Instituting or maintaining these feedback systems during the transition period provides a clear model for the organization of the future and provides the new leadership important information with which to begin. Carefully documenting the work of the team will provide a starting point for transitions of the future.

Discussion Questions

1. How can the transition team juggle the competing priorities of day-to-day operations, the change process, and the CEO search?

2. What skills and experience does the transition team need to provide the oversight, stewardship, and creative change management mandated by the anticipated change?

3. What ongoing evaluation systems will be used to assess whether the transition plan is sufficient to meet the requirements of its charge?

8

Managing During the Transition Period

It becomes an act of juggling eggs and golf balls. Some of the daily maintenance has unyielding weight, and sometimes when you toss the eggs of change one or two splatters on your face; but all in all, you know that your organization will grow through this courageous act of transition.

Poor Transition Management

One of the major causes of leadership turnover is the poor, crisis-oriented management of the transition period. Few organizations have clear, written succession plans to fall back on in the face of a CEO's rapid departure. Boards are frequently disorganized; transition management falls to one person or to small cadre of people who are soon overwhelmed by the magnitude of a task that many engage in for a first time. In their rush to resolve the transition crisis, boards do not establish explicit plans, do not communicate clearly to the larger community, and severely underestimate the amount of time, energy, and resources needed for the search and transition. The person they find to fill the role is more often an excellent program director or administrator than an experienced big-picture leader, fund-raiser, and community developer, the hallmarks of the successful CEO of a nonprofit organization.

More often than not, leadership transitions are poorly managed. From the time a leader's departure is announced (whether forced or chosen) until a new leader is selected and integrated into the organizational culture (usually a much longer period than expected) there tends to be ad hoc, unplanned management. Search and selection are frequently rushed and reactive. Instead of defining the strategic directions they want the new leader to take—in effect, a job description for the incoming executive—boards focus on finding an outstanding person and hope that she will take the right path. Exhausted by the search and selection process, boards frequently fail to carefully introduce and empower the new leader. Nor do they carefully guide the early performance. Generally, there follows a brief honeymoon period between board, leader, and managers, and everyone sighs with relief and exaggerated optimism. Then the unstated or confused expectations of the selection process emerge in tensions and conflict, and the process of turnover begins again.

Once the inexperienced manager is hired, one of two scenarios generally unfolds. In the first, exhausted board members hand over the organization's leadership abruptly and completely to the new CEO while announcing in euphoric tones that their hard work has culminated in a perfect choice. No one could be that good, but new CEOs are reluctant to admit that. After a lengthy, unsupervised honeymoon between CEO and board, the board discovers that the CEO is flawed. It panics and exaggerates the problems, and a struggle begins between board and the CEO that is difficult if not impossible to resolve.

In the second scenario, the board has gotten used to day-to-day operational management during the transition period and finds it hard to hand control to the new CEO. The micromanagement renders the CEO less competent, fulfilling the board's fears, carried over from the failure of the last CEO, and a battle ensues that leads to turnover. In both scenarios, vicious, downward cycles create a culture of uncertainty and the probability of one leadership turnover after another.

The Potential

On the positive side, well-managed transitions generally lead to successful leadership tenure, which in turn leads to well-managed organizations and the possibility of optimizing growth toward achieving the organization's mission. What does good transition management require?

- Strong governance.
- Clear transition planning.

- Strategic leadership recruitment and integration into the organization. This includes strategic planning, search, selection, open communication with the community, careful handling of the exiting CEO's departure, and the new CEO's introduction.
- Patience. The average, effective transition effort takes from 12 to 18 months from announcement to the full empowerment of the new CEO.

To date, as many as 83.3 percent of nonprofit organizations have not created a succession plan.[1] The potential to limit damage and increase organizational strength by building these plans is immense.

Two Intertwined Management Challenges

During the transition period, there are two intertwined but distinct lines of management. The first concerns the transition itself and includes the clarification of the mission, the vision, the strategy, the search, the departure of the old CEO, and the introduction of the new CEO. The second concerns the everyday business of the organization. This includes orientation to program services, financial and information management, fundraising, and communication systems. Both are vital; neither can be subordinated to the other.

The development of the transition plan is described in the previous chapter. Now we will discuss the act of implementing the plan in a thoughtful and careful way that honors the culture of the organization and the strategic priorities and works to prepare the organization for the growth in its life cycle.

Implementing the Transition Plan

Planning is one thing. Implementation—no matter how good the plan— is often harder. In some ways, it is like implementing a strategic plan. Because we can hardly discuss all of the implementation challenges in one chapter, here are some that are particularly important and potentially difficult.

Time and Commitment

The time required to lead an organization through transition would be daunting to someone who had full time to devote to the process. Seldom do members of the transition team have this type of liberty. Usually they hold demanding jobs and serve the community in several other areas. Therefore, it is essential that the team divide the tasks and areas of stewardship and leadership throughout the entire group. The team also needs to look for places to bring multiple stakeholders into the process. The easiest way to convert people to a new vision or strategy is to give them a meaningful role in making it happen. In this way, the team can keep their heads above water as well as recruit converts to the strategic process.

Managing Day to Day

This is an important and vital focus that is often ignored and replaced by wishful thinking—we hope things work out during this period but don't have the time to pay attention.

But day-to-day management presents a huge opportunity. As we have suggested, the transition team has to look at what went before the transition and evaluate how and why leadership failed or succeeded in major areas of work. More often than not, especially in grassroots and entrepreneurial organizations (and others), the CEO was far better at inspiration than management. So here is the opportunity to begin reorganizing any undisciplined or chaotic areas of work and putting in good management practices. If, for instance, the organization hires an interim, a primary focus of her job can be to put systems in shape, clarify accountabilities in and across departments, ensure clear communications, and so forth.

Here are some particular challenges during the transition period.

Playing It by Ear

The lines between governance (board), leadership (staff), and management (staff and operational volunteers) naturally blur during the transition period, largely because the board—or transition team—must take a more active, even operational role. The CEO is either missing or on the way out. The supervision of staff must come from somewhere. If there is an interim CEO, the transition team can largely delegate much of the everyday responsibility and authority to that person. However, not everything can be delegated to the interim. The interim CEO will not have relationships with key stakeholders such as funders, and the transition team most likely will have to be more active in maintaining relationships with the larger community. The same may be true with organizational partners and key community and political figures.

In short, the transition team and the interim CEO roles will not be crystal clear. The interim CEO's tenure will be projected to be brief. As a result, it does not make sense for her to develop extensive external relationships. The team and interim will have to play a great deal on the fly until they have worked out an effective division of labor.

Delegation

Where possible, the transition team will want to delegate as much authority and responsibility as is prudent and possible to staff: the interim CEO, senior management team, and other assigned staff. To an extent, either the transition team or the interim CEO will have to monitor the delegation of responsibilities throughout the organization more than is their custom.

Delegation in the right balance is hard. People generally delegate too little, but sometimes they delegate too much. Too much leads to neglect. Too little leads to all kinds of problems, including burnout, not grooming people, and to turning people off. Here is the opportunity to get that right, to set an example, to put a new approach into place.

Delegation is an art that varies situation by situation, but here is a sequence of activities that breaks delegation into constituent parts:

- Frame the task with its sense of urgency or regularity. This is what I need from you. Here is the objective, the time frame, the importance of the task.
- Wherever possible, give room for people to come up with their own solution and plan.
- Review the plan with inexperienced employees. That is, ask them to develop a plan for accomplishing the task. Then review their plan and, if necessary, help revise it before they set it in motion.

- Let experienced and trusted employees go right from plan to implementation. This kind of autonomy is a sign of respect. It also saves the manager considerable time and energy, recognizes the high performance of employees, and provides skill development.
- Hold people accountable for completing tasks in a high-quality way. The approach to accountability will vary from person to person and team to team. Again, inexperienced people might be monitored more, whereas experienced people should mostly be evaluating the quality of their own work.

Reporting

One of the main reasons the CEO's job is difficult is that she does not often receive a clear statement of expectations and how they will be measured. Boards need to determine the criteria in such areas as financial growth or stability, program improvement, establishing management best practices, and evaluation of services.

The transition period, with all its potential neglect and chaos, is an excellent time to be clear about what kind of information is needed. The transition team should describe how information should be reported. This is an opportunity to develop clear reporting systems that provide information in the form best used by the board rather than asking the board to transcribe operational data into future projections in their head.

For example, monthly financial reports are often presented to the board with expanded operational details required for departments to manage themselves. That level of detail does not communicate future trends well. The transition team can design balance sheets, cash statements, and cash flow projections to assist the board in future casting. Rather than receiving reports of the number of clients in programs by geographic area, the transition team can help the staff translate the detailed numbers into charts in the form of a dashboard of important trends that need to be analyzed on a regular basis to observe movement toward mission achievement. Pre and post tests of children's quarterly growth in reading or decision making as attributed to program activities might be added to the dashboard. The transition team can design how the strategic plan will be monitored by how they require reporting during the transition.

Transparent reporting is necessary for good management and governance. Clarifying it during the transition will make it much easier and more effective when the new CEO comes in.

Accountability

Accountability can get loose or lost when organizations focus on "getting by" and hiring the new CEO, who will then save the organization—and the exhausted transition team—like a knight on a white horse. This is all the more reason for the transition team to establish very clear rules about who reports to whom, how that reporting will take place, and how people will be held accountable for clearly stated objectives including maintaining effectiveness and morale during the transition.

Stakeholder Relations

Stakeholders are often attached to the CEO. It is essential that the board and the transition team make connections with stakeholders in preparation for leading in the interim period. This should occur before the departing CEO leaves if possible. Introductions should be scheduled with the departing CEO and the leadership of each stakeholder group. Logistically, it makes sense for the transition team and senior management to divide the assignment for stakeholder relations. Obviously, any ongoing relationships should be leveraged. At the same time, with a reasonable plan, the team can stay connected, particularly with funders. Members can oversee any obligations the organization has to the stakeholders, and they can involve the stakeholders in the process of revising or developing the strategic plan.

Funders often fund leaders. Therefore, funders dread change because they have a significant investment in the organization through the current CEO. They are concerned that this investment be protected during the transition. The relationship needs to be nurtured, so they buy into investing in and supporting the transition activities. After all, they, too, want to see the organization grow to achieve its mission. That is exactly why they are banking on it.

Likewise, community members are seeking ways to connect with the organization. The broader the strategic planning group, the greater the opportunity will be for the transition team to explore joint efforts throughout the community. This also helps to communicate the mission of the organization and the strength of the board in supporting that mission.

Mission-Strategy Focus

As suggested, transitions offer the opportunity to clarify and consolidate the organizational mission and to make sure all is aligned to it. However, with all that is going on, there is a tendency toward a crisis orientation. The transition team should resist moving through the transition too quickly. This will result in losing sight of the mission and strategic direction. If the transition team is unable to stay connected to the strategic plan, the entry of the new CEO will be much harder. The transition team should keep an eye on the interim process and manage in a manner that sets up the organization for the positive entry of the new leader.

Grooming

During the lead up to the CEO's departure, some staff will have stepped up; others may have fallen away. It is important to identify and nurture the talent that is present. There are three reasons to keep everyone focused.

1. This will result in maintaining day-to-day functioning to maximize movement toward the mission.

2. Identifying and developing staff strengths and talents will provide the incoming CEO with the best possible team to get the strategic plan accomplished.

3. Engaging the staff in steering the agency during the interim keeps them committed to the mission. They will be motivated to stay and perform well through the transition in a manner that excites them about the new CEO's entrance.

Dealing with Uncertainty and Resistance

Change is hard, and those implicit or explicit in transition planning will almost invariably be resisted to some degree. Change can threaten vested interests and make people anxious. It poses a threat even when it means leaving behind painful or dysfunctional ways of operating. Resistance to change takes many forms, from direct opposition to foot dragging to apparent agreement accompanied by inept plan implementation. Indirect resistance is particularly difficult to deal with. Upon the suggestion that lethargic efforts, unusual mistakes, or pessimism that inhibits action might reflect an unwillingness to change, most people deny such motivations. In such cases it is difficult to find ways to reassure or motivate people.

When conducted in the manner we have been discussing, leadership transitions require significant organizational change. Often, because it professionalizes the transition process, the organization catapults itself into a new and generally more professional stage of its development. Reviewing, renewing, and updating the organization's mission, vision, objectives, and strategies will almost certainly precipitate major organizational changes. So, too, may the introduction of interim leadership, even if it is only temporary.

The process of organizational change is challenging, one that people find confusing and anxiety producing. Consequently, they often react by resisting. They do so by pulling into themselves, acting lethargic, expressing skepticism toward interim leadership, and reacting to every little setback.

Managing the change process is one of the transition team's major challenges. It helps to break down the process into more manageable steps, each one to be accomplished before moving on to the next, while keeping focused on the endpoint the organization is moving toward. Following are some tactics for creating mission-driven teams.

Leading the Organization Through Change

As Franklin Delano Roosevelt once said, "It is a terrible thing to look over your shoulder when you are trying to lead...and find no one is there." The first step for the transition team to lead the organization through change is to make the decision to do so. This requires a consensus among all the key stakeholders whose wisdom and goodwill might affect further organizational development. The transition team should endeavor to detail the problems that have been found in the old ways of work and communicate the cost to mission achievement of not addressing the problems. Members can put together a concise rationale for needed changes and why they are necessary to the organization's success. As the new strategic plan is formed, the team can assess people's level of trust in its efficacy.

To begin the move toward the decision to change, there must be a clear perception of the need to change—and of the changes already in motion. Through revisiting the strategic plan, the transition team, board, and senior staff will get clear on the mission and develop a perspective of what needs to happen to move more efficiently in the direction of achieving the mission. The key is to help the army of stakeholders become comfortable with these needs.

As soon as a board starts leading the organization through the transition, or change process, chaos will emerge. Actions that have been the norm no longer seem to fit. Everything the organization does is less rote and more in need of direct attention. The transition doesn't create chaos. It is the large number of stakeholders encountering psychological stress. Transition is a process people go through as they internalize and come to terms with the reality of new situations that are brought about by both the subtle and large changes that are needed to realign the organization's perspective of the new horizon.

The transition team will have to help people through three critical steps:

1. Holding people together as they let go of the old ways of doing things and deal with the losses they feel because of those changes.

2. Helping people hang on through what William Bridges calls the "neutral zone"—the time when the new isn't fully operational, but the old is gone.

3. Assisting people in making a new beginning, reinforcing their first steps in new systems and ways of work, showing appreciation for people's willingness to learn to change, and helping them celebrate what and who the organization is becoming.

In the first phase—letting go of the old ways—some will temporarily lose their sense of competence. They will feel uncomfortable and need to be assured the new ways fit with the rules and values of the organization. People may feel a loss of peers and peer groups as departments and ways of working shift. Some things will be over for everyone—this chapter in the organization's history; certain volunteer and employee expectations; perhaps even some program that the organization has been known for throughout the community.

There inevitably will be a chain of cause and effect collisions. When A changes, B no longer works and a new C needs to be developed. The transition team will want to identify and discuss who is losing what and try to foresee what secondary changes will probably occur and what will be different when each change is completed. The stakeholders together need to accept the reality of what is changing, and everyone needs to appreciate the importance of the subjective losses each is accepting for the good of the whole organization. The transition team should expect overreaction from some people in the initial phases of the transition. It is the team's job to express concern and sympathy openly while gently turning people's attention to the future.

The transition team may want to develop a transition management dashboard. Just as in a car or an airplane, a correctly situated and properly laid out dashboard will allow team members to keep their eyes on the road and monitor how the organization is moving through the transition. Is it going too fast or too slow? Is the organization's energy on empty, or can it go many more miles without worry? Do people feel that the transition leadership is pushing too hard into the red zone, where people may blow up in frustration, or is the transition smooth and steady? What are the key performance indicators?

The organizational dashboard may include key financial data, program services and operational movement toward benchmarks, a gage of the funding plan, and so on. The team will need a disciplined schedule for reviewing the components of the dashboard. They will need to have a list of control measures that have been put in place, along with key dates so that in reviewing the dashboard they can ensure that nothing essential is getting lost.

During this time of transition, the team will need the patience of Job as they give people information over and over until it is heard, understood, and acted upon. This is how new realities are built in organizations. The team will need to define what is over and what is not. This will prevent the overload of trying to do things the old ways in the back office as team members perform the new ways—the ones they don't trust—in the front office. The clear and continual communication of transition information will also prevent people from individually deciding what to abandon, by preference rather than by the need to realign. It will prevent people from tossing everything out and losing essential pieces of the organization.

During transition there is a need for rituals or ceremonies that dramatize the things that are ending, such as burying past or old ways of work. It is always important for the team to treat the past with respect. The past is the platform on which the organization has grown to be able to move to the next level of performance. In keeping with the need for ceremony, give people a way to take a piece of the old ways with them, whether it is symbolic or more concrete. The team needs to show stakeholders how what has come before will endure in the continuity of what really matters: the mission.

A subset of the transition team will need to focus continually upon communications. It will communicate clearly and transparently and often to the broad spectrum of stakeholders. The entire team needs to stay on message: This is about aligning everything we do to move the mission forward.

Leading people through the second step, the neutral zone, is difficult. They know things are changing, but they do not yet have all the details or perhaps even a clear sense of what new way will come. As French novelist André Gide said, "One doesn't discover new lands without consenting to lose sight of the shore for a very long time." When an organization goes through major transition, clear sight of land may not be obvious to everyone for one to three years. This is why strongly committed leadership is so necessary.

People in organizations are seldom practiced at being "in between." We Americans in particular dread the time it takes to get where we want to go. That is why we are fascinated by any type of instant transporter in science or fiction. Marilyn Ferguson, an American futurist, described the feelings at work during transition in this way. "It's not so much that we are afraid of change or so in love with the old ways, but it's the place in between that we fear...It's like being between trapezes. It's Linus with his blanket in the dryer. There's nothing to hold on to."

The transition team has to become what people hold onto when they doubt whether they can do what is necessary to take the organization to what it can become. In creating things for people to hold onto during the transition, it will be necessary for the team to create temporary systems.

They will need to strengthen organization-wide connections so that they create champions of change at every level of the organization. They will need to encourage creativity at every level to find the right fit in all of the systems.

In the third step, as the organization moves toward the introduction of the next leader, it is important for the team to encourage people to ask questions. If people don't understand why changes have occurred, they won't be able to absorb them. Now is the time to get it right. Whenever possible, connect changes to storytelling. That is the easiest way for people to remember the importance of their actions. Although everyone wants to feel good during the introduction of the new leader, it is more important that the team help the organization face both the good and bad facts about what the organization will need to do. Otherwise, stakeholders will attribute financial cutbacks or eliminated programs as the whim of the new leader rather considered action in alignment with the strategic plan.

As the new leader takes the steering wheel, the team needs to be consistent in how it reinforces the new beginning of a leadership cycle. It needs to ensure that systems have been reorganized for the "new beginning." Both internal and external resistance is to be expected. People will feel that this is the only way to express loyalty to their past leader. The new leader won't look quite the way team members expect him to look. His words and language will not sound like the former leader who was embedded in the organization's culture. The transition team will need to assist the incoming CEO in finding ways to ensure and celebrate some quick successes without wandering from the path of the strategic plan. The team will also assist in identifying the organization's life cycle and how it fits with the growth of the organization. It can help stakeholders recapture the dream that brought them into the organization and see how the new leader will connect them to future successes while reconnecting the organization with its venturing spirit.

As the new leader begins, the team can keep the board on track with the transition strategy and help to paint the big picture for their new leader. It can provide the new CEO with key information necessary for initial decision making. The more information that is conveyed in a way the new CEO can grasp the organization's culture and ways of work, the sooner the board will begin to see how it can partner in this leadership pact.

It is the job of the board and the transition team to work to build stakeholders' trust in the new leader. There may still be some old baggage that needs to be thrown out so people can move forward. It is important for everyone in leadership to have a clear sense of priorities and to reinforce stakeholders who achieve them with attention and rewards.

As the new CEO settles in, the team can step back and take stock of new opportunities.

In reinforcing the new strategic direction, the transition team should highlight the outcomes that change, no matter how difficult, will produce for the organization.

The team members must remember that they are farther down the path of change than other stakeholders, so they will need to be patient and understand the outlook from others' positions. Now is the time to take stock of how the organization fared during the transition and to look for lessons in "transition ability" for the organization. Everyone should celebrate the organization's enhanced ability to deal with change so that next time they can say, "Hey, we've done this before. We know how to do it."

With consistent leadership from the transition team, the board, and, eventually, the new CEO, the organization can move out of the transition period. When a transition is successful, there is much greater alignment of all of its core dimensions: leaders, stakeholders, and community. The board and new CEO form a partnership during further planning and implementation of change. They have a broader, better organized constituency—because all were included in the transition process.

A professional leadership capability has been achieved in several ways. First, there is a new CEO, with better and new skills, and perhaps managerial, financial, or marketing skills. At the same time, the board has come to terms with the reality that all leaders have flaws, as does the board. During a transition, the board is sorely challenged and frequently divided, often doubting its own ability to pull the organization through. In this trial by fire, it implodes or matures. If the transition was successful, the board has generally matured. Its members, too, have become more professional. Individual roles are more clearly defined and more closely related to skills than to alliances or "filling in." Board committees have become better ordered and more functional. Hopefully, board members have learned to manage the new CEO with a light hand and given her considerable autonomy, even as they hold her accountable through regular monitoring and evaluation.

As it consolidates the new organizational processes, however, the board must take into account both the difficulties of the recent past and the need to move assertively into the future.

Sustaining or Reintroducing Creativity and Spirit

How often have organizations, in the name of efficiency and order, killed off the spirit of adventure that built them? After the transition, organizations will still have to recruit and enroll clients, as well as design and implement the best possible programs and services in the best possible way. They will have to raise funds, bolster their staff, bring in new board members, and all the rest. If they set about this task in a mechanistic way when a passion for the organization's mission, ethics, and practice were what animated them in the first place, they will stagnate and eventually slide downhill. The professional management, which is now such a relief, will grow officious, conservative, and sluggish—in short, bureaucratic. The continuing challenge is to put the new management processes and style in the service of the organization's mission and vision.

Discussion Questions

1. How can the transition team divide the work of accessing and changing systems and processes on one hand while providing day-to-day oversight of the organization?

2. What are the "soft" changes needed in the organization's culture or ways of work? What are the linear process changes that will reinforce movement toward the mission?

3. How will the organization know that the transition team has successfully brought the organization through the transition period?

Endnotes

1 *Executive Director Tenure and Transition in Southern New England*, 2004, Maas and Randall, for The New England Executive Directors Partnership.

9

Managing the Search Process

I have been on a board through the transition of the CEO twice. The first time, the board didn't step up to make the transition plan happen after the departure of the CEO. After going nowhere for three months, we ended up hiring a consultant one day a week for $500 a day to manage the transition and the search.

—*Community Leader*

The Desired Outcome: A Great Fit Between the Organization and the Leader

Before turning to the search process, let's ask what kind of outcome we are looking for. This is a question too often taken for granted. "Let's get the best person we can," people think; but it's not that simple.

The essential challenge is not finding exactly the best CEO, but finding the right CEO for a particular organization at a particular time. There are stories of CEOs succeeding with some organizations and failing with others, or succeeding with organizations at certain stages in their development and failing at other stages.

Even the best leaders will fail in the wrong circumstances. To take an example from the international stage, Winston Churchill, often acknowledged as one of the great leaders of the twentieth century, was a failure by almost anyone's standards during his pre-World War II efforts to lead England. He was a far better war than peacetime leader. Overly bellicose in times of peace, he came across as brave and to the point once the war started.

So it is with CEOs. Some are effective in the formative stages; others in stable, well-established organizations. Some are good at stabilizing organizations in times of turmoil but lack innovation, an important competency when substantial change is required. Some may be wonderful with staff, volunteers, and constituents, but less effective when it comes to administration and relations with the board. If the organization can afford support—the equivalent of a chief operations officer—it can hire inspirational but less technically experienced leaders. If, however, the organization cannot afford to provide such help, not even in the form of an efficient board member who can take the time to manage some operations, even the most inspirational leader and brilliant manager will run into tremendous problems.

Fit and the Internal Candidate

One person who often is both well known and likely to fit well with the organization's mission, vision, strategy, and culture is the internal candidate: a chief operating officer, vice president of programs, chief administrative and finance officer. The fit may be far from coincidental but, instead, the result of being groomed for organizational succession. This kind of candidacy, however, presents both advantages and disadvantages.

Internal candidates have several primary advantages:

- The candidate is present, a fact that may permit the board to skip a lengthy, seemingly disruptive, time-consuming search process.
- The internal candidate is already familiar with the organization, its culture, and community, and he can start right in. Relationships with board members, staff, and constituents can be continued rather than created anew. Extending current loyalties can help the organization proceed confidently.
- The board is familiar with the internal candidate's capabilities and is able to support and compensate for any limitations.
- An internal candidate's compensation and benefits package can be adjusted incrementally and may represent something of a bargain compared to the current market compensation.

However attractive and convenient the internal candidate, it is best to conduct a search. There may, after all, be a better candidate out there. Furthermore, the internal candidate's credibility or stature will rise if he comes through such as search and remains the best choice for the job. Then too, internal candidates bring disadvantages as well as benefits.

- External candidates are more willing to listen to the priorities the board wants to set, whereas internal candidates may be inclined to continue running things as they have always been done or less able to motivate other staff to consider new approaches.

- When the departure of the current CEO has followed schisms among board, staff, and volunteers, and especially when the internal candidate has played a role in the struggles, the search is even more important. It is unlikely that choosing the internal candidate will lead to healing.

- Paradoxically, the candidate who is a valuable staff member presents a serious problem, because the organization probably does not want to lose her in her present role, particularly during a time of instability or conflict.

- The board or staff may have seen the internal candidate at less than her best and may be clear that she is not the right candidate.

- Rejecting the internal candidate means in many cases that she will leave the organization either immediately on learning she will not be chosen or in a short time. The embarrassment of not being selected or the sense that there is "nowhere to go here" is likely to open her eyes to other avenues. Going through the search process may increase her confidence and convince her she is ready to be a CEO, even if that means changing organizations.

It is important that the board treat the internal candidate with clarity and tact. The leader of the search process should keep the internal candidate informed of the search plan and progress. If the committee decides at any point that she is not a candidate, it should inform her immediately that, despite respect for her, the inclination is to hire an outsider. Some search committees believe any internal candidate deserves an interview, but if the committee truly believes the fit is not appropriate, the candidate may realize the consideration is disingenuous. The sooner she knows the process is over, the less expectations build and the less disappointment there may be. When the new CEO is chosen, the board should guide her in taking a particularly respectful approach to the internal candidate, allying and consulting with her if possible. This kind of entry behavior signals a general respectfulness to the staff and increases the likelihood of healing past wounds.

Components of the Search Process

Once the transition team has been named, many of the key components of the search process will sound familiar. The search committee should be a separate group or at least a subset of the team. This committee will have a separate and distinct function, selecting the future CEO. Here we will summarize the executive search process.

Clear Mandate

The search committee needs clear direction from the transition team that defines its responsibility, authority, resources, and operating methods. The search committee needs to know if it has the mandate to make an offer or whether it should present the top candidate to the full board for approval and whether the transition team or the whole board should develop the compensation package. Consulting with a professional transition consultant before making these decisions may give the transition team a realistic sense of effective practices so that members don't charge the search committee to operate in problematic ways.

Any possible conflict or overlap with standing committees should be clarified. Often, members of a standing personnel committee are not the right people to constitute the search committee. However, preparing the personnel committee conceptually for the need to constitute a separate search committee builds a stronger alliance. The personnel committee may conduct an assessment of the organization's human resources policies to assist the process. Board and committee input is important to building the new CEO profile. It also helps board members in preparing to work with new leadership.

Leadership: Naming the Search Committee

Search is a board function. It is the board's primary job to hire, manage, and, if necessary, fire the CEO. As with the transition team, the search committee should be led by a key board member—either the president, president-elect, or a member reporting directly to the transition team and president. The search committee chair should be present at every commit-tee meeting and confer between meetings with consultants and members. Where possible, there are several qualities for effective committee leader-ship: experience in managing group processes and working collaboratively with consultants, a respectful manner with other members, and, if possible, some experience with the search process.

Search Committee Membership

The search committee chair should appoint the search committee mem-bers after conferring with the transition team leader, the president, and other key leaders and stakeholders. Potential members must commit to prepare for every meeting, including a great deal of "homework" when needed, good-humored deliberation, and sharing of opinions collegially. They should also be able to tolerate disagreement and come to common (compromise) conclusions without being in total agreement. Because the search process may take between three to six months or more, mem-bers who anticipate long absences during the period ahead may not be appropriate. As much as possible, every member of the search commit-tee should be in attendance at every meeting. Otherwise, ownership of decisions and the ability to resolve issues as they arise are jeopardized. Conference calls or joining meetings by phoning in are options, but only in a pinch.

Some writers feel that search committees should represent the entire organization: board, staff, volunteers, and community members. It is essentially the board members' role to employ the CEO, and they will supervise and work side by side with the candidate they hire. However, nonprofit cultures are frequently participative, and staff members cer-tainly have an investment in the person who will be selected. The com-position of the search committee should reflect the organization's dominant culture. If staff are normally consulted frequently and have close relationships with the board, the search process should have a sim-ilar flavor. If staff and board roles are more distantly defined, it may be appropriate to delegate this work to board only.

Including staff on the search committee presents several benefits:

- Staff presence may make it easier to gain buy-in from staff when a candidate is selected.

- Staff members bring a perspective different from the boards and may be able to comment on the candidate's likely acceptance and appropriateness in day-to-day roles.
- Staff may be willing or able to provide certain administrative functions to the committee when a professional consultant is not leading the process.
- Staff members have a high investment in the success of the search.

There are also challenges:

- Human nature might tempt staff members to lean toward hiring a person whose style they particularly like or who might favor their particular viewpoint about the organization's direction. If board members are seeking a different profile, conflicts may arise.
- Staff choosing their eventual supervisor may favor a comfortable rather than challenging plan of action.
- Staff chosen to serve may have to defend a course of action not pleasing to peers and may be subject to pressure to talk about confidential aspects.

If staff members serve on the committee, several guidelines are advised:

- Maintain a majority of board members to retain the clear understanding that the hire is a board responsibility.
- Select staff one level removed from direct responsibility to the CEO so that staff on the committee will not be directly supervised by the successful candidate.
- The board members may confer without staff presence regarding issues of compensation, supervision, review of board concerns, or other issues considered confidential.
- Staff may be asked to serve in an advisory rather than voting capacity.

Including volunteers and community members has several advantages:

- They may develop closer ties with the organization as a result of their service.

- They may bring a valuable perspective that differs from an "insider" view.

- They may bring experience with search processes in other organizations.

Disadvantages of including volunteer and community members in the search include these:

- A lower level of knowledge of organizational history, issues, and personalities

- Less commitment to participation due to other allegiances or pressures

- Less stake in the outcome of the search

- Other agendas that might be served by particular choices

Some commentators assign a role on the search committee to the departing CEO, although it is usually limited and defined in advance. Others (Neighborhood Reinvestment Corporation, 1998; Adams, 1998; and these authors) advise firmly that the outgoing CEO not be involved at all.

Search committees often want to include the departing CEO as a member of the committee, either because they are used to looking her way when making decisions or out of a desire not to offend someone they hold in high regard. However, it's important for the board and its committees to begin to face the future without the perspective the departing CEO may represent, merely because they may have grown dependent over time and they need to be able to function when that leader is gone.

One departing CEO of an arts organization serving on a search committee was enthusiastic about the process and played a constructive and active role until each candidate came for interviews. Then candidate after candidate was deemed to be lacking in some essential element. It was difficult for her and the search committee to see how she feared a successor that might be seen as stronger than or more appropriate for the organization than she had been. This is another reason why the outgoing CEO should refrain from serving on the search committee. The committee is searching for a candidate that meets today's needs and the current strategy. This is not likely to be the same charge that the previous CEO held.

The departing CEO also has other work to do. Involving her on the search committee will divert her from tasks that only she can do in preparing the staff and constituents for her departure.

The board members should ask the departing CEO for an organized plan to transfer fully documented files. They should invite observations of the current status of operations, and they should engage in dialogue of what the CEO would do differently in her partnership with them. Much has been written about the first 90 days a CEO is on the job as the head of a new corporation or organization. Equally important to the transference of a healthy corporation is the agenda of a CEO in the last days at the helm of an organization.

Checklist for the Outgoing CEO

While much of the board and committee work is future focused, it is essential for the board to also charge the outgoing CEO with responsibility for preparing the organization for new leadership. The outgoing CEO can best identify and assess the current status of operations. They can assure that up to date operating procedure manuals exist. They are best qualified to document the current footprint of the organization: staff and departmental status, organizational commitments that are not yet fulfilled, and relationships that must be fostered in the community.

The outgoing CEO uniquely can

1. Reinforce stewardship for the organization's strategic plan.
    a. Assess the current status with the board and staff.
    b. Identify short-term commitments to implementation.
    c. Reinforce strong, distributive leadership throughout the organization.

2. Document processes and practices, and openly identify strengths and weaknesses.
    a. Create a guidebook that identifies activities that have been directed out of intuition and turns them into disciplined, documented, and replicable action steps.
    b. Identify personal strengths and talents that the organization may need to replicate or replace from other resources.

    c. Review personal weaknesses and identify particular skills and actions that are a priority for the organization.

3. Pull any skeletons out of the organization's closet.

    a. Are there difficult problems in the organization's history that have not been dealt with?

    b. Are there hanging legal issues?

    c. Are there outstanding fiscal issues that need to be pursued?

Considerations in choosing board members for search committee service include these:

- "Representation" of certain constituencies—geographic, program components, board committees, long-time members or newcomers, and so on
- Gender, age, racial, and personality balance
- Reputation for hard work, and acceptance of the level of work required
- Availability for meetings, ability to schedule without great difficulty, and flexibility when changes in plans are needed
- Ability to listen, understand, discern, and communicate cordially
- Leadership qualities

The search committee should be relatively small to maintain efficiency and confidentiality. Scheduling can be one of the most difficult tasks of the committee when more than seven members are involved. Odd numbers work well, although a committee would rarely take a vote and proceed if a significant number disagreed. Having an uneven number keeps movement in any conversation.

An administrative person will be needed to support the committee's scheduling, copying, mailing, and meeting logistics if a consultant is not taking this responsibility. This person needs to agree to strict confidentiality.

Although small search committees may be more efficient, they may not fit well with all organizations. A community that emphasizes wide participation and broad-based decision making may find that a small committee violates its principles and culture. When the search follows community conflict, a larger, more inclusive, and less efficient committee is more successful if it can bring together divergent groups and help heal old wounds. In other words, the search committee, like the leader, should align with the particular needs and values of the organization. Just keep in mind that not everyone can serve on the committee. By asking some to serve, others are inevitably excluded and must be given other ways to contribute.

Confidentiality

To attract a high-quality pool, candidates must be able to trust that their interest not be shared outside the search committee. Current jobs may be at risk in certain situations, and candidates may be unwilling to risk embarrassment if they are known to be rejected. Every search committee must agree not to divulge candidate names or ask friends, spouses, partners, family, neighbors, coworkers, or colleagues for information regarding candidates. If the committee chair learns of a breach of this agreement, the committee member must be terminated, and apologies and repairs should be made as possible in an attempt to retain the candidate.

Developing a Timeline

The first event triggering the search timeline is an organizational meeting of the search committee. At that meeting, it's important to list and discuss each of the tasks ahead and to put meeting dates on the calendar. Busy committee members sometimes find this the most challenging part of the search. Establishing dates for each event within the search as milestones will help create momentum and keep a sense of progress before the group. Although the names of the candidates must always be held in confidence, there is no reason for the process to be secret; therefore, putting into the calendar periodic reports to the committee's stakeholders (the full board, staff, funders, others of importance to the organization) is wise.

Stakeholder Input

Each organization has many stakeholders, including clients, partners, funders, and major players in the communities that the organizations serve. Naturally, they have opinions about the organization's needs, and listening to their input early in the process will not only provide the committee with valuable information, it will demonstrate a genuine sense that the committee is listening to its "partners." The search process is generally a time of anxiety as well as hope. Stakeholders will be concerned about the future of the organization and what it will be like to work with the new CEO. Providing a venue to talk about these hopes and anxieties and to offer suggestions can make it easier to obtain buy-in later in the process. Valuable names of referral sources or potential candidates may also be gained.

Obtaining stakeholder input may be done through a simple survey, either online or on paper, or through well-designed conversations in meetings. Strategic one-on-one conversations by phone or in person may be helpful as well, depending on the number, location, and role of the stakeholders.

Communication

Throughout the process, keeping stakeholders informed is well worth the time and effort. Regular board and staff meetings provide natural times to update the groups on progress and anticipated next steps. As discussed previously, the names of the candidates should be held confidential, but knowing that the search committee is meeting its milestones will be reassuring and create goodwill for both the board and the incoming CEO. One of the most important people to keep in mind through the search process is the outgoing CEO. Personal communication by the search committee chair, board president, or consultant will assist the outgoing CEO in his process of leaving the organization well.

Nonprofit governance consultant Nancy Axelrod provides a step-by-step prescription for communicating during the search.

Search Communication Plan: Help Build a Learning Community

1. Announce why the CEO is leaving. Manage, but do not distort, the message. The spin should be light, emphasizing directions and opportunities and drawing lessons from past problems.

2. Describe the CEO's tenure, accomplishments, main initiatives, and progress on the strategic plan. Describe how these successes fit in the long-term development of the organization. For example, the outgoing CEO got us through the launch and was very good at that phase, but we need different skills for our current phase.

3. Announce the formation of a search committee.

4. Circulate the CEO profile to the community; involve it in attracting applicants.

5. Keep the community informed throughout the process.

6. Announce the hiring decision to the organization and to the larger community through local and professional media.

7. Describe what has been learned about the organization during the search process: for example, from candidate observations and self-reflection. Explain that, when you are selling something, you get to know it in a different way.

8. Describe the new CEO and likely early activities in office.

What About a Search Consultant?

If you decide to retain a search consultant, do so early in the process so you will have a partner and adviser in all aspects of the search. If search committee members are chosen first, they can assist in interviewing and hiring a consultant; however, if you hire the consultant first, she can provide support and advice in selecting the committee. Most experienced consultants are aware of many effective practices and have preferences for ways they believe the committee can be most productive.

If resources permit and strong consultants are available, search committees can benefit greatly from the services of a consultant. The process is too time consuming for most board members who are volunteers with other commitments. Searches can consume as many as 200 administrative hours, and few volunteers are ready, willing, or able to add such a large project to their busy lives. Most volunteers will be involved in one search, at most, during their tenure, and they may have little experience in creating strategies for making the most of the committee's time and resources or handling difficulties that may arise, such as frustration over process or a shortage of viable candidates.

Pros

There are many good reasons to engage the services of a search consultant.

Consultants Know the Process

The consultant can educate the board about the search process: the time and resources it will take, the stages and practices to reach desired outcomes, and the potential pools of candidates to draw from. The latter consideration, in particular, is critical. There is an acknowledged shortage of qualified candidates for nonprofit CEOs. Broadening the potential pool from which to draw may mean the difference between an excellent and a mediocre choice.

Consultants Can Conduct the Search

The consultant can set up or personally conduct the process, which, minimally, includes an understanding of the following:

- Organizational readiness for the search
- The transition process happening around the search
- Structuring the search process
- Group decision-making processes
- Communication with stakeholders, candidates, and committee
- Advertising and outreach for the position
- Acknowledging and tracking applicants

- Screening applicants
- Effectively marketing the organization to appropriate candidates
- Creating effective and legal interview, reference, and background check protocols
- Making the selection
- Researching and structuring the compensation package, including terms of employment, benefits, severance, and relocation
- Negotiating with potential candidates and getting the "yes"
- Helping the board and the selected candidate get a good start

Consultants Offer Perspective

Experienced consultants add not only specific expertise but perspective. They have a clear sense of how long the search process should take. They can prepare the organization for the intensity of the process and the bumps and curves of transition. Consultants watch for pitfalls in the process and keep expectations in check by emphasizing the kind of talent likely to be available.

As we have already discussed, many boards look for rescue from their current situation. They want a CEO who combines all the qualities that rarely, if ever, exist in one person: visionaries with great public presence along with superior entrepreneurial and financial, program, and staff management skills. A consultant can support the committee's coming to grips with the real versus the ideal.

Consultants Help with Integration

Good search consultants know how to manage both selection and integration as a seamless process. They can lead the leadership transition team and the entire board in discussions of potential "onboarding" scenarios and assist in creating a plan to meet each scenario. If, for instance, a visionary candidate with few managerial skills is found, what kind of support can the organization provide? What kind of support will be necessary for a manager with a program background? By thinking this way, the organization can substantially increase its pool of candidates.

Cons

Search consultants can become a mixed blessing. Although they bring experience and structure to the process, their use can delay the committee's own development. It is important that the committee maintains control of the process and does not defer to the consultant. Just as attorneys provide advice with which you make your own decisions, the search consultant can advise and enlighten the committee; however, in the end all decisions are the responsibility of the search committee. There are several benefits to boards doing their own searches:

- The new CEO needs the commitment of the board. This may be enhanced if board members have carried out the selection process themselves because they have more invested in the CEO of their choice.

- Search specialists can lead to homogenized candidates. The desired qualifications may be consolidated into packages that can fit a number of organizations. Local diversity is essential to organizational success, and boards who do their own searches inject that diversity into the search process. If this is a concern, selecting a local search consultant may solve it.

Increasingly, nonprofits can benefit from consultants with technical skill plus knowledge of what makes nonprofit organizations unique and valuable. A specialty in nonprofit organizations has developed, and experienced consultants to nonprofits are able to support the search committee without making decisions for them. A skilled consultant can help the board develop its capacity to be a strong and capable partner to the CEO it proactively chose from among highly qualified and appropriate candidates.

Hiring a consultant requires financial resources, and planning ahead for transition is one way for organizations to be able to afford assistance. Wise budgeters know that transition costs are as predictable as the need for a new roof, and allowing for an annual allocation to a transition "fund for the future" will keep the organization in good stead when a CEO change begins. Funders who are committed to the organization's success may be another source of funds. Some boards reallocate the amount previously budgeted for the CEO's salary to pay the consultant or interim costs after the CEO has departed.

The cost of hiring a search consultant will vary according to geographic region, seniority and experience of the consultant, seniority of the candidate needed, and size of the organization. The scope of the project is also a significant factor. Some consultants will work with the organization throughout the entire transition; others specialize in the search process exclusively. A range of 30 to 33.3 percent of the base annual salary of the candidate recruited, with expenses additional, is common, but other arrangements may be offered by consultants.

Guarantee Versus Warranty

Search consultants to for-profit companies frequently "guarantee" that the candidate they recruit will stay in place for at least a year. If the candidate departs for any reason, the consultant will repeat the search process, charging only expenses. Although this arrangement may be offered for nonprofit searches, it is less common for several reasons:

- Consultants to nonprofits are willing to work with committee members who may not be experienced in hiring.
- Consultants to nonprofits generally work in a participative way and modify their practices to meet the cultural norms of organizational decision making.
- Consultants working with committees generally present options and then support the decisions made by committee members. Their decisions may not be those the consultant would make if asked to present more limited numbers of candidates.
- The total dollar amount charged by consultants to nonprofits is often lower due to the lower salaries of nonprofit CEOs.
- Unless the consultant is retained long term, he has no control over organizational processes that can promote success or undermine a good hire.
- Search assignments are generally accepted with the understanding that the candidate's personal circumstances may change and are not under the control of the consultant.

A "guarantee" may not be offered, but the organization has the right to expect a "warranty." The consultant should offer references that assure the committee he is thoughtful and conscientious and has a record of positive results for other organizations. He should also demonstrate due diligence and strong communication as well as a clear understanding and technical expertise in the process of recruiting excellent candidates for nonprofit CEO roles.

How Much to Use a Consultant

It is up to the board to decide whether and how much to use a consultant's services. These services can range from advice/guidance to a hands-on, soup-to-nuts full search process. Determining the amount and type of consulting help needed will depend on at least a few key decisions:

- How much money does the organization have/want to spend on consultation?

  The search may be one of the most important processes the organization undertakes for the foreseeable future and should take appropriate priority in budgeting. Thinking of the process as an investment rather than an expense may be useful, and amortizing the cost as the organization would a capital purchase may be in order.

- How much time are board members—perhaps with staff assistance—willing and able to put into the process? The administrative side of the search can be time intensive, and volunteers and staff may not have the time for outreach, careful record keeping, and handling inquiries from prospective candidates or referral sources.

- Some search consultants are willing to provide partial search services such as screening applicants, checking references, or simply guiding board members in how to conduct the search; however, splitting responsibility may lead to each party blaming the other if the results are less than positive. Having multiple parties in charge sometimes means no one is really in charge and may create a fragmented process where things can slip through the cracks. It's important, too, to be sure there is one standard for judging candidates.

- How much experience with search processes do board members have? Do they have networks in appropriate fields to attract high-level candidates? What is their level of confidence that they can conduct the process professionally and expertly?

- How much preparatory work, as outlined in earlier chapters, has been done? The more extensive the preparation, the more apparent the object of the search and the more doable the task.
- How united is the organization? In a divided community, the use of a professional can help prevent factions from prejudicing the choices. Is the process complicated by board or staff members applying for the CEO's job? Considerable skill and tact are required to avoid alienating important people. In such cases, the objectivity of the selection process must be beyond question.

Selecting a Search Consultant

Maintaining a list of consultants available to assist the organization in various ways is a wise practice for both CEOs and board presidents. Management assistance centers or associations for nonprofits may provide search services, and community foundations often maintain consultant listings. The best referral source is another organization happy with the services provided by its consultant. Internet listings can also connect the organization with experienced nonprofit search consultants.

Depending on the availability of experienced consultants, an initial phone contact by the board president or search committee chair can ascertain the consultant's style, process, availability, and fees. If a tentative match is perceived, the consultant may be asked to provide a written proposal for review by the transition team or search committee.

Interviewing two or three consultants then can assist in determining if the chemistry is right between the consultant and the organization. Being courteous in scheduling and taking care not to ask for large blocks of the consultant's time go a long way in beginning a relationship of respect with the consultant. At this stage, the consultant's time is provided without charge, and it's less than ethical to use him to solve problems or provide advice when he might not be hired. Most consultants are small business people or individuals, and their time is literally money. They remember organizations that follow through with a courteous response.

Detailing the Agreement

Once a consultant is chosen, a clear letter of agreement needs to be signed by both parties. The agreement should detail services to be provided, the amount and terms of payment, and the obligations of the organization to the consultant.

Budgeting

In addition to the consultant's fees, the expenses managed by the consultant are generally additional. They may include advertising, consultant and candidate travel (airfare, hotels, ground transportation, parking, mileage, meals, and so on), postage and couriers or other delivery services, telephone and fax, printing, copying, and supplies. The search committee will have latitude in the amount and types of advertising needed and determining whether candidates will be considered who may need relocation assistance. An out-of-town candidate may need assistance to bring family to see the area before reaching a decision. The consultant can develop an outreach plan for review by the committee depending on its decision regarding acceptance of local or out-of-area candidates. In the electronic age, even committees anticipating only local interest are likely to receive inquiries from throughout the country and even internationally.

Advertising and Outreach

One of the first tasks of the search committee will be preparing the job announcement. A job announcement can only be written once a job description has been agreed upon by the board. The job description is an internal document used to inform the CEO of the board's expectations. It can only be developed by the board once the transition team has clarified the organization's vision, objectives, and strategic plans and performed a current-state or SWOT analysis (described in Chapters 3 and 4). Bear in mind that the aim of the search is to find a CEO who fits the particular circumstances of the organization. This means taking an unblinking look at both the dreams and the realities of the organization and its community. The development of the job description can concretize the board's deliberations around fit; it should specify exactly the type of CEO to align with the organization. See Appendix C, "Sample CEO Job Descriptions," for sample job descriptions.

Using the job description for essential information, the search committee should develop a position announcement that is used for the following purposes:

- To inform board, staff, constituents, and the community that the search has begun and to share the perspective of the organization on the leadership it is seeking
- To inform potential applicants about the organization, the job, and the qualities needed and to encourage appropriate applicants to apply
- To encourage referral sources to share news of the search with potential candidates
- To create an open application process
- To serve as a foundation document for the search committee to use in screening applicants, to help form questions asked of candidates, and to evaluate and choose finalists

A position announcement may cover many pages; at other times, it may be a pithy two-page document including the following:

- A description of the organization and the community, highlighting current and future needs. At its best, this description would include a historical overview, with an assessment of the organization's current developmental phase. For example, it might indicate that the organization is just emerging from its grassroots stage and needs to enter a more professionally managed phase. The description might indicate that it is a long-standing, stable organization, wishing to sustain its traditions and program services; or that it has become stagnant and wishes to enter a new phase of innovation and growth.
- A description of the responsibilities, authority, and reporting structure the CEO would assume. This is the place to indicate the kind of partnership the CEO should build with the board, current administrative staff, volunteers, and constituents. Don't hesitate to include a description of the organization's cultural preferences and to indicate where on the spectrum from democratic to autocratic the leader should be.

- A description of the qualities of leadership the organization believes will meet its needs, including competencies, character, experience, and professional qualifications. This is the place to define the organization's wish for an entrepreneurial or a highly orderly CEO, or for one steeped in a particular pedagogy or management style. Being specific about measurable skills or experience is helpful. It's easier to assess whether a candidate brings more than 10 years in a senior leadership experience in a substance abuse prevention organization than it is to determine whether he has outstanding communication skills.

- A description of the compensation package may be included depending on the search committee's strategy. Listing a salary range will encourage all candidates to advocate for the top of the range. Listing a modest salary may discourage candidates who do not yet have an emotional connection with the organization or reason to consider lower compensation than they may have presently; yet it can establish realistic expectations and eliminate the need to review resumes of candidates expecting a higher salary. Saying the salary is TBD (to be determined) may be to the advantage of the organization wishing to review a range of candidates but is less helpful from the candidate's perspective.

- A clear, simple description of application procedures. Asking for a cover letter, resume, and salary history generally provides enough information to initially screen the applications received. Candidates are sometimes reluctant to answer the request for salary information, but many will provide it. Asking for it up front can eliminate the need for a screening call later in the process.

Once the position announcement is complete, committee members should be encouraged to share it with friends, colleagues, and neighbors, taking it to meetings and sending it to individuals and organizations that can spread word of the search. Board members and staff can be valuable in sharing the announcement widely as well, and a mailing to the organization's members will produce referrals.

Brief copy, perhaps a paragraph, excerpted from the position announcement can be used in organizational newsletters and in print form where there's a charge per word.

A key objective of the search process is developing a rich pool of candidates so that the choices are many and varied. If you think of the search process as a funnel, with many applicants in the beginning being narrowed to fewer well-qualified candidates and finally to a successful finalist, the volume at the top becomes a critical success factor.

Because job seekers increasingly use online postings, successful searches can be accomplished with modest advertising budgets. Expensive print ads can be avoided, but it's important to use some amount of print advertising to make the search an open process. If the organization is known for valuing diversity, local or neighborhood newspapers that don't yet offer online postings can provide access to candidates who don't have easy access to computers and can increase the response of specific candidate groups. Asking which edition will reach the highest number of job seekers will help determine the cost benefit of the ad price. Some take care to avoid holiday weekends when job seekers are likely to travel and miss the weekly print help-wanted section. Others feel holidays are the right time to capture the attention of otherwise too-busy executives.

Online job sites abound, making it important to develop a targeting strategy to reach specific types of job seekers. Online postings generally remain accessible for 30 or 60 days and can be much more cost-effective than print ads. Professional and sectoral (for example, youth development and child care) associations often provide job listings on their websites, and using list serves (a membership of a number of people who simultaneously send messages to all members of the group) in particular fields may be particularly effective.

Finally, nothing is more effective than one-on-one calls, asking if the recipient of the call is aware of the search. That's where the name "headhunter" comes from. The search consultant will begin with appropriate candidates already known to be seeking a position and will generally target a database of referral sources and professionals in the field and peers to the position. He will also use suggestions by the organization's staff, board, and committee and will contact community leaders for ideas and recommendations. If the committee is managing the search without a consultant, this time-consuming task should be divided among committed committee members who will follow through without fail. Having a "captain" to assemble a list, make assignments, and make sure the calls are made in a timely fashion is helpful.

Screening and Tracking Applicants

Careful record keeping is essential in an effective search. Without complete data, it will be difficult to evaluate the breadth of the outreach, to treat candidates with courtesy, to provide information on the search's progress, and to keep in touch with candidates appropriately during and after the search. There can be a substantial volume of detail work in a professionally managed search process.

Acknowledging Applications

As applications are received, acknowledgements are at minimum a courtesy and more an enticement to well-qualified applicants. One person on the committee, the consultant, or a staff person providing confidential assistance to the group should be the point of receipt so that applications are treated quickly and uniformly. Applicants who have seen only a brief posting should receive the full position announcement at this time to be sure they feel they are qualified and remain interested.

Developing a Database

Keeping a database of applicants' names, addresses, and date of acknowledgement will allow for duplication checking, responding to candidate inquiries, analyzing the effect of the outreach, and reporting to candidates when the process is complete. Many applicants have been treated poorly or ignored in other processes, and the organization can really shine by being friendly and professional at every point of contact.

Carefully Screen Applicants

As applications arrive, the consultant or committee member designated for this purpose will likely save each one electronically, review each one for basic appropriateness according to the criteria established in the position announcement. Using a screening tool can make this process easier, and a simple worksheet listing each of the qualifications desired will allow the screener to separate unqualified applicants. Often three piles are helpful at the beginning: definitely not, definitely yes, and need more information. Brief calls to candidates may be required to clarify information such as the size of the organizations they have served, budget or staff sizes, salary requirement, or ability to relocate.

An agreed-upon number of applications can then be provided to the full committee for review. It's generally difficult to have each committee member review a different group of candidates because each is likely making decisions based on different experiences in life and work. If every committee member reviews the same group, a discussion about which applicants each prefers can focus the group on its values and the needs of the position.

The number to be reviewed is subjective. As a rule, committee members may find it difficult to find time to review even 20 resumes without losing interest or the ability to distinguish between a variety of characteristics. Reviewing only 10 or fewer may leave the group with no one to consider when they have resolved their differences. As a rule of thumb, having about 15 resumes in the first review by the group as a whole leaves room to eliminate those who catch the interest of only a few in the group yet create an interesting and viable pool for further consideration.

One tool for making the initial comparison of committee member opinions productive is to ask each one to rank the resumes in order. Often one person will choose a #1 who is someone else's #12. That provides rich ground for discussion about differing expectations and desires. Some committees prefer to create groups—perhaps high interest, medium interest, and low interest—and then negotiate about which candidates move between the categories. At any rate, a method needs to be found to manage agreement on which candidate to pursue. This may be a low emotional point in the search.

The committee will be confronting the fact that there is unlikely to be an ideal candidate. Members may realize they have held a picture in their minds similar to the well-loved departing CEO or just the opposite. Encountering real flesh-and-blood candidates who are available at this time and place and are interested in this opportunity requires an adjustment. The necessity of making decisions between priorities can be a sobering realization. If the committee began with 15 to 20 resumes, selecting approximately 10 for further consideration is a good step forward.

Interview Applicants and Select Finalists

Screening the group of candidates selected through the committee's first round of discussion is an opportunity to "flesh out" the impression the candidates made on paper. Once again, it's vital not to divide the group and have some interview certain candidates and others the rest. The standard by which each is judged will inevitably vary, and the group as a whole will not be able to discuss the candidates they have not experienced. Either the consultant can interview all the candidates with questions developed by the committee and provide a transcript or detailed account of the conversation, or the entire group can interview all the candidates by conference call. Although time consuming, the candidate's attitudes, sense of humor, ways of describing her work, and reasons for decisions come to life through this process. Care must be taken, especially in group interviews, that questions asked of the candidate are legal and relevant to learning about their appropriateness and fit for the position.

Once again, ranking the candidate's interviews can be a good device to enable the committee's conversation and selection of finalists. Taking care to listen carefully to everyone on the committee is vital; often in groups there are people who are reticent to disagree or to raise issues that could take the process in a different direction. An experienced consultant or facilitator can guide the group to include all viewpoints as it makes what can be difficult choices. Emerging from this part of the process with as many as 5 to 6 candidates can allow for choices as candidates are met in person.

Taking a Step Back

If at this stage the committee is not confident that an appropriate candidate remains in the pool, going back to the outreach stage is the next step. Gathering new applicants may require giving an update to the community, but it will send a message that quality is first in the minds of the committee. Taking more time may be inconvenient, but in the long run, choosing a candidate who is less than a great fit will create hardship for the organization at a later time.

Provide Information for Applicants

Candidates selected for an interview in person will want information that may not be provided on the organization's website or in the position announcement. Each applicant should be provided with a consistent package of information that may include the annual report, strategic plan, by-laws, board list and meeting minutes, most recent audit, current budget, several recent financial statements, organization chart, brochures and program descriptions, benefits description, personnel policies, board manual, and so on. Including news articles, anniversary publications or special events programs, invitations, and videos can enhance the package and provide a great recruiting tool.

Keep in mind that the organization may be recruiting highly qualified candidates who have choices of their own to make. Providing these materials will help the candidates come to interviews well prepared and able to ask questions and converse at a serious level about how their experiences and abilities could fit organizational strategy, culture, and objectives. Because assembling these materials is time consuming and may be expensive or include proprietary information, supply may be limited to a small group of finalists just before meeting the committee.

As the field narrows, the consultant can be a friendly and safe person with whom the candidate can test her questions and observations about the organization. Knowing if the candidate is under time pressure with other decisions or whether there are misgivings about any part of the process can help eliminate last minute withdrawals or other disappointments. Committees without consulting help are at a disadvantage at this point. Candidates may be reluctant to share their concerns when they are simultaneously trying to impress the committee with their confidence and fit.

Conduct Reference and Background Checks

As the number of finalists narrows, learning what others have to say about the candidates in addition to representation of themselves will assist the committee in choosing the most appropriate candidate. A committee discussion of the issues they feel are most important will guide the development of questions that are asked of each reference. Each candidate will provide a list of suggested references that the consultant or committee representative may call. Candidates often want to contact each one prior to receiving the organization's call. At this stage, candidates may not feel comfortable providing the name of their current board president or supervisor, and it can be important to keep their application confidential.

Following an in-person meeting with the committee, if there continues to be mutual interest, the committee can ask for the candidate's permission to "go offline" and talk with references of the committee's own choosing. At this point the candidate will have to assume the risk of the current employer learning of her search and may even have to ask for permission to have the organization call for a reference. The committee that hires a candidate without a conversation with the candidate's current direct supervisor does so at its own peril.

Once the candidate becomes a finalist, certain background checks are wise, whereas others are mandated by law. Organizations working with children may have state requirements for criminal records checks, and others may find this to be a wise checkpoint. The organization may ask candidates who will have access to the organization's funds to agree to a credit check. Educational credentials and professional licenses can be easily verified. Consultants and other third parties will be required to have the candidate's written authorization before conducting these checks, and in every case, asking for permission to do so shows respect. If permission is denied, the organization must weigh whether the candidate's desire for privacy indicates any cause for concern.

Interviews

Before inviting finalists to meet with the committee, having the consultant or a committee representative meet in person with the candidates can allow the committee to take feedback from that meeting to further assess style, ability to engage and develop rapport, charisma, and consistency. This is also a good opportunity to enhance the candidate's interest in the organization and share information with the applicant about the anticipated interview process. Having the committee confirm the invitation list for committee interviews after this step is a safeguard to make the best use of the committee's limited time.

As many as four candidates can be interviewed in person by the committee during a single day. Spreading candidates over different days creates a risk that different committee members will see different candidates and then be unable to compare. Seeing more than four candidates in one day is difficult due to inevitable fatigue and even confusion about which candidate had what to say. If the committee has a genuine interest in fewer candidates, of course fewer should be invited, but seeing a range of candidates generally provides a richer choice.

The committee should develop an interview protocol before meeting the candidates so it can gather information about consistent topics. Having an interview format doesn't negate an informal and friendly atmosphere where committee members can pursue issues of interest that arise during the interview. The consultant's role may be to observe the process, both of the committee members and the candidates, so that he can better advise the committee regarding fit.

Following the interview, while memories are fresh, committee discussion will lead to one of several outcomes:

- One clear favorite emerges, with an enthusiastic decision to take the next steps.
- More than one candidate is suitable and will need further investigation.
- None of the candidates fits the bill.

In the case of a clear favorite, the committee or consultant may complete the reference process and provide an opportunity for the candidate to meet other stakeholders and to become more familiar with the organization. In the case of the need to know more, the consultant or committee representative may seek out additional reference information and schedule a second interview as appropriate. If no candidate is of interest, the outreach process begins again, but often with a clearer and more cohesive committee. If the process is repeated, it may be quicker or generally more satisfying as a result of lessons learned in the first process.

Stakeholder Input

When the committee introduces a candidate to stakeholders, it may be for several purposes. The committee may present a candidate informally and ask stakeholders for input rather than a vote. Bringing stakeholders into a process at a late stage and taking their opinions then as an "up or down" vote can be disastrous—stakeholders who have not been involved in the discernment process to date rarely have sufficient information to veto a candidate vetted so far by an informed and attentive search committee. However, they may have observations that the committee would do well to heed. If the feedback is less than positive, the committee may have another candidate in waiting that they also feel is a strong choice. If the feedback is affirmative, the committee will proceed to negotiating an agreement.

If the committee is uncertain between two candidates, stakeholder feedback can help settle the question. However, for reasons discussed earlier, it is just as likely to further confuse the committee. Due to human nature, a brief meeting inevitably leads some people to prefer the one while others prefer the second candidate, and then a whole new dynamic is created that demands resolution. It may be more useful to present candidates in sequence rather than as a panel of two. If the committee truly has a preference between candidates, acting on that preference creates fewer complications than deferring the choice to another group.

Negotiate and Make the Job Offer

From the earliest contact with the candidate, it's vital to listen for issues of importance that can make or break the offer from the candidate's perspective. Asking about salary needs early on can establish whether the candidate's expectations are within the range of the organization's abilities. Discussion of benefits also should not wait until late in the process. Some candidates need health insurance at a low cost for the entire family; for others, health insurance is provided by a partner or previous employer. The readiness of the family to move can be the difference between acceptance or withdrawal, and tactful attentiveness to this factor during the process can assure it is addressed. Organizations sometimes have to use the occasion of this important hire to debate changes or addition of benefits, and a candidate can be lost after great investment if this is left to late in the hiring process.

Draw Up a Contract or Letter of Agreement

The president of the board should prepare and sign a letter of agreement or contract clearly stating the organization's offer. It can be drafted early in the search and go through any approval process needed before a candidate is even identified so there are no unnecessary delays when a finalist is ready to accept.

Issues to be clearly stated include these:

- Title
- Starting date
- Salary and benefits
- Reporting structure
- Method and dates of evaluation
- Duties
- Terms of employment (at will or for a specific time period)
- Terms of termination of the agreement.

A consultant can be helpful in negotiating small points or unexpected issues that may arise, and care must be taken that the parties don't fall out of favor at this late stage over a point that is important to one but not anticipated by the other. The board president may need to talk with the executive committee or with the organization's legal counsel during this process and may help the board anticipate the decision that they are approaching. Having each party agree to the terms before formal action by the full board can avoid a failed offer.

The Board Makes the Offer

When the candidate agrees that the proposed offer will be accepted, the full board should vote to extend a formal written offer for the candidate's signature. With that signature, the communication plan should be activated for the announcement process.

Notify Unsuccessful Candidates and Stakeholders

Candidates who have given their time and met personally with the consultant or committee deserve a personal call letting them know another candidate has been selected. With this careful consideration, the unsuccessful candidates can become friends of the organization going forward. All applicants should receive a sealed letter letting them know the search is complete. Postcards or emails run the risk of being seen by someone other than the candidate, violating confidentiality.

Stakeholders are waiting for news and will appreciate timely and personal communication by the board president about the outcome of the search and the plans to welcome the new CEO. First among those informed should be the outgoing CEO.

Potential Pitfalls in the Search Process

The Neighborhood Reinvestment Corporation's 1998 report, *Managing Executive Transitions*, provides an excellent summary of the potential pitfalls in the search process. They are summarized here.

Five Danger Zones in Hiring a New Executive

1. Poorly structured hiring process
   - Poor strategy or work plan
   - Unclear job definition/candidate requirements
   - Inadequate recruitment/pool
   - Rushing to hire
   - Ignoring employment laws
2. Money issues
   - Letting money be the key issue
   - Noncompetitive salary/compensation package
   - Picking the bargain candidate
3. Internal board conflicts
   - Lack of board clarity
   - Polarized board
   - Deceiving the candidate about organizational health
4. Special interest pressure
   - Undue pressure from insiders
   - Discriminatory practices
   - Partnership power plays

5. Personality traps
- Being "snowed" by fast talk
- Ignoring bad chemistry
- Looking for a savior

Although a well-executed search is not "rocket science," it does require planning, care, and consistency. Search committee members often develop a camaraderie that carries into the future. The hours of work are quickly forgotten, and they often feel a closeness to the CEO they have selected. A professional search process strengthens the organization and leaves committee members feeling glad they participated.

Discussion Questions

1. How should the board of directors and the search committee develop an open and transparent search process that both recognizes members' potential conflicts of interest and utilizes the most experienced members?
2. How can a broad range of stakeholders' input be elicited during the search process while keeping the organization focused on the strategic plan of the organization?
3. What systems need to be developed to keep the board, the search committee, and the transition team working effectively together?

10

Using Interim CEOs During Transition

In an ideal world, CEO transitions would occur with plenty of notice, the organization would be perfectly aligned, and the hardest decision would be deciding whom to select among a raft of perfectly fitted experienced candidates. However, in the real world, CEO transitions do not usually occur without a significant time frame between the exiting CEO and the organization's readiness to appoint a new person.

As noted previously, a commitment to the process of revisiting the organization's strategic plan prior to engaging in a CEO search is essential to selecting a new CEO with an appropriate fit with the organizations' values, culture, and life cycle. An organization's adherence to process may appear time consuming, unless the expense of time, money, and forward movement is considered when a CEO search is not successful. Because the hiring of a CEO is so costly in money, resources, and strategic movement, it is essential that organizations refrain from making a hasty decision about who should be hired without doing the necessary work to prepare the organization for new leadership and to engage in a thorough and thoughtful search process.

Yet, seldom is a nonprofit staffed for redundancy, particularly in the CEO role. The lean staff structures of the current economy stretch staff and volunteers about as far as they can go on a daily basis. Often organizations look internally at the board or staff for a potential quick fix. Although there may be an internal candidate (either staff or board) that seems like the appropriate person to serve during the interim, this is generally not a good idea. It can take the objectivity out of the selection process and create confusion throughout the organization if this person decides she would like to be considered for the long-term position. Having been in the interim CEO position can be a deterrent to establishing a working relationship with the new CEO, and it sets the organization up to lose one of its most valuable staff members if that candidate is not selected for the CEO position and has hard feelings.

Increasingly, nonprofits are finding it necessary to contract with an interim CEO to lead the organization during the transition and search process. Interim CEOs are available who have training and experience in leading nonprofits through a leadership transition in a manner that fully utilizes the "in between" period. They are prepared to assist the board in readying systems for new leadership.

Advantages of Using an Interim CEO

The transition of the CEO creates an opportunity for the organization to conduct an in-depth analysis of all of its systems and ways of work. A professional interim CEO often comes with greater experience than the CEO who may ultimately be hired. The interim also comes with an objective eye. He can look at the systems, structure, and operations of the agency without knowing the particular circumstances that led to their development. As agencies progress through their organizational life cycles with changes in leadership and funding, resources, and personnel priorities, they often "jury rig" systems and to make do on a tight budget, to utilize current personnel or respond to funders' objectives. Over time, quite a chaotic house of cards can be built.

By hiring an interim, the organization can maintain forward progress in achieving its goals. The board receives assurance that operations are being sufficiently and effectively maintained while they focus on their governance role. The interim can help the board evaluate in a planned and mindful manner the effectiveness of the previous CEO as well as review staffing, programs, and methods in light of the organization's goals.

At the same time that the board is engaging in the complex process of preparing to select new leadership, a skilled interim can make needed changes in the organization. Interims do not have to build alliances for the long term, nor will they suffer from the long-term effect on their popularity from those changes. A board can charge an interim CEO with jump-starting a major change that is expected to bring short-term resistance from volunteers and staff. The interim CEO can afford to "take the hit" of implementing an initially unpopular strategy for significant long-term gains to the organization exactly because he is only in the organization for a short time.

The interim CEO can also provide an objective, deep-level analysis of structures and systems. She can do stakeholder interviews to determine the satisfaction of community members and funders with the organization's programs and can put her findings into context for the new CEO. A president of a community hospital described how the interim CEO's internal scan served as his primary orientation to the organization. He particularly trusted the information from this assessment process because of its objectivity. As he met with stakeholders and staff, he presented the assessment's findings and initiated discussion at a level that allowed him to take a clear measure of systems and goals in the first six months of his tenure instead of having to spend that time getting up to speed. He reported that the interim CEO had cleared the "dead limbs" off the path so that he could move more quickly to lead the organization into the future.

Sometimes the departure of a CEO leaves major tasks undone, such as the end of a capital campaign, major construction, or external certification review. The board can hire an interim with significant experience in a particular area to complete the remaining task, knowing that the longer-term incoming CEO can be recruited for the broader leadership and expertise needed to move into the future. The interim can also initiate focused development efforts on members of the senior team to prepare them for new strategic efforts.

Finally, and often, most importantly, hiring an interim CEO buys the board valuable time to create a pool of candidates that fits the organization's unique needs. Board members can separate stakeholders from the experience of the departure of the previous CEO and fully revisit their strategic plan as a basis of assessing their requirements for the next CEO.

Situations When an Interim Is Particularly Needed

Sometimes the use of an interim CEO prior to employing a longer-term CEO is imperative. There may be a need to grieve a beloved CEO's death or unexpected departure before the organization is able to move on. There may be a need for remedial work on systems or mechanics that have fallen into disrepair. Organizations under great stress may be well served by creating a defined space between their departing CEO and the incoming CEO. The charisma or the impact of the departing CEO may be overpowering. The current health of the organization may need intensive care from a short-term leader. Also, both the board and CEO may no longer have the trust of the community. Following are key scenarios suggesting the use of an interim.

A Turnaround Is Needed for the Organization to Survive

Organizations sometimes lose their focus. Board members stay in their positions too long and begin to take the health of the organization for granted. CEOs get lulled into complacency after years of being at the helm. Monitoring systems are taken for granted, and slowly the organization drifts off course. Perhaps funding decreases at 10 percent a year and the number of clients served decreases at a slightly slower rate. Everyone consoles each other that this is an anomaly. They cite external causes such as recession or declining population in the community, or they tell themselves that the press just isn't giving any attention to "good causes."

Then, slowly, the organization is jolted into reality. It receives a management letter with its audit that identifies weaknesses in the checks and balances of its financial systems. Funders the organization has depended on for a decade question their efficacy. Constituents complain of inattentive staff and shoddy services. The final blow occurs when an oversight agency delivers a qualified performance audit that speaks of mismanagement. In this situation, significant strategic planning and operational review will be necessary prior to engaging the search process.

A courageous board may need to bring in an interim CEO who can confront difficult issues, expose areas that need immediate change, and make unpopular decisions. The board may need a ruthless assessment of "sacred cow" programs that have outlived their viability and need to be closed. They may need an objective assessment of staff performance to weed out the "dead wood," and they may need to examine long-held partnerships that are going nowhere. This type of work can be handled most efficiently by someone who does not need to build long-term alliances and does not hold anything sacred because of past allegiances. An experienced interim CEO can work closely with the board to realign operations while helping the board to refresh itself, its membership, and its practices.

There Are No Currently Functioning Systems to Sustain Maintenance of the Organization

When an organization lacks the basic systems required to provide a platform of success for new leadership, it is advisable for the board to engage an interim with the skills to design and implement financial management systems, outcomes evaluation, human relations policies for employees and volunteers, and basic governance policies. The interim's work will build a platform upon which the new leader can lead to the achievement of the organization's mission and goals.

Also, when the organization is mired in a dysfunctional culture, it is best for an interim to assist the board in reframing the culture, the ways things are done throughout the organization. The interim can work with the board to reconnect the organization to its core values and beliefs. If the organization's membership or constituency has expanded or it needs to be opened to subcultures, the interim can work with the board and staff to acknowledge, respect, and discuss differences between core values and beliefs. In times of crisis, interims may work to uncover problems within the organizational culture that are just below the surface of awareness for long-term members of the organization.

Retirement of a Long-Term CEO or Founder

When the current CEO's image is one and the same as the organization within the community, it is unrealistic to expect that person can immediately be replaced. In addition to the strategic process described earlier, the interim may need to support the organization through a time of change, including the following:

- Going through a sense of loss of what was
- Experiencing doubt about the future
- Feeling uncomfortable about what is going on
- Discovering there may be light at the end of the tunnel
- Understanding the value of the change

People contribute their time, commitment, and psyche to the mission of an organization they choose to join. As a result, they often experience the departure of a founder or long-term leader with a sense of loss. The CEO represents the agency to them, and the organization needs to find a way to celebrate that leader's contribution as well as to grieve for the loss of their leadership before they attempt to hire a new CEO. An interim may need to allay doubts about the future of the organization and give people permission to move forward. This is hard, especially with a founder who is suffering a sense of loss of identity herself. The interim can provide breathing space for the organization to travel the cycle of change with leadership that is not immersed in the cycle so deeply herself.

A CEO of a community development agency told of immediately following the founder of the organization. This community organization had been started in the 1970s at a time when community development was changing and expanding. The founder convened the leadership of churches, health care facilities, family organizations, youth groups, and civic leaders. He led a year-long strategic visioning process to develop buy-in about how this community of 60,000 people should be developed. Then, over the next 30 years, he became known as the father of the town. When he decided to retire at age 70, the board of directors allowed him to take control of the search process, and ultimately he selected his successor.

Unbeknownst to the newly hired CEO, the founder also decided to stay on at the agency as the CEO Emeritus. When the new CEO arrived at the agency for his first day of work, the founder had not vacated his office, although he had graciously cleared the office next to him for what he saw as his protégé.

The new CEO hurriedly set up a meeting with the board members who had been involved in the search. They reasoned that, although it was not the best circumstance to have the founder remain for a short time, it was best for the agency to allow him to leave on his terms. They were sure that would be within a month.

Seeing no immediate alternative, the new CEO decided to make the best of the situation. He accompanied the founder to meet funders and community leaders, which certainly helped in his orientation to the position. However, he also spent hours listening to the founder's detailed descriptions of how he managed operations, which did not dovetail with the new CEO's management philosophy. The new CEO became aware that the founder had controlled every aspect of operations and that all the operational detail was in the founder's head. There were no records.

The new CEO began the laborious process of reconstructing the information he received into reports. He then developed systems to monitor operations. However, the founder would not allow him to implement anything because he had not let go of the reins. Over what became a three-month period in which the founder came to the office every day, the new CEO slowly came to be his anointed person. At the same time, the process exhausted the staff, confused constituents, and weakened the organization's standing in the community. After the third month, the founder was diagnosed with a major illness and had to leave after all, but without the celebration that was due him.

The new CEO was happy for the opportunity to know this legend in the field. However, a year after he began his leadership position, he still grapples with how to strengthen his relationship with the board, which he saw as an instrument of the founder. He sees himself as a placeholder while the organization emotionally finishes the last era. This CEO feels that significant strategic movement will happen only when he has put more systems in place in the organization and he moves on, to creating the opportunity for truly fresh leadership.

An interim can enter an organization when the board, employees, and constituents are feeling discomfort about the departure of a long-beloved leader and want to expand their comfort zone about what is possible for the future. He can help them hold on to the vision for the organization long enough to construct new ideas about the leadership needed for the next phase of the organization's life cycle. By working with the organization to clarify what needs to continue and what no longer serves a sufficient purpose, the interim begins to help the board set a new vision and discover what challenges lay in the future. Once the board members are drawn into this creative process, they will no longer need to keep the organization stuck in its past. Rather, they can own the development of their strategic plan for the future. This is the point at which the selection of longer-term leadership is most effective.

Immediately Following a Crisis That Has Shattered the Organization's Confidence in the Board and CEO

Perception becomes reality in this media-laden world. When an organization faces a crisis of confidence from the public, whether fully accurate or not, there may be a need for a wholesale change of leadership in senior management, the board officers, or both. Scandals in nonprofit organizations hurt everyone in the industry. Of course, we as people make mistakes. That is our nature. Nonetheless, we have a cultural expectation of near perfection of leaders within the nonprofit sector. The very practice of putting nonprofit leaders on a pedestal ensures that they will inevitably fail unreasonable expectations for perfect performance.

When an organization is faced with a major scandal, it may not be sufficient to put greater checks and balances into place. There is a need to assess the attentiveness of the board. The board may need to regain the public trust by bringing in a high-profile interim who can clean house appropriately and align the organization to more conservative practices. Public trust, once breached, cannot be rebuilt easily. Nonetheless, a public and transparent plan of reformation enacted by interim leadership can set the platform for a new beginning.

How to Find an Interim CEO

There are a number of places from which to secure an impartial and effective interim CEO. Foundations, nonprofit associations, associations of nonprofit consultants, and capacity-building organizations often have a recommended list of trained consultants, former CEOs, and community members with the professional experience necessary to lead an organization during a transition. National organizations often offer interim personnel to affiliates, as do some search firms, and associations of professional in the organization's field are an excellent place to look. It is essential that an interim be selected who can start working immediately upon hire.

Ideally, this interim CEO will have experience in the specific field of the organization's mission; however, this is not essential if she has excellent management and strategic skills, is a good listener, and is willing to work with the board to put the organization's house in order. The candidate needs to be available immediately. She should have significant management experience and expertise in consensus building, systems analysis, and fund development to be able to supervise the organization's staff and make useful assessments. She will also need to be a calming factor for the board, staff, and constituents.

It is generally not advisable to use a board member as the interim CEO. A board member stepping into the interim CEO position upsets the balance of governance and operations and reduces the objectivity with which assessments will be conducted. It may result in adherence to the status quo rather than exploring new perspectives on the organization's goals.

No doubt, in the assessment process, any interim CEO will find things she doesn't like or which she might have done differently. It is essential that an interim have a reputation for the ability to keep her counsel. There is a time and a place for sharing objective assessments of the issues with the board of directors. This is the only forum for the interim CEO's communications about what she would have done differently.

The skills needed to turn an organization around and bring it back to sound footing are quite different from those needed to stay the course. The board members can determine the opportunities they want to direct the interim CEO to take advantage of as they prepare the organization for its next growth spurt.

The Role of the Interim CEO

The secret of an effective interim CEO is that she is generally in and out in no more than 6 or 8 months to lay the groundwork for new leadership. However, she may serve in this interim role for up to 12 months in extraordinary circumstances such as a failed search. It is the board's job to keep the transition process on its timeline. When the board feels no urgency to move the search process forward because it has an interim, it is risking bringing the organization to a halt. Interims lose their effectiveness with an extended stay. There are strategic decisions that they should not be making. Furthermore, the community loses the stability of leadership that is fully engaged and leading the movement.

The interim's role is not to redirect services, change programs, or create personal alignment between the staff and herself. A good interim CEO is neutral regarding personal style and preference. Rather, she reflects the board's strategic governance priorities in every level of operations and seeks areas that are out of alignment or in need of refreshing. The best interim process is one in which the board is specific about what the expectations are for the interim period. The interim is advised through the use of a contractual agreement of the specific tasks that will be pursued.

Certainly, the interim will provide daily leadership of operations, including managing the financial picture and implementing the funding plan. She will work with managers to keep all staff focused on their work and will keep the board on track strategically. She must also hold the organizational culture together and keep constituents satisfied and engaged. She can assess the skills and tenure of staff, determine potential structural weaknesses, and assemble information for the incoming CEO. This includes pulling together contracts, checking compliance, and measuring outcomes. In effect, she will set the stage for the organization's rebirth that comes with new leadership.

Primarily, an interim should be focused internally within the organization. However, one key external task of the interim CEO is to maintain relationships with funders and to keep them apprised of the organization's status and the status of the transition to a new CEO. In preparing the way for new leadership, the interim engages staff and constituents in letting go of old ways of work and beginning to explore new options, perhaps for greater efficiency. She helps people connect to their aspirations for the organization, helps the transition team develop the transition plan, and assists the staff in integrating their work to the board's direction. The interim also works with the search consultant or search committee to facilitate communications with candidates about the organization and with staff about the search.

Managing the Interim

To effectively use an interim CEO, the board needs a clear understanding of what it expects to be accomplished. The board should develop a performance contract that lays out expectations of the interim, and the board president or an oversight committee (such as the executive committee) should meet with the interim regularly to discuss progress and respond to new findings. The board should devote a section of board meetings to dialogue and discussion of the plan of work, an update of accomplishments, and a consideration of further work that is required.

Managing the Transition from Interim to Newly Established Leader

Once the new CEO is hired, there is usually a short overlap in which the interim can share his findings and assist in the orientation. It is often sufficient for this period to be less than two weeks. Rather than risking the confusion of "two heads," it is preferable that the board contract with the interim to be available as needed to provide further assistance to the CEO. Effective practice dictates that the interim provide a report of his work and recommendations to the board at the close of the assignment.

Using Interims for Leadership Positions Other Than the CEO

Increasingly, nonprofit organizations are utilizing interims in other senior management positions. If the board's duty and care required in oversight of financial operations is sufficiently intense, it may want to consider an interim when the CFO position is open for any length of time. A similar argument can be made for any senior leadership position that requires extensive expertise when the expectation of the search for a replacement employee is expected to approach several months.

When nonprofits are asked why they decided to use an interim, their response tends to center on these reasons:

- The board was committed to conducting a significant strategic planning process and wanted to take the time to do it well, providing for sufficient input from multiple constituents.

- A search consultant found the organization not prepared to identify the skills and assets needed in their next leader or not prepared to welcome and incorporate new leadership without significant preparation.

- The organization had experienced problems in management and operations that indicated a need for retooling of systems.

- The cultural health of the organization was unstable, and the board wanted to reconnect with its core values and purposes before formulating a new strategic plan.

Just as hiring a CEO is more of an art than a science, the placement of an interim CEO does not guarantee success. However, because of the focused nature of the interim's plan of work, there is much less risk in exchange for the greater reward of starting the new CEO in a healthier organization that is clear about its strategic goals and prepared for movement toward its mission.

Discussion Questions

1. What will the organization gain by engaging an interim during its transition process?
2. What opportunities exist for significant progress in achieving the organization's goals by utilizing an interim?
3. How might board and staff receive guidance and development through the use of an interim?

11

Introducing the New Leader

"The board courted me throughout the search process. They met my every need. Yet, three months after my arrival, we weren't meeting quorum requirements at board meetings, and no one had time to meet with me between meetings."

—*CEO considering leaving after her first year at the organization*

Integrating the New CEO into the Organization and the Community

The integration of a new CEO is an often-neglected activity. Generally, search committee and transition team members are exhausted. They just want to hand the organization over, often leaving the new CEO to sink or swim on his own, diminishing his chances for success. Alternatively, boards that have grown accustomed to their increased leadership role have trouble letting go. The inevitable result is a lack of early guidance, in the first case, or a power struggle in the second.

Yet another scenario has the board and transition team playing out their ambivalence. They confuse everyone by alternately pulling back and then reclaiming leadership. Once again, struggles for control are the result. If the CEO gives in and cedes too much responsibility to the board, he will hardly be thanked. The board generally considers a new CEO who relinquishes control so easily to be irresponsible.

The transition team is charged with the vital task of introducing the new CEO and orienting him to the organization's mission and strategic plan. This activity should continue until the new CEO is well integrated and the board is comfortable that this new leader can represent the organization's values, maintain its culture, drive operations, and manage the organization's place in the larger world.

Among the central tasks is holding a major planning meeting to articulate or clarify mutual expectations between the board and the new CEO. Individual or group meetings with the entire board should be scheduled so that talents and potential contributions can be explored. If possible, a board retreat by the end of the first six months will help to solidify the leadership team of board and senior management. Primary elements of this retreat will be a review of the organization's strategic plan and a discussion of its implementation through governance and operations.

The transition team should work with the board to establish a disciplined method for evaluating the CEO's ongoing progress of the CEO's performance and his integration into the organization. The method should include creating action steps that are specific and measurable.

Here is a sample of performance accountabilities for a new CEO:

- **Finance**—The CEO will produce a budget that is built to accomplish the year's goals and objectives as presented in the strategic plan.
- **Fund development**—The CEO will collaborate with board members to develop and implement a fund development plan that will support the organization's budget.
- **Membership**—The CEO will develop a membership recruitment and support plan that engages staff and operational volunteers in implementing the strategic plan.
- **Integration**—The CEO will develop a service delivery plan to provide services to constituents in alignment with the strategic plan.

Time should be scheduled during board meetings to discuss the CEO's introduction and areas in which he can request greater—or less—assistance from the board. When necessary, the CEO and the board should jointly redesign the tactical plan to align with the strategic plan, and the board should have ongoing exploration and dialogue with the CEO about the effectiveness of systems and services in furthering the mission.

Before the transition team can hold a new CEO accountable, it has to make sure he is oriented, particularly to the organization's mission, vision, and strategic plan. This can be done in two complementary ways. The first is didactic, telling him, "Here is our mission, vision, and plan."

The second is narrative and experiential. Introduce him to the best storytellers—those who can make the words and instructions come alive with images of well-served clients and well-functioning staff. Then take the new CEO on tours of programs and services. During the tours, he will be able to speak to clients and hear, firsthand, how they have benefited through participation in the organization. There is an entirely different level of understanding created when one witnesses the difference made in people's lives. The mission comes alive and the strategic plan comes into more vivid focus.

Among other things, the transition team should do the following:

- Assist the CEO in developing his partnership with the board.
- Help him build credibility internally and externally by providing a forum to speak at board meetings and in key community arenas.
- Teach him about the internal and external political environment that is of particular importance if he has recently moved into a new community.
- Discuss strategic areas that have been given priority status by the board.
- Review the information and metrics the board needs to receive to fulfill its oversight and governance responsibilities.
- Review reports currently being received by the board, and discuss where different information or analysis might serve the board's oversight in the implementation of the strategic plan.
- Make sure the board reviews its own effectiveness in managing to the strategic plan.
- Encourage the CEO to review key deadlines to ascertain whether they are in sync with both the board strategy and deliverables.
- If appropriate, request a presentation of the organization's achievement of certification and licensing requirements at a board meeting in the first three months. This will create agreement about any remedial work that may need attention as well as bring the CEO up to speed on the organization's legal requirements.

- Require that the interim director and senior staff brief the new CEO on high priorities.
- Empower the CEO to set up ways of working with his staff team that make sense to him rather than referring back to "how it has always been" when operational changes are made.
- Support the CEO in establishing his authority with the staff.

Utilizing an Organizational Development Consultant

The board may need to allocate resources for the CEO to bring in a consultant to assist in building her relationship with the staff team. The consultant can assist in determining if the right people with the necessary skills are on the staff and can provide an objective balance to the many (perhaps unintentionally) biased assessments individuals will be providing to the CEO. A good consultant can also help the CEO discover and respect the expertise and ways of work of the current staff.

A guided staff retreat can help the CEO to organize and understand the wisdom and experience the staff brings to the organization. The intensity of a retreat will help the CEO negotiate a clean slate with staff, dispensing with rumors and fears that floated prior to their arrival. The consultant may also need to help the staff resolve or bury past issues, conflicts of style or grievances, enabling them to move into the future with their new leader. By utilizing an external facilitator, the new CEO can concentrate on listening to her staff and learning about operational systems and can use the retreat to begin building trust and establishing her preferred ways of work. Together, the newly configured senior staff can develop a shared synergy for moving forward on the mission.

Here are some additional goals for such a retreat:

- Acknowledge that, as a new person in authority, the new CEO may require more formal channels of communication between staff and board members than the previous CEO.
- Encourage the new CEO to develop her own style of and means for communicating between operational and policy-making groups.
- Help the new CEO articulate an appreciation of staff and volunteers for their ongoing leadership, particularly during the transition period.

- Thank staff in advance for their assistance in orienting the new leader.

- Review and praise everyone's work throughout the transition and look for ways to assure them that the change in leadership is supported by the board and will continue to fully utilize the long-term staff and volunteers' significant talents and resources.

- Keep an ongoing dialogue with a broad cross section of the organization about how the board intends to utilize the new leadership to accomplish everyone's objectives and, ultimately, the organization's mission.

After the retreat, the CEO will need to do the following:

- Work with department managers to assess operations.

- Support department managers in uncovering any issues that have been swept under the rug without looking for blame.

- Encourage truth telling even when it may imply a need for staff and board development or a change in ways of work. The introduction of a new CEO is an excellent time to encourage a "fresh air" analysis of systems.

- Ask questions when she doesn't understand the implications of what she sees, and face the good and bad facts of where the organization stands today. As the new CEO and the board review the organizational red flags, plans can be established to improve performance objectives across the entire organization and ensure they are aligned with the strategic plan.

- Pay particular attention to health and safety issues that may have been overlooked.

- Conduct a review of financial systems with the finance committee of the board, and determine that checks and balances are being utilized in an attempt to segregate duties appropriately.

- Review the stability and effectiveness of technology used throughout the organization.

- Report to the board on what she thinks may be priorities compared to the current strategic plan.

- Assess actions she would like to champion that are not currently in congruence with the strategic plan.

The New Leader's Agenda

In launching a new CEO, it is vital to challenge her to select priorities that will take the organization to a higher level of performance and leverage the current deliverables of the organization. Ask her, for example, to provide a "confidence rating" for each priority she establishes so that board dialogue can explore and compare options for strategic action effectively. Through dialogue with the CEO, the board can help determine where the introduction of new leadership can best leverage her energy for the greatest return to the organization.

Expecting to receive a leadership agenda that expresses how the new CEO will implement her tactics to bring life to the strategic plan within six months to a year can discourage her jumping in too soon to make her mark on the organization. First, she needs to immerse herself fully in the day-to-day operations. Many new leaders believe their board expects signs of their "brilliance" immediately and, as a result, they act impulsively to prove how they are different from the past leader. They initially don't fully understand the board and CEO partnership in leading the organization. Unless the new CEO becomes grounded in the partnership and the board's strategic plan for the organization, she will not understand the need to act in alignment with the board's vision and may make capricious changes to prove her authority over operational issues. When actions are not well thought out, unnecessary stress is created, and the leader is likely to lose followers, at least temporarily.

When the CEO has had time to become reasonably grounded, ask her to create a tactical plan that provides benchmarks for the board's evaluation of her success. Encourage her to identify opportunities for quick, meaningful "wins" so that people will easily see the advantage of following the direction of the board and CEO. Negotiate the goals and priorities for the first six months of the CEO's tenure with clarity and transparency. The greater the understanding of common expectations, the more likely all will be in alignment in terms of goals. It's useful to craft a process for delivery of outcomes to the board and develop a two-way progress evaluation between the board and the CEO for the first six months. This will form the basis of communicating and measuring success on an ongoing basis. Working with the CEO to identify and implement her own professional development plan to bring her skills to a higher level will provide meaningful learning experiences that will serve the entire organization.

Meeting Volunteers

In an organization that utilizes a strong volunteer component, it is essential that the new CEO be introduced to volunteer constituents in a formal and supportive manner by the board. This can be accomplished at an annual meeting, at a special reception, or at regional or constituent group meetings. The important issue is that the board provides the introduction of the CEO to the community and in the process shares its respect for the CEO and communicates the organization's mission to the entire community.

Media Opportunities

The introduction of the CEO to the community creates a great public relations opportunity. Combine media interviews of the new CEO with announcements of the strategic plan and how it will impact the community. Utilize events to shine a spotlight on the mission of the organization. It is important that the board and staff coordinate their messages so that one clear and transparent image of the organization and the new CEO's role will be broadcast repeatedly. Even with our oversaturated communication channels, the process that best disseminates the organization's story is committed people talking to one community member at a time. The new CEO will be representing the organization's brand throughout the community. First impressions are powerful, so be sure to provide enough orientation for the CEO to tell the organization's story effectively and in alignment with the board's vision.

Community Introductions

Take advantage of the introduction of the CEO within the community to highlight your organization's mission and the partnership your board is developing with the new CEO to move forward in new ways. Make sure your message is clear, strategic, and consistent with how the organization is moving forward. Share the board's conviction that this new leadership will contribute significantly to the community and assist the CEO in getting invited to community groups and conversations that will make this assertion reality.

Board members need to assist the CEO in making appropriate connections, particularly if he has come from outside the community. This is a time for board members to use their contacts for the organization and to introduce the CEO to the leadership of peer agencies, surrounding affiliates, community and business leaders, and the funder community.

For integration to succeed, the new CEO needs to form partnerships with members and groups in the organization and community. The board will want to introduce him to external constituents that are likely to maximize the organization's effectiveness.

Board members can often stabilize the marriage between staff, constituents, and the CEO by showing visible support. They can introduce the CEO to key clients and vendors, initiating a dialogue with each group about their vision for the organization and their attendant needs. The time dedicated to getting the CEO off to an effective start will be one of the best investments the board can make in the CEO's success and retention.

Most importantly, both the board and the CEO need to hold onto the realization that this partnership is for the long haul. Just as the board did not acquire its knowledge and expertise about the organization and its mission in a short period, the new CEO cannot expect to grow into his leadership position without significant seasoning. Everyone needs to be patient, expect missteps, and anticipate more than a few rough spots as the CEO learns about the organization's culture in a trial by fire. Without board support, the CEO could become frozen in fear of overreaction to the steps he sees that need to be implemented for the betterment of the organization.

Beginning to Implement the Strategic Plan

Organizations should assume that a new CEO will supplement the strategic plan reviewed by the board with the knowledge, skills, and experience she brings to the organization. After all, the CEO was hired because her skills, values, character, and personal objectives fit with the organization and its plans. If she fails to take the strategic plan seriously or diverges widely from its major directions, the board must step in immediately to guide or to insist that the plan be implemented. If the board fails to confront a new CEO who has taken her own direction, problems will build with time.

The Personal Side of Integrating the New CEO

The integration of the CEO to the organization's internal community and to the larger external community is important to establishing a satisfactory environment for the CEO to establish roots and begin to make this new organization his "home." If the CEO is unable to find appropriate housing or sell his previous home, he is likely to become dissatisfied and return to his former community, leaving the organization with a failed search. A CEO also needs assistance in finding schools, places of worship, health and fitness facilities, and opportunities for family members to pursue interests and hobbies. The board can assist in this process by showing the CEO and his family the options available and introducing them to key members in each field. While there is a delicate balance between helping and intruding in the CEO's life, offers of assistance in the new community will help him to feel welcome and be able to focus his energy on the organization. A school in Atlanta exemplified this approach. The school's complete leadership transition plan is reproduced in Appendix B, "Sample Leadership Transition Plan."

Using a Mentor or Executive Coach

The integration process is complex. However welcoming the organization and the community are, the new CEO is likely to encounter many problems, some of which he would prefer not to share widely. It is helpful to have a sounding board and problem-solving partner accessible during such times. At least four options come to mind:

- **Board president**—There is no one more helpful than a particularly compatible board president. There is a limitation to this choice, however. Even the most compatible president has opinions and a separate stake in almost everything the new CEO does.

- **Executive support team**—Because the board president has an important, formal relationship to the CEO, he is often not the best problem-solving partner for the CEO. Some organizations appoint, instead, a group of three or four board or community members who can put aside their own and institutional interests to serve as collective mentors. In fact, it helps if this group has a limited institutional role in the organization.

- **Mentor**—Many new CEOs rely on mentors from their old communities. These are trusted advisors who know the CEO well and who take his interests, rather than the organization's, to heart. Their limitation is their lack of knowledge of the new organization.

- **Executive coach**—It is a wise board that provides a new CEO with an executive coach, a professional dedicated to the CEO's, and therefore the organization's, success. Like the mentor, the coach is limited in familiarity about the organization but rich in organizational experience, management skills, and objectivity.

Reducing Isolation and Increasing Integration

Often, boards neglect the post-hiring period, which increases the incoming CEO's isolation and can bring out the authoritarian aspects of the CEO. The following strategies decrease isolation and speed integration:

- **Involve the new CEO before the start date**—Use the time between hiring and the start date to give the incoming CEO a feel for the organization. He can review reports, handbooks, and audits, for instance. He should attend all interviews for new staff members as well as a staff meeting, department head meeting, and board reception.

- **Welcome the new CEO**—The board president should meet with staff before the incoming CEO's arrival and express enthusiasm for the new hire. If an interim director has been appointed, she should stay on for a couple of weeks to transfer knowledge of the organization's current status. Often, a series of introduction ceremonies and social activities are planned to welcome the new CEO.

- **Include the new CEO in planning and evaluation**—When the incoming CEO starts, it is time to revisit the plans made in the prehiring stage and involve the new leader in the process. It is extremely important to get the board and new CEO working together right away. This is the time to review long- and short-term goals and establish an evaluation process. There may be a 90-day check-in followed by more in-depth 6-month and 12-month evaluations. During the same period, the board should not only evaluate the new leader but its own role in leadership of the organization.

- **Use the authority of the board**—When the CEO starts, all eyes are on his every action. Early actions will be overinterpreted. To mitigate this effect, the board president should be as visible as possible during the first few months. The honeymoon period only lasts so long, and every change made by the new CEO will upset some constituency, especially the ones who supported a different candidate. Board members can take some of the heat off the CEO by making it clear that the organization's priorities are their own, and the CEO's job is to implement them. This strategy is particularly important for founder successions in which the new CEO's every action will be compared to the myth of the founder.

- **Schedule interviews**—The CEO may want to conduct a series of confidential early interviews with staff, volunteers, and individual board members to gain multiple perspectives of operational issues. Organizations tend to develop complex relationships within their leadership. The interviews will allow the new leader to learn about the organizational culture and act to align it with the mission and values where change is needed.

The new CEO must understand organizational culture before moving in new directions. Otherwise, incoming leaders may find themselves trying to fix things that are not broken. The board and transition team must curb their impulse to dump the organization and its challenges in the new CEO's lap and run. Only with careful integration will the incoming CEO succeed in a new community. Integration is the first step in leadership retention.

Realities That New CEOs Face

The new CEO quickly learns some pretty frightening realities. First, she finds out that although she is responsible for the overall success of the organization, there are enormous limitations to what she alone can accomplish. Sometimes, for the first time in her life, she realizes that this job is all about what she can do with and through other people. She has to absorb the reality that she's ultimately responsible. The power to get almost anything done long term lays *not* in her authority but in her power of persuasion. She begins to realize that everything looks more complicated when she is at the top looking down. Perhaps in the program director position or as the fund development director, she believed she had all the answers. This perspective may have even driven her decision to apply for the CEO position. Now, when she sees the whole picture, often for the first time, she realizes that the linear solutions she held onto no longer fit the total needs of the organization. She also begins to realize that the whole picture that is now more apparent to her is still not seen by the department heads and other key constituents. It is the role of the CEO to paint this picture with sufficient clarity to gain the trust of others to follow her lead.

In some ways, the new CEO does have great authority as long as she doesn't resort to using it unilaterally. People are looking for her to lead, often after a long period of a lack of leadership. However, every time she rules through perceived dictation, she loses a little of that positional power base. Also, second-guessing senior managers pulls operational authority away from them and creates a quagmire in decision making that decreases respect for the new CEO. In the long run, any need for undue wielding of authority creates a bottleneck for timely action within the agency.

The second frightening reality the CEO may encounter is that the skills she used to get the CEO position will not necessarily transfer to the new position. The best course of action is to turn the tool box for managing and running things over to the senior managers. In many ways, rather than "running things," the CEO's primary job is to paint the doorway to the future of the organization so that staff and constituents move through it to the next level of achieving the mission.

The third reality is that the CEO's authority is counter-balanced by the board of directors. The CEO has an entire board of big picture bosses, or at least we hope so. More likely, there is a mixture of big picture thinkers, people wedded to a specific program, opportunists looking for a new place to wield power, and a significant number of high-level experts who care so much about the organization's mission that they willingly spend huge blocks of time doing everything within their power to assist in achieving it. The CEO can never forget two things:

- The board hires, evaluates, supports or overrules, and has the power to fire the CEO.
- Boards are composed of experienced, capable people who know how to wield power but don't necessarily know the organization's business.

Another rude awakening for the new CEO is that her life and schedule are often driven by both internal and external people's needs, which forces her to wedge her agenda between and within constituents' priorities. This can be particularly difficult for a CEO who likes to believe she is in control of everything. In addition, it becomes obvious that, as CEO, she cannot personally know everything or even everyone on whom she depends for success.

So, what is a new CEO to do? The first task is to hone effective communication skills. She will also need strong muscles for indirect influencing to sell her vision for the organization. Rather than keeping a closely held strategy that she shares in small steps, the CEO needs to share her strategic vision broadly, eliciting support across all levels of constituents. She should develop a process of bringing everyone onto her team by empowering them with an understanding of the strategic plan, the structure she intends to use to propel the organization in that direction, and some basic guidelines that communicate the core values that will be held sacrosanct in getting there.

New CEOs are often surprised at how much their actions are scrutinized and overinterpreted. In previous positions, the new CEO may have almost envied the attention given the CEO who often appeared to do little more than share the accomplishments of others. Often, new CEOs expect to enjoy living in that spotlight. However, living under a microscope quickly becomes a real killer for many. Nothing is off the record. Misinterpretations of the past or actual missteps in previous jobs often precede a new CEO into office. As a result, the new CEO can be forced to defend herself before she even gets to work in the new organization.

The best tactic for combating incorrect information is to continue operating in as transparent a manner as possible. The more information shared broadly in real time, the less chance fiction can hold up. Different constituencies respond to information from their differing perspectives. So, the CEO learns to speak to constituencies in their preferred language and to use reflective listening.

Leaders who are used to brainstorming out loud can end up with managers leaping to enact half-baked ideas. CEOs' names are easily co-opted for other people's purposes, and time and resources can be wasted trying to set the record straight. A CEO's actions and words may be magnified and distorted, sometimes beyond recognition, and people may try to second-guess her, communicating information that needs to be clarified later. Finally, people who used to tell the CEO the truth in their previous position may now endeavor to tell her what they think she wants to hear.

Mitigation

The new CEO should share his strategic priorities early and often, staying absolutely focused on strategy. All too often, in an attempt to win friends, a new CEO may agree to anything and everything that is brought to his attention. He ends up making promises he cannot deliver and communicating to constituents that he has no set agenda. Often it becomes necessary for a new CEO to put a stake in the ground to assert the direction in which he intends to lead and to show staff that he is indeed in charge, regardless of the long tenure of the managers. However, this needs to be done tenderly and with respect so that the new CEO doesn't overstep the managers' responsibilities. It is important to keep staff motivated and moving forward with operations. Also, winning the respect of long-term staff comes with a significant set of constituents who have placed their faith in the staff member who is most closely aligned with the delivery of services to them.

The CEO who has moved up within the organization faces a unique set of realities. Suddenly, the view of the trees he nurtured for so long is obfuscated by the big picture of the forest. He may feel that he used to know everything that was going on in the organization, but now every bit of information received, even from former colleagues, is filtered by someone's agenda or perspective. Often, long-term relationships become at least temporarily tilted as colleagues try to make sense of the change in status. Informal sources of information may dry up, and people who have worked with the new CEO for years want assurance of exactly what he intends to do with the information provided.

Wherever possible, internal CEOs need to use indirect power. By recruiting senior managers to assist and developing a disciplined process to communicate with and through them, the new CEO brings the organization into sync with his strategic thinking. The internal CEO has an advantage in creating a learning organization because he is demonstrating all the skills he acquired throughout his career-long learning process. Now, through working closely with his former colleagues to maximize their individual expertise, the CEO continues the learning organization rather than pursuing the much less useful "domination" of an obedient organization. Clearly, the most powerful CEOs expand the power of those around them.

A CEO who has come up through the ranks will need to develop new sources of information. He may need to create external channels of communication with constituent groups to find out what is really happening throughout the organization. Sometimes it works to develop a group of independent advisors who agree to truth telling regardless of how they think it will help or hurt the new CEO. As discussed earlier, it may help to hire an executive coach who is paid to specifically push the CEO to higher levels of performance. CEOs who have come up through their organization will need to work particularly hard to develop structured support from other CEOs or organizational associations because of previous relationships.

Discussion Questions

1. How can an organization effectively introduce new leadership into both the internal and external communities?

2. Who should orient new leadership, and what content areas need particular attention?

3. What "realities" of the organization need to be communicated to new leadership in preparation for their representing the organization in the larger community?

Part
4

Attending to New Beginnings

12

Succession Planning

"Our board attempted succession planning as a quick fix just before the CEO announced his departure. It was a very awkward process. We passed over many issues very quickly. The CEO felt that he was in an embarrassing and exposed position. The plan just scratched the surface, and there was a lack of total board involvement. It made us feel torn about the division between the board president and the CEO."

—*Board member of a community health center*

Reconciling Models from Our Corporate Experience to Nonprofit Life

Succession planning has traditionally been thought of as identifying a person within the organization or hiring an associate who will at some time assume the current leader's position. This model is often used in corporate settings, and when an announcement is made of one CEO's departure, a new CEO is named in the same press release. This is possible when the organization is large enough that potential successors are groomed for many years, running divisions in different parts of the business or even sections of the world, often becoming part of a management team where it is understood that one will "rise to the top." It is also the setting of power struggles that result in corporate splits and the departure of highly talented and driven individuals who may go on to run competitive companies. An unintentional outcome of this model is developing talent for the wider corporate field.

How does this model apply to the nonprofit sector? The advantages of home-grown leaders are obvious. They are well known to the staff, board, clients, and community. They, in turn, know the organization and its setting and are demonstrably dedicated to it and its mission. In a support role to the CEO, many programs may have actually been generated and implemented by the second-in-command, and staff may already report to this familiar leader. The CEO may have told the associate explicitly that she is being trained to succeed her. She may have gotten that message through years of unspoken signs or signals.

The primary flaw in the corporate scenario for nonprofits is that the nonprofit board—not the CEO—holds the organization in trust for the community in perpetuity, and as a result holds the responsibility for replacing the CEO when necessary. Contrary to the corporate setting where the CEO has been tasked with establishing leadership continuity, it is not the nonprofit CEO's responsibility or right to name her successor. The board may see a need to take a new direction that the departing CEO does not see or agree with. Although it may be tempting to see moving the COO or a VP of a significant area of operations automatically into the CEO role as a low-disruption strategy, it is also likely that the associate has been in a complementary role and brings different skills than those of the CEO. Often one has been externally oriented while the other is focused internally. Unless an organizational shift of focus is in order, it's likely that someone with similar skills to the departing CEO, rather than different ones, will be needed.

A leader from within may not be favored at the time of the transition. Board and staff will have seen her bad days as well as her best qualities, so there is less romance about an internal candidate than there often is about an external possibility. The second-in-command may not have a broad base of experience from work in other organizations or settings and may not bring a fresh perspective to the job. If a deeply committed member of the organization is installed without an open and broad-reaching selection process, some may wonder about favoritism or missed opportunities for new ideas and energy.

True Succession Planning

Nonprofit succession planning is more authentically the process of preparing the organization for leadership change. That is done by keeping strategic planning up to date, by continually evaluating the effectiveness of the organization's programs and staff, and by keeping a vital and active board appropriately engaged. It includes careful hiring and support of professional staff as well as proactive relationships in the community. It demands explicit conversation about how the organization will manage leadership transition when needed in the future. When the CEO departs from the organization, the organization is then ready to move into a new phase of leadership with healthy systems in place. Although it seems simple and perhaps not worthy of the volumes that have been written about succession planning, this is the surest way to ensure healthy continuation of the organization's mission through inevitable change.

Each nonprofit can accept the responsibility and opportunity to develop its leaders not just for its own organization but for the rest of the nonprofit sector. Investing in staff development means that another organization may benefit from that work while your own organization can draw upon a leader developed by a peer organization.

The question of developing staff for future CEO roles within an organization or within other nonprofits may not seem that relevant—and certainly not urgent—to many organizations, particularly those that are too small to have a significant pool of potential leaders among staff. When there is even one manager with clear leadership potential, however, allowing and even encouraging a career ladder for staff rather than jealously guarding them and trying to prevent their departure at all costs can engender an open environment where work contributions are freely given. Creating a strong pool of future leaders benefits all.

Identifying and Training Future CEOs

Grooming young leaders can take place in a number of ways:

- The CEO can mentor potential leaders on his own staff or encourage the development of a mentor relationship with another organization's CEO.
- The organization can fund coursework or individual instruction to build skills and leadership abilities, such as general management, finance, writing, or fundraising.
- CEOs can place potential leaders in low-risk opportunities for ever-increasing responsibility and expose them to community leaders. Evolving leaders need exposure to those tasks and relationships that are part and parcel of the CEO's job: fundraising,

volunteer relationships, financial management, board support, and management. This can be a sticking point, either because the staff is stretched thin and can't afford duplication of focus or because sharing these tasks may imply succession that is not intended. Explicit professional development plans can be the answer.

Networked Leadership Development

A National Association of Independent Schools (NAIS) survey found that even though only 23 percent of new heads of school had previous headship experience (Orem, 2002), little attention has been dedicated to the development of leaders. The same NAIS survey found that the majority of heads felt they were unprepared to deal with legal issues, business administration, fundraising, and working with the board of trustees, indicating a clear need for programs that develop these skills.

Some public school districts have responded to the shortage of principals by developing ongoing succession processes that train leaders before they are needed. These programs provide school districts with a systematic way to identify, evaluate, and train future leaders, creating a leadership pool that can be drawn upon as the need arises.

Nonprofits like the national YMCA have also placed significant emphasis on development programs for new CEOs.

Many communities and universities offer leadership development programs, and professional associations can offer emerging leaders exposure to challenging opportunities. Providing a budget for memberships, experiences such as conferences and internships, and materials such as books and DVDs can support reading and learning for young leaders. Certification programs through organizations such as the Association of Fundraising Professionals or the American Society of Association Executives may be useful as well.

Although it would be difficult to create an entire leadership training program within a grassroots organization, pooling resources and developing collective, hands-on training programs for a group of small nonprofit organizations might prove invaluable to nonprofit communities and are not beyond their capabilities.

One option is for ten or so organizations to join together to implement mentoring programs. In these programs, an apprentice would be assigned to an organization for an entire year, spending five or six weeks working in each of the organization's major administrative areas of finance, development, and program as well as in two service delivery departments. Apprentices immersed in each of these areas would do real work, not simply observe. They would also attend board and board committee meetings. Some days they would shadow the CEO, and the CEO and apprentice would hold weekly meetings. Both the Neighborhood Reinvestment Services in San Francisco and Maryland Nonprofits have had some success with such collective activities, and there are myriad nonprofit support groups for various levels of staff.

Board Succession Planning

The transition from one board president to another can be as momentous or disruptive as the departure of a CEO. Such transitions may signal different policies on service provision, board leadership, and the management of the CEO. In fact, these changes can lead to the voluntary or forced departure of a CEO.

Some associations change board presidents every year. Frequently in nonprofits, board officers serve multiple-year terms. When term limits are in place, succession planning is often more commonplace and seen as normal than is the case of a CEO with indefinite tenure. But if the board has not instituted term limits, the president may have served longer than the current CEO or even with multiple CEOs over many years.

In one affordable housing organization, the founding CEO and initial board president served together for 27 years. Suddenly the president died, leaving the CEO without his long-time partner. The board had long since deferred development of the vision and direction of the organization to this duo, and no one on the board was prepared to step up. With some pain, a new president was selected, but he too fell ill and was unable to serve long term. He was able to help the board thoughtfully select its third leader before stepping down. The impact of having three presidents in only three years echoed through the organization for many years.

It is important, then, for boards to establish orderly succession procedures and to select and groom new presidents, as well as committee chairs, in a timely and thoughtful manner. Ideally, the board will use a modified version of the process to identify, select, and integrate a new CEO.

The following tasks should be familiar by now:

- Forming a selection committee. This gives the process weight and seriousness of purpose and an understanding that multiple voices will be heard.

- Writing a job description. Although the president of the board is a volunteer job, it demands certain skills, has specific responsibilities, and carries with it significant authority. Thinking about these qualities and seeing them explicitly detailed will assist the selection committee and potential candidates to assess an appropriate fit. It can also lessen any political expectations that any particular person will ascend to the position without assessment of skills needed.

- Developing an interview protocol. What do you want to know about a potential board president? How will you compare candidates?

- Making the process clear to the entire organization. Even more than the CEO role, the selection of a board president needs to avoid accusations of cronyism and backroom politics.

- Introducing the new president to the community.

- It is vital for the new president to form a successful working relationship with the CEO. Facilitating this relationship can be part of the selection committee's portfolio.

- Transferring information from the incumbent to the new board president.

- Thanking the outgoing president ceremonially and assisting in his departure from the board at the end of the term. Staying on the board may lessen the personal separation pangs, but continuing to occupy a seat that might be filled by a new board member creates an insular board and lessens the impression that newer members can contribute significantly. As with a departing CEO, when it's time to go, doing so gracefully is a major gift to the organization's future. Even when the departing president has been a strong contributor both financially and with his time, converting him to a friend rather than board member is part of creating an ever wider universe of support.

This process may seem idealistic, especially to new and small organizations that hustle to find almost anyone who will give of time and funds. In that case, perhaps it is best thought of as a transition process to aspire to—one that will become increasingly possible and relevant as the organization grows. Beginning wise processes and procedures early is easier than beginning them when there are established poor habits later on.

In some organizations, a board president comes to the role through a succession of other responsibilities. In many associations, the VP of membership will progress to the VP of programs role and then become the president. One church elected a moderator and a moderator-elect each year, and these two served with the past moderator as a rotating three-member board leadership team with various responsibilities. Such systems create a sense of stability, but it's necessary to be sure that each officer with the potential of becoming the president has the characteristics needed in that role. Otherwise, significant swings of priorities and personalities can take the board and the whole organization in entirely different directions or create the need for support of the board's varying strengths and gaps.

Emergency Succession Plans

With the introduction of a new CEO, it may seem that the transition process is complete. But all CEOs leave eventually—some voluntarily, some through the board's insistence, some by taking better jobs elsewhere, and some through illness or death. In each of these cases, the departure may be sudden. To prepare for this possibility, experts stress the importance of creating an emergency succession plan. These plans differ, but most include six core tasks.

Create the Job Description

Identify the primary functions of the CEO. This process not only defines the priority tasks that must be accounted for if a CEO suddenly leaves either permanently or temporarily due to illness, accident, or other personal crises, but serves as an opportunity to reflect on the CEO's role. Assuming the CEO and board are working in partnership, the CEO can and should be a full participant in this process. This description may be shorter than a permanent CEO's position description. Some tasks—for example, fundraising or strategic planning—may not be in the list of duties to be cared for in an emergency.

Short- and Long-Term Challenges

Determine what needs to be done in case of an immediate or long-term emergency. For example, the plan may temporarily elevate a senior manager to serve as CEO or create an executive team of administrators and managers.

Potential Interim CEOs

Keep a list of individuals or groups who could take over in case of emergency, and make that list public. If the United States government can do this for the presidency, so can a nonprofit organization. If there is already an executive team, it can be designated as the interim leadership.

Training

The designated replacement should receive training in the CEO's essential tasks and be made privy to all basic information about the organization before an emergency occurs. This approach argues for considerable transparency about financial, personnel, and other matters of the organization.

Accessible Information

All relevant information about the organization should be readily accessible to the board and the interim CEO. This approach argues for documentation and, if possible, navigable information systems.

Communication Strategy

The emergency succession plan should have a communication strategy, including how to describe the CEO's absence and nature of the interim leadership to staff, volunteers, constituents, major donors, and key community leaders. It should also designate a spokesperson for the emergency transition period.

Communications should focus on straightforward information that leaves little room for misinterpretation. Timely disseminating and reporting what is happening will mitigate the stress created by not knowing what is transpiring. People abhor a lack of information and are likely to fill any gaps with creative speculation. While many informal channels are used to communicate an organization's information, during times of leadership change a predictable method and timeline should be established for informing constituents about board plans during the transition.

Retaining CEOs

We discussed retention as one way to avoid a transition early in our discussion of the leadership cycle. We have now come full circle. This is when retention must be considered again. Leaders who are effectively supported by the board of directors are more likely to stay in office for longer periods. When they experience a partnership in fund development efforts and share challenges with a group of volunteer leaders and staff, CEOs can "lead from the middle" rather than feeling that they are standing on a deserted field. In 2009 the American Express Foundation funded a study by The Bridgespan Group, "Finding Leaders for American's Nonprofits." The study found a number of areas that boards can focus upon in order to develop and retain CEOs, including the provision of professional development. CEOs thrive best when they have access to networks with other leaders, when they have opportunities for continual learning, and when they have or can acquire the needed functional skills.

Another requirement for retaining leaders is for the organization to hire a candidate who fits within the organization's culture. For instance, if an organization invites great discussion of multiple perspectives, a CEO candidate who does not easily share authority and allow dissention is not likely to thrive. Board leadership should provide a thorough orientation to the culture of the organization. They should also be willing to discuss potential changes that may be needed in the organization's culture with their new leader. Over time, with a concerted effort leaders can extinguish negative or out-of-date attitudes and ways of work in the organization. A CEO who endeavors to change the culture of an organization without the leadership and support of the board is not likely to remain at the organization for long. Members' natural resistance to change will be channeled as disapproval of the CEO, who is endeavoring to align the culture to the strategic directives of the board.

The CEO is more likely to have increased tenure when board members stand behind her during the difficult tasks that are the CEO's responsibility. For instance, it is never easy to remove a volunteer from a job that he enjoys and has held for many years. However, it is necessary for the CEO to release a volunteer whose actions result in safety violations or who consistently contradicts the operational guidelines. It may be easier for to board members to be silent during such a difficult time, but their courage in adding their endorsement to difficult operational actions on the part of CEOs may result in their staying with the organization.

Regardless of the quality of the search process, CEOs are likely to enter their role in the new organization with a few significant gaps in functional expertise. It is incumbent upon the board to help them develop a plan for acquiring such skills or structuring other staff positions to fulfill those functions. It is also incumbent upon the board to support leadership development throughout the volunteer and staff structure in order to grow new leadership that can step forward into operational areas that have been stabilized by the CEO in order to clear time and attention to developing new systems and programs. Finally, the board should give public praise to the CEO when it is earned and refrain from blaming or overreacting to the inevitable mistakes that will occur as the CEO endeavors to fulfill broad responsibilities.

The Continuing Cycle

Leadership is best conceived broadly, not so much as a moment but as a cycle. Events leading up to a transition set its tone, producing orderly transitions in some cases and crises in others. Skills, structures, processes, and ongoing leadership influence the nature of transitions. The development and nurturing of these skills and processes before a transition and in the months and years after the selection of a new CEO are as critical as the management of the transition.

Discussion Questions

1. Who should participate in the succession planning process? How will they create a framework for new leadership without eliminating leadership options for the future?

2. How are future leaders best identified and developed in the organization?

3. What resources are in place to support stability in the event of an emergency transition of leadership?

13

Leadership Continuity and Long-Term Governance

Back to the Beginning

The goal of leadership transition is to establish new leadership that will be effective and sustained. It is a goal that can only be measured with time, certainly not during the three- to six-month honeymoon almost always granted to new leaders. This chapter will quickly review the pathway toward good transitions, and then it will propose a set of activities aimed at sustaining and amplifying the gains made during the transition.

Where We've Been

Passing the Torch has focused on five ways to deal with the ill effects of rapid, frequent leadership turnover and, more importantly, how to turn the crises that are generated by the turnover into opportunities to advance the missions of organizations.

The first step is to put a new frame around the turnover and transition process, to see it as a powerful opportunity to further organizational ends. This is not to minimize the risks and destructive power of the turnovers—and poorly managed transitions. Rather, we emphasize the opportunity to review and revise purpose and planning to set the ground for new leadership.

The second step is to review and revise the organization's general sense of direction. To be an effective opportunist, you have to know where you're going. Only then can you transform all the random and destructive elements that shake loose during crises into forces that move you toward your objectives. That is the point of Section 2, "Fundamentals of Effective Leadership," which distills the art of leadership and organizational effectiveness: how to align an organization's human and financial resources in the service of its mission and vision, as articulated by its strategy.

Often when we talk about alignment, we mean aligning staff and perhaps volunteers to get work done. But here we are talking about a broader alignment. We mean that leaders, boards, and external stakeholders, such as community groups and funders, must be aligned to mission and strategy. Take the leader. His skills, values, leadership style, and personal objectives must fit with the culture, structure, objectives, and resources of the organization he leads. The goals, culture, and decision-making style of the board of directors must be aligned with those of the CEO and the organization.

In fact, during the transition period, boards have two preeminent goals: to align their organizations to best receive the new leader, and to select a new leader best aligned with the organization to move it toward its objectives.

The third step again presents a philosophical shift to go with organizational change. The transitional goal is not to replace one person with another. In fact, that idea by itself is so misleading that it creates a bad transition. It leads to the idea that you can simply find the most talented person, give her a general orientation, and hope that she leads the organization in the right direction. But she may be a mismatch to the organization's culture and find it impossible to find enough allies to move the organization in any direction. Or her personal goals may be at odds with organizational goals, and she may not be motivated to move the organization toward its mission. Leaders are only effective with followers with whom they share beliefs, with whom they are credible, with whom they share, at least to a point, a common idea about the method by which you move toward goals.

Leaders and leadership are different; leadership is a web of relationships that move the organization forward. The third step then is to reconceive the transition from the replacement of one person with another to the replacement of one *form* of leadership—a team and a way of thinking—with another.

Fourth, we have insisted that the transition period not only be well and professionally managed, but managed in a style that serves as a model for all future management: build a strategic plan, manage it, communicate with stakeholders, select a leader who fits with the plan and with the organizational culture, and introduce and position the leader for success.

Finally, we propose that the way to go about doing things during the transition period should serve as a model for future leadership: for volunteer leadership, for professional leadership, and for the relationship between the two.

The shift from one CEO to another is only one of the many important and potentially difficult transitions that mark organizational life. There are many others. For example, there are the regular—or irregular—changes of the guard among board presidents, each of whom can challenge the stability of the CEO and the organizational style he has presided over. There are comparable changes among key staff people, chief financial and operating officers, for example. There is the need to adapt to major external changes, such as major increases and decreases in funding, new competition, and new technology.

Among all these forces, the board generally exerts the greatest influence on CEOs, and it is the relationship between the board president and the CEO that most observers agree is the key to sustained and effective nonprofit leadership. The remainder of this chapter focuses on how to build and sustain an effective working relationship between boards and CEOs—after the official transition is complete.

Building Bridges and Authentic Relationships

During transition, the board often has become entangled in operations and is reluctant to turn the operational reins back over to the CEO. If the board has been virtually steering operations for six months or longer, as the new CEO transitions into leadership there is a need to balance roles and relationships, both with the total board and between the board president and CEO. Organizations often assume that their new leader will automatically be in sync with the board and the president. In reality, the partnership more likely starts with two leaders with type A aggressive personalities who enjoy being "in charge." Another possible scenario is that the board president has taken his position as a source of status. He doesn't expect to do the heavy lifting of making other volunteers in the community unhappy over difficult decisions. He anticipates the CEO standing alone in these situations.

An organization could also have hired a CEO from the external community who views her new role as being hands off. She doesn't choose to learn about the operation of the organization. She believes she can steer the ship from afar while focusing on fund development and external relationships. If the president and the board expect the CEO to display a thorough understanding of deliverables in each department, this may cause conflict. The final misfit partnership is one in which the board president and CEO are in sync as a pair, but out of sync with the rest of the board.

This section explores methods for enabling the board to move back into its oversight role and to build a working partnership between the board president and the CEO.

The Board Returns to a Partnership and Relative Background Position

During the transition period, the board steps from the background into the foreground, from a place of clear partnership with the CEO—and, often enough, service to the CEO—and into the primary leadership position. To complete the transition, the board has to step back and let the new CEO take the primary lead again as the face of the organization and its chief executive with responsibility for decision making and the implementation of strategy.

As the board steps back, it should review how it had positioned itself before the transition period. Had it been too close, too involved, too controlling? Had it been so hands off that there was little accountability for the CEO? Was it sufficiently involved in its ambassadorial role? In fundraising? In policy making? Generally, this kind of review can be greatly aided by a consultant, someone with both perspective and a good general idea about effective board function and effective board-CEO relationships. Excellent self-evaluation tools are available online from organizations such as Board Source and The Drucker Institute and are discussed in Chapter 5, "Good Governance."

The objective of this self-evaluation is twofold: to organize for optimal effectiveness, and to determine the optimal relationship with the incoming CEO. We already discussed "good governance" in Chapter 5, including the primary responsibility—fiduciary, policy/strategy, and management of the CEO—as well as the functioning of effective committees. In particular, the governance committee must be strong. Its job is to continually replenish the board with new blood and to insist that the board maintain discipline. In the case of a high-functioning board, committees meet and report, meetings are lively and respectful, the CEO is given candid, respectful feedback, finances are closely monitored, and individual board members do not intrude on staff functioning, talking and acting as though they speak for the whole board.

The change from the transition to the "normal" period is a little like the shift from war to a peace-time army. It must recede into the background yet maintain readiness and discipline at all times.

Building an Effective CEO-Board President Relationship

The single most important determinant of CEO effectiveness and tenure may be the relationship with the board president. The introduction of a new CEO presents an ideal opportunity to create a strong relationship between the two. Here are three key steps, best facilitated by a consultant or a local neutral and respected party.

First, the facilitator meets with each party for a couple of hours. The objective for each is to envision what the ideal relationship with the other can be regarding how they will share authority, face outward to the community and inward to staff, and relate to the strategic plan's formulation and implementation. There is a formal side to this kind of vision: the president agrees to an annual performance review for the CEO and insists that the strategic plan must be passed by the board; the CEO may insist that all staff hiring decisions, implementation plans, program development plans, and so forth are hers alone. And there is the informal side of the plan. "While you, the CEO, have final say on hiring, I'd like you to consult with me on major hires. While you, the president, have final say on the strategic plan, I will have to implement it and have considerable knowledge about the subject matter. So I would need to be a full partner in any strategic planning process."

After each party has had an opportunity to elaborate his idea of an effective relationship, it is time to bring the two leaders together. There is hardly a single way to conduct such a conversation, but one way begins with each, without interruption, laying out his vision. That way the full contours emerge, the relationship of the parts can be clear, and the general personality is more transparent. After each has communicated a vision, it's time for questions. The questioning can be free form, back and forth, but we recommend that each take a turn questioning the other. This supports the habit of respectful listening so that each actually understands the other before negotiations and jostling begin.

Once the individual visions have been elaborated and the responses given texture and explanation so that each knows what is behind the initial vision, it is time for conversation. Here, too, it is important to build habits of productive conversation. When, for example, one person wants something different from what the other wants, it helps to point to the difference, not to demonstrate how the other is wrong. Getting to common ground is a lot easier when compromising differences than when licking the wounds created by attacks or having to overcome the desire to build barricades.

During the conversation, even more informal agreements can be sought. Each can learn about how the other learns: Do you prefer a phone call, a written report, an outline and a conversation? Do you like to meet regularly—say weekly for an hour—or mostly on an as-needed basis? What percentage of our conversations should be by phone? In person? In other words, the leaders should decide on some rules of the road in their relationship.

One of the most important subjects contained in these road rules is confidentiality. It helps if the two say explicitly who else will be privy to information shared in their conversations. No one? Then the conversations are strictly confidential except what they agree to share with others. The board vice president and the deputy director? This kind of conversation can only thrive with candor, and candor can only thrive with confidentiality, which is one of the vital elements of trust.

If the two leaders can trust one another, share information, develop the capacity to make high-level decisions together, and make sure to limit the backbiting from their respective constituencies, they are in a position to seek common ground on the major policy decisions that form the basis of their relationship. If they can focus on these substantive decisions and not on trivia—the way people walk and talk or who their friends are—they can set a behavioral example that will be picked up throughout the organization. Within the culture built on this relationship, long and productive leadership tenure is much more likely.

Negotiating Effective and Authentic Roles

A key part of the negotiation concerns roles. Roles are a negotiated set of behavioral expectations, but they are more than a list of activities. They are vessels that hold the expectations that leaders and organizations have for one another and define the relationship between the two. The expectations are mixed together and negotiated and then emerge as consistent, almost ritualized forms of behavior. In one case, the outcome will be very much like the patriarch of a traditional family. In another, the role will be like an expert, offering guidance. Another will become a "servant leader," whose primary role is to facilitate the activities and effectiveness of others.

Roles bring out some but not all of who we are—our boldness or our capacity for accommodation, for example, our creativity as an entrepreneur or our steadiness and orderly ways as a manager. Just as leaders bring only part of themselves to their jobs, so organizations select and nurture certain qualities and emphasize particular behaviors. In response to an organization's wish for a managerial form of leadership, its newly chosen CEO may try to be more than usually orderly and planned—and play down the more free-wheeling tendencies that had led to success in her former organization.

It is rare that leadership roles are well negotiated. Even with elaborate search and selection processes, organizations rush to fill the void created by departed or discarded leaders. They look mostly to the character of the leader and to past experience and ignore the fit between organizational needs and the leadership style of an incoming CEO. The focus is primarily on finding a great leader, not a great fit. It is also rare that leadership roles are explicitly and carefully renegotiated when organizations grow or change course. This lack of careful negotiation, alone, is responsible for much of the mismatching and disappointments that have led to the rapid turnover and increase of leadership transitions that now plagues both the corporate and nonprofit worlds.

When the role—and the way the organization monitors its execution—departs too far from who the leader is, she cannot play it effectively or authentically; neither she nor the organization will be satisfied. More often, she will find herself failing to live up to expectations or find that what seemed like initial expectations have shifted. In such cases, the leader almost inevitably finds herself in a struggle with her board of directors or with the senior leaders who report to her. There will be no alchemy. On the other hand, if the role unites powerful and effective aspects of the leader's character with the organization's practical needs and cultural preference, the chemistry is strong.

A Contract and a Covenant

At the conclusion of their negotiations, CEOs and board presidents form a complex social contract with one another. It consists of three basic elements. The first is formal: The CEO agrees to perform the following tasks for a period of time and for an agreed-upon salary. The second is informal: Here is how we believe we can work most effectively with one another, supporting one another.

The third is what we will call a *covenant*. Both formal and informal contracts between people are essentially quid pro quo agreements that say, "I'll do this if you do that" and can be severed at each person's will. A covenant is stronger because it involves a third "party"—a shared mission, shared principles, and revered witnesses. It has a moral or sacred quality to it, and it cannot be broken lightly.

With leaders and followers who share a fierce devotion to a common cause, the covenant may be equally fierce, and both may be vigilant in their attention to any deviation. With others, the covenant may resemble the powerful bonds of family members. With still others, the covenant may center on mutual respect and a belief in collective decision making. The values, images, and mutual expectations embedded in these covenants differ dramatically from organization to organization, as does their ability to bind leaders to followers around their shared purposes.

As roles may be written in job descriptions, so covenants can be written, but covenants mean much more than the explicit terms suggest. Leaders and followers are bonded together to serve not only themselves but a higher purpose. The covenant creates stability with a touch of magic. It represents a sacred trust.

So it should be between CEOs and board presidents. Much in the relationship is about business. The shape of the relationship varies between hierarchical—the formal role of the board is to hire, fire, and manage the CEO and to establish the strategy that the CEO is charged to implement—and reciprocal and equal. Many CEOs and presidents relate this way. And, in many cases, the formal hierarchy is upended: CEOs put presidents in place and manage them. In any of these arrangements, however, the most distinguishing and powerful quality is the covenant that brings them together in common purpose.

Identity Narratives

In some important ways, the identity of the CEO is a story that the leader and others must agree upon. How the CEO is known and, therefore, how people relate to him is a narrative that links the board, CEO, organization, and community. If, for example, he is commonly known as a good but ineffectual person, people will relate in one way. If he is known as good, strict, detail-oriented, and generous to those who are especially loyal, people will relate in another way.

This might sound like reputation, but it is a little different. It includes the leader's own story about himself and others. In conversation and public talks, he may say that he was drawn to the work because he so identified with the trials and tribulations of the people in the neighborhood. In his eyes, he is one of them. But these people may feel that he is not one of them, that his long residence in Ivy League colleges has made him different, and they may let him know about the difference. He may counter that under the skin he is still the same person, that he deeply understands their situation. They may point to this or that action to show he does not. The "conversation" may go on for a while until, most of the time, a common ground is reached. In effect, the leader and stakeholders agree on a story about who he is, how he leads, and how he should lead.

As bridges, these narratives are negotiated, modified, and even transformed in the interaction between leaders and their organizations. And leaders may be changed as they interact with the organization's story. Take Margaret Leonard of Project Hope in Boston. She characterizes herself as a skilled and hard-working servant leader. But many followers have a more exalted view of her. Here, for example, is a statement by a foundation president: "Margaret reminds me of the Dali Lama: fearless and always kind in the presence of others...She is fearlessly reaching out every moment. And her generosity is joyful, not heavy or burdensome." Margaret is aware of these portraits and dismisses them with regularity, but she knows not to fight them too hard, because they might help "move the mission" of ending homelessness, and that's what is most important to her. The stories draw even more people to her, and she responds, not just to the people but also to the stories. In part, she *becomes* the stories. When this happens, when the leadership story is owned equally by leaders and followers, the chemistry between them is at its most powerful.

In their most exquisite forms, stories portray leaders as the embodiment of their causes and organization. One thinks of Gandhi, who virtually became Mother India, and Martin Luther King, who is indelibly identified with the Civil Rights Movement, but also of Steven Jobs in the world of computers.

What's interesting is that these identity stories are both fiction and nonfiction. They bring to the fore certain qualities of the protagonist that fit the leadership situation, and they push into the background qualities that interfere. For instance, Gandhi was not always kind, certainly not to his family. Churchill's powerful will could and did during peace time look like willfulness, stubbornness, and grandiosity, all qualities that held him in good stead during World War II and for which he is almost entirely known.

Leadership identity narratives are not exactly the same as individual identity narratives. Individual identity stories cover more ground. They include our self-images as men and women, mothers, fathers, sons, daughters, and friends, as well as our experience of age and spirituality. Leadership identity stories focus on the character we bring to work, the roles we assume, and the way that others respond to us.

Leaders and followers don't always agree on a narrative that satisfactorily links them. When that happens, it is somewhere between difficult to impossible for leaders to lead or to get things done; and more than likely, the relationship will come to a disputed end.

This may seem unfortunate, but it is also necessary. As we suggested, leader and led must be aligned. To do so, they need a story to suggest how and why the leader is the right person in the right place at the right time for this job. And that kind of alignment will seem not just correct but good—meaning authentic and hopeful. It provides the promise of a productive leadership relationship.

Closing the Gap Between Espoused and Lived Values

The very best of leadership relationships foster alignment at the deepest levels. In their organizations, there is an often fierce desire to close the gap between espoused and lived values. Organizations take on this challenge with many different degrees of seriousness, from those who pay lip service to their values to those who are doctrinaire and permit members little room for independent action. When the desire to close the gap is promoted equally and over time by board and CEO, it will become embedded in the organization's culture, its DNA. When this happens, the desire to close this gap lends intensity to each action, an intensity that deepens the relationship among people and between everyone with the leader. The commitment to close the gap is not built in a day or a month, and it is a rare achievement.

Feedback

In addition to well-negotiated roles, expectations, and stories, sustainable relationships among volunteer and professional leadership are based on regularly shared information and interpersonal candor. Broadly speaking, this means feedback, which comes in a variety of forms.

Regular, Candid Conversation Between CEOs and Board Presidents

First, as we suggested, CEOs and presidents must meet with one another on a regular basis to share information and come to conclusions in areas they have agreed to share. The information can range from the mundane to the dramatic, from the gist of the monthly financial statement that will be presented in a week to the possibility that an employee will be investigated on ethics charges. In well-functioning CEO-board relationships, each agree to "have the other's back" and never to "blindside" the other. If, for example, a group of board members have begun to grumble about the CEO or one of his principle policies, the president should make that known. If there is a good possibility that a key staff member is failing or leaving, the CEO should make that known. And, where the relationship is good enough, president and CEO can give each other feedback about their effectiveness and limitations.

Second, a set of formal feedback mechanisms should be established and administered.

Regular Reporting on Agreed-Upon Information

The most important feedback is provided during regular board meetings. The feedback should cover organizational basics: finance, human resources, program development, and marketing. The method for providing feedback determines how well the information can be received and utilized. The board is responsible for explicitly stating what kind of information it needs to carry out its fiduciary and strategic responsibilities, the kind of financial information it needs to hold the CEO accountable. What level of detail, for example, do we need to know about programs? How are staff doing? Is the program hitting its goals: this many clients reached, that many making progress, and so forth? In effect, a "dashboard" is established, consisting of key informational indicators of organizational effectiveness.

When boards are explicit in this way, the CEO knows the objectives she must reach and how her effectiveness will be judged. It becomes less likely that she will be judged by how she talks, dresses, or relates to individual board members and more likely that she will be evaluated on the basis of mutually agreed-upon goals.

Once shared expectations are aired, negotiated, and decided and the contracts, formal and informal, are "written," they must be reviewed and revised and monitored with regularity and seriousness of purpose.

All too often, boards do not specify what they need to know and in what form they need to know it. At some point they may get concerned: Revenues are down; rumors are circulating about declining program standards; there will be tighter state regulation about some aspects of finance or programming. Concern leads to criticism or to a demand for some kind of information that the CEO and organization has not been collecting. This can lead to some problem solving and solutions, but often enough, it leads to conflict and impasses.

Regular CEO Performance Review

It seems obvious, almost not worth saying, that the board needs to regularly review the performance of the CEO—its "one and only employee." Many organizations do so in a variety of ways, from formal to informal. Sometimes the board president conducts the review and delivers the message. Sometimes a separate board committee is established to construct the review and deliver its results; sometimes the committee develops the review and delivers it with the president present. We do not favor a separate committee that also serves as an informal advisor to the CEO, because it seems hard for the CEO to believe in the neutrality of advice from people who also judge her and determine her salary and tenure. We prefer a method that allows input from the entire board before decisions are made about what issues will be discussed with the CEO.

The form of review varies. Some boards simply deliver impressions, whereas others use an elaborate questionnaire. Organizations like Board Source provide excellent templates for this process.

The key points are as follows:

1. The board should perform a regular performance review.
2. The review should be based on well-established effectiveness criteria, agreed to by both the board and the CEO.
3. The CEO should evaluate himself based on the same criteria.
4. The results should be delivered in the spirit of partnership and support—"We want you to reach these goals"—rather than simply or strictly as a report card.

The reports should emphasize both accountability and a shared sense of purpose, and they should be attentive to discrepancies between the CEO's and the board's evaluation. Serious discrepancies signal a lack of alignment between expectations, roles, and narratives. A similar evaluation by each party might still note serious problems but would mean that the board and CEO were aligned, on the same page, and could work together to make improvements.

It is rare that boards evaluate their attitudes and behaviors toward CEOs. For one thing, it is often one person or a small group, the board president or the executive committee (made up of board officers), that has the lion's share of the contact. This kind of privacy has limitations. If for no other reason than for board morale, it helps to have greater transparency and participation in board-CEO activity. Perhaps most importantly, board leadership needs evaluation, too, and information supplied by the CEO should be included in that evaluation.

Regular Board Self-Evaluations

Even boards that take the time to review the performance of their executives rarely review their own. Yet, as we've made as clear as we can, board performance is critical to organizational effectiveness, and it's particularly important to the effectiveness of CEOs.

The simple act of reviewing its performance against clear standards of effective performance introduces a whole new idea into board life. It says, in effect, that there are standards to which we can and should hold ourselves accountable, and we need to think about the structure, processes, values, cultural norms, skills, and behaviors that align with our mission and strategy—and about activities that do not. It introduces the idea that we need to empower people to hold us to our own rules and our purpose. For example, a well-functioning governance committee is often charged with both refreshing the board with new membership and establishing disciplined behavior.

Regular and Predictable Tests

No matter how good the relationship between boards and CEOs, there are tests of its stability and adaptability. In effect, these are regularly occurring events that hold the potential for organizational crises in the best and worst sense. When an organization loses funding for a cornerstone program, experiences a serious accident of a client or staff member during an activity, or experiences misuse of funds, the partnership of the board and CEO is sorely tested. These are random and unpredictable tests that measure the organization's effectiveness. The ability of the board and CEO to stay on message together about the mission of the organization and the remediation of the crisis will demonstrate to the larger community that the mission will be served at the worst of times. Scheduled events also provide tests of the organizations ability to deliver on its mission. The introduction of a new board president, the renewal and restructuring of the strategic plan, and the decision of the CEO to depart all create visible tests of the organization's effectiveness. This book focuses on the transition periods specifically because preparation for them can be accomplished only through managing the whole cycle of leadership. Boards must pay attention to strategic movement throughout the entire cycle if they are to be ready for effective transitions.

Managing the Whole Cycle of Leadership: Managing for the Long Term

Although organizations naturally focus on the narrow period of transition, the nature and quality of leadership transitions are determined at least as much by what happens before and after. Transitions that follow the graceful, long-anticipated departure of a revered CEO, for example, are entirely different from those following scandal or prolonged and acrimonious conflict between the board and CEO. CEOs that are introduced with dignity and care and provided the support they need—a good partnership with the president, an executive coach, for example—are more likely to succeed and have longer tenure than those abruptly dropped into an organization.

Even within the transition period, one event influences another. For example, good transition management enhances the likelihood of a good search process. Comprehensive searches enhance selection. Careful attention to fit between organizations and candidates increases the likelihood of the CEO's early success. Support during early tenure enhances the stability of leadership.

Leaders will come and go—as they should. Partnerships among the CEO and board presidents come and go as well. The need for serious strategic planning comes with powerful changes in constituencies or clientele. As they shift, organizations must avoid quick, narrow responses; they must reject the short-term view, the crisis orientation, a reaction only to events of the moment, and focus instead on the long view. In the long view, leaders and partnerships among leaders may be said to cycle through relatively predictable phases. By identifying and planning for this regular march of phases, organizations give themselves the best balance of continuity and stability, on one hand, and adaptability, on the other. Together, intentional continuity and adaptability provide organizations their best shot at ongoing excellence.

We have identified a cycle of leadership transitions common to organizations. In this section, we would like to sketch some of the keys to managing each phase of the cycle. These sketches should seem familiar because they represent brief summaries of recommendations made throughout the book.

We could begin the cycle during any phase: the moment of departure, the moment of selection, and the period of stability that, if sustained, would support longer leadership tenure. The cycle would be the same. We begin here with the stable period because the best way to decrease leadership turnover is to prolong effective leadership tenure.

Management Challenges, Phase by Phase

We tend to assume that management challenges only rear their heads during difficult times. However, every phase of an organization's life cycle presents unique challenges. During times of stability, boards and CEOs are at risk of falling asleep at the wheel, assuming there is no need for change. In reality, if an organization is not growing, it is shrinking. Assessment, evaluation, and planning are what moves the organization toward its mission. During difficult times, strategies and plans are tested in real time. This also requires assessment of how effective the planned strategy was, and lessons are learned that shape future strategy and planning. During times of transition, everything is examined thoroughly to establish a base line of where the organization is and what needs to occur under the future leadership.

Periods of Relative Stability

When leadership is stable and at least relatively effective, boards and CEOs relax; they often don't want to think about the future. But this may be the most important phase of the cycle. Here are the particular management challenges during this phase:

- **Assessment**—Make sure that the organization is on track: true to its mission and strategies; operationally effective; financially sound; functioning with up-to-date systems, from hiring to evaluation to data management; providing adequate support to the CEO; and nurturing the partnership between the board and the CEO. The assessment can be internal or with the assistance of a consultant.

- **Performance review**—Provide the CEO and the board president with clear, regular feedback about accomplishments, strengths, and areas in which growth is essential. Base the review primarily on the leaders' implementation of the strategic plan.

- **Succession planning**—This includes the following:
  - An emergency succession plan to provide guidance in case of illness or sudden departure of the CEO.
  - A regular way to bring new presidents into partnership with the CEO: for example, being elected six months to a year before taking office and participating with the current president in meetings with the CEO.
  - A transition management plan to take effect during the months the organization is without its professional leader.

Times of Difficulty

When difficulties with the CEO or between the board and the CEO emerge—and this is a normal, regular event—there should already have been developed the habit of conversation and problem solving between the two to stave off escalating conflict and other problems. Here are the management challenges:

- **The habit of conversation and problem-solving**—Insist on regularly scheduled meetings between the board and CEO, in which the partners build a history of negotiating tense or perplexing issues, so that new difficulties fit into a partnership culture of skill, success, and confidence in their ability to solve problems, resolve conflict, and compromise on issues.
- **Utilizing outside expertise**—Designate an outsider—volunteer or professional—to help negotiate and resolve differences if they seem beyond the capability of the CEO-president partnership and before they grow too large. A consultant on retainer, who knows the leaders and the organization, may be best for this purpose.

Decision to Depart

There are many reasons for the CEO to leave an organization. The CEO may want to retire or take another job; the board may ask the CEO to leave; staff and executive conflict may have reached a point of no return; or the CEO may have contributed what she knows best, and the organization may advance to a developmental level for which this CEO is not suited. In any case, management challenges include these:

- **Developing a transition plan**—Who will manage during the interim between the departure of the old and the introduction of the new, and how will she or they manage?
- **Building a transition team**—It is generally best to form a transition team with specifically designated roles to spread the work and to represent various constituencies in the community.
- **Building a communication plan**—Alert the community of the upcoming departure, and assure them that there is a stable management team in place to guide the organization. The message is managed so that the departure is seen as part of the organization's effort to stay on course with its mission, objectives, and strategies.

Transition Period

Transitions generally take between 6 and 12 months, or, if one begins when a departure notice is given and ends when a new CEO is well integrated into the organization, the period can take as much as 2 years. During this time, the management challenges include these:

- **Maintaining a well-functioning transition team**—The transition team acts as the rubberband that holds the organization together so that it can run smoothly while assessments are occurring, the search is in process, and new leadership is being introduced.
- **Create job descriptions and strategic plans**—Among its tasks, the transition team must create a job description that should mirror the organization's strategic plan. The new CEO will be hired to carry out that plan.
- **Sustain communication**—Sustain communication about strategic, financial, and search efforts with the community—staff, funders, constituents, and referral sources—so that all constituencies trust that an effective transition process is in effect, and organizational stability is assured. Make the decision-making process for search and selection as transparent as possible. This will build trust and avoid rumors and worries about favoritism and power plays.
- **Conduct a highly professional search and selection process**— Some boards contain members familiar with these processes and with the time and ability to lead. If they don't, it helps to enlist the aid of a professional search consultant.

Introduction, Early Phases of New Leadership

Once a new CEO is hired, boards often give up too much control too quickly because they are exhausted or believe they should immediately turn the reign over. Alternatively, they hardly give up control and operating responsibilities within the organization at all. Both approaches interfere with the early effectiveness of the new CEO. Management challenges during this phase include these:

- **Effective introduction and support for the new CEO**—The transition team must introduce the new CEO in an enabling way: praising but not exaggerating his strengths; clarifying his role(s) and mission; and providing administrative support, where possible.

- **Disband the actual functioning of the transition team**—The transition team must set a time to disband, letting go of operational management within the organization.

Introduction of New Board President

New presidents tend to shift policy and relationships according to their beliefs and comfort—and, too often, just to mark their territory. The management challenges include these:

- **Clarifying the organization's mission, vision, values, objectives, and strategies**—Like the CEO, the president will embody the mission and vision and will be asked to hold the CEO accountable for realizing them.

- **Orientation**—Often new presidents are elected and left on their own. The executive committee, the out-going president, and the CEO can form a committee for the purpose of—and should spend a good deal of time in—orienting the new president to his duties, including advisor to the CEO; employer of the CEO; community representative.

- **Nurturing the CEO-president partnership**—It is vital to nurture the incoming president's partnership with the CEO. This can be done informally by the outgoing president. It is often done more expertly with the help of an executive coach who is charged with helping the new partnership form in an optimal way.

- **Clarifying CEO-president roles and expectations**—The two should meet to clarify formal questions of authority and responsibility as well as informal expectations about support, autonomy, leadership style, and how they generally like to work in partnership. This meeting should take place as soon as possible, and then agreements should be reviewed three to six months later.

And then the cycle begins again.

Discussion Questions

1. What are the essential elements of maintaining an effective partnership of the president and chief executive officer?
2. How can volunteer leadership transitions be supported throughout the organization's life cycle?
3. How can boards utilize annual evaluations of themselves and the chief executive officer to prepare the organization for leadership transitions?

Epilogue

The purpose of our discussion has been to describe the skills and processes that can best guide nonprofit organizations not only over the bumps and curves of leadership transitions, but through the entire leadership cycle. No leader stays forever, and even good partnerships can dissolve. Each organization passes through a life cycle characterized by stages, and each transition point may require new leadership. The challenge is not to ward off or deny these growing pains, but to create a professional culture and the skills to support it. Only then can the organization weather these transitions with the least disruption and the greatest creativity.

Having read about the pitfalls of transition and the many things that can be done to effect productive change in organizations, it may be tempting to focus on the tremendous effort it takes to create a healthy cycle of organizational leadership. Why do nonprofit CEOs undertake positions that require incredibly long hours and soul-level investment in organizations and communities for modest salaries? Why do volunteer leaders add the responsibility of holding organizations in trust for the community in perpetuity to their busy lives, taking time away from lucrative jobs, families, and leisure?

It is because the rewards are so great. The nonprofit sector is sometimes called the Third Sector. As the "not business" and "not government" institutions in our society, nonprofit organizations are the "third leg of the stool" that binds communities. If nonprofits went on strike for even a day, communities would grind to a halt. There would not be sufficient child care, elder care, or care for the sick. Education would come to a stop, and the traditions and legacies of our cultures would cease to be shared. Recreation and preservation of the environment and public discourse would suffer. So much depends on nonprofit leadership.

Through the work of committed, caring, and educated leaders, our communities continually seek to make progress. It is worth it to create enduring relationships that empower neighborhood development. It is worth it to create the music that comforts the human spirit and inspires achievement.

We offer the lessons we have learned in leadership transition in respect of the amazing nonprofit CEOs, staff, and board members we have served and in gratitude that our careers have been alongside theirs.

Part 5

Tools

Notes on Research and Research Methods

Research Sources

We have taken a few different angles in researching this guide:

- Seventeen interviews with nonprofit board presidents who had led their organization through the transition of their CEO.
- Twenty interviews with CEOs who had experienced two or more transitions during their career, as well as two or more transitions of board presidents.
- Thirty-three interviews with leaders of Jewish day schools who had experienced transitions.
- Seven interviews with management consultants who had worked with nonprofits during transitions.
- Three focus groups about the transition process, with a total of twenty nonprofit CEOs.
- Observation and guidance of more than two hundred leadership transitions in nonprofit organizations, Jewish day schools, and corporations.
- Providing executive coaching to eight CEOs and board presidents as their organization went through a leadership transition.
- Researching the literature on leadership transitions in independent schools, nonprofits, and corporations.

- Researching and practicing related topics, such as executive search, professional development for nonprofit CEOs, and succession planning.
- Review of effective-practice literature on transition management and related topics such as the executive search process.

Prescriptive, Not Descriptive, Research Literature

Although the body of literature is growing, there is yet a limited amount of research on the leadership transition period. Consulting firms and coalitions of nonprofit organizations provide much of the research and recommendations that exist. You can find an archetypal example of this literature in Transition Guides' "Founder Case Studies," which stress the role of transition consultants.

It is not surprising that articles on a transition or search firm's Web site would emphasize the need for paid consulting services, but it is important to note that this perspective currently permeates the nonprofit transition literature. For example, Tom Adams of Transition Guides, Tim Wolfred of CompassPoint, and Deb Linnell of Third Sector New England have been published in *Nonprofit Quarterly* and are cited in numerous other publications. Similarly, two of the more comprehensive studies of leadership transition were conducted by the Neighborhood Reinvestment Corporation (1998) and CompassPoint, intermediary organizations with their own transition services.

This is not to suggest that transition services are being oversold. Many transition consultants come from years of experience as nonprofit leaders, and their motivation is to enable increased capacity and fulfillment of mission in the sector. Transition studies are still in their infancy. Research by independent parties is needed to expand the pool from which ideas about leadership transitions are drawn.

B

Sample Leadership Transition Plan

Transition Plan Draft: A Community Organization

This is an example of the planning process for one organization as they introduce the new CEO to their membership, staff, and community. It is important for a cross section of members and staff to participate in this planning process so that the new CEO is integrated into the organization with a full understanding of its operations, programs, expected outcomes, and current tactical plans. The CEO then can begin to take up the leadership mantel in a congruent manner with the history of the organization and the current needs and opportunities before him.

What Does Success Look Like?

1. During the first quarter, administrators, staff, and board members get to know the new CEO and feel confident and excited about the future.
2. Department managers will engage in and feel ownership for the organization's strategic plan.
3. The CEO will "hit the ground running" when he arrives on April 1.
4. Members will feel comfortable and confident that the CEO is capable of leading the organization into the future.
5. Members will get to know that the CEO is approachable, knowledgeable about the organization and its mission, and will recognize members' needs.
6. The new CEOs' family will become well adjusted and happy in their new home and community.

7. The new CEO will build successful relationships and work well in the community.

8. Programs and initiatives that are time sensitive (for example, decisions that need to be made between now and June 30) will continue on course.

9. Timely communication about the transition process will occur with board members, staff, and constituents. People will feel engaged, able to voice their concerns, and aware of what is happening.

10. Members will recognize the new CEO as their new leader and know him by name.

Key Factors

1. The organization will pay attention to the emotional factors of the transition: loss of attachment, turf, structure, future, meaning, and control.

2. The transition team will provide clear communication to board members and staff to create reasonable expectations for the transition year.

3. The transition team will provide clear communication to clients to create reasonable expectations for the transition year.

4. Leadership will work to strengthen the staff's ability to cope with ambiguity and uncertainty during a time of major transition.

5. The board and staff will recognize that uncertainty and ambiguity will lead to people assigning meaning and interpretation to words and actions that may or may not be true.

6. The board and staff will use regularly scheduled events and routine activities as the vehicles to address transition issues.

Transition Structure

The transition team will be composed of the following:

- Team chair
- Chief Operating Officer
- Board member with professional experience in human relations
- Board member with professional search experience

- Incoming CEO
- External consultant

Sample Leadership Transition Timeline

Lakes Region Girl Scout Council

Date	Action
December	CEO announces to executive committee that she plans to retire next
January	Board meeting to discuss the transition process
March	Board retreat to revise strategic plan and design transition
	Charge to the transition team and search committee discussed and developed
	Transition timeline developed
April	Roles and responsibilities assigned to president, board, and outgoing CEO
May	Request for proposals from search consultants issued
June	Transition team appointed and oriented
	Search committee appointed and oriented
	Selection of search consultant, who will meets with the transition team and the search committee to plan the process
	Search consultant meets with entire board to discuss strategic plan, organizational culture, and key experience and skills needed for new CEO
	Stakeholder's survey and focus groups about key criteria conducted

Date	Action
July	CEO position announcement posted
	Advertising occurs
	Outreach to potential candidates
	Transition team and executive committee of the board meet with CEO to discuss interim options and to define outgoing CEOs task list
August	Search committee begins screening process
	Transition team meets with senior management team to design plan for oversight during the transition
September	Area delegates meet with representatives of the board to discuss needs during the interim period
	Committee to lead the party and fundraiser for outgoing CEO begins work
October	Search committee interviews candidates and selects finalist
	Board receives search committee report and meets with finalist
	Board endorses candidate and completes the hiring process
	Invitations for departing CEO event are sent
	Board reviews status report of transition plan
	Board conducts CEO evaluation and the board self-evaluation
November	Incoming CEO comes to town for reception and annual meeting
	CEO assisted with housing and family move support
	Board and CEO review status of the strategic plan
December	Outgoing CEO event held
	Incoming CEO begins orientation
	Board retreat with the outgoing and incoming CEOs to reach consensus on priorities for the next year in the context of the strategic plan
	The plan is developed for introducing the new CEO to key stakeholders, funders, and community leaders

Date	Action
January	Outgoing CEO exits
	Incoming CEO meets with transition team and senior management
	Annual financial audit begins
	Community introductions begin
February	New CEO and president attend national meeting of chief executive officers and chief volunteer officers
	President introduces new CEO to national leaders
	President and CEO receive training in shared leadership
March	Transition team attends all board committee meetings with the CEO and discusses priorities and ways of work
	Officers and CEO conduct constituent meetings in geographic areas
	Transition team begins to hand over the reins more fully to the new CEO
April	At the board meeting, the transition team leads a discussion on the agenda for the board retreat in June
May	CEO partners with the president in presiding over the large volunteer recognition event
June	The annual board retreat is held, where the strategic plan is reviewed, the status and movement toward achievements are noted, and the CEO reports on her organizational analysis and perceptions about any needed changes, the transition team is thanked and disbanded
	An advisory panel is constituted to serve as external advisors to the organization and to assist the CEO in operational issues

The new CEO and his family are happy and well adjusted in their new home and community.

Outcomes	Events/Activities	Who's Involved	Who's Responsible	Timing
The children are tested and placed at a community school. The family is comfortable with the way the school works.	Electronic "back packs" sent to them each Friday Admissions testing and placement Send new family package	External Consultant Technology staff		March February/March
Expectations and boundaries CEO are defined.	Conversation with Senior Managers		Appropriate department managers	August
The entire family knows their way around town resources, shopping, contacts, and so on.		Real Estate Agent	Real Estate Agent	
New CEO and family develop new friends and feel comfortable in the community.	Play dates arranged by the organization			
New CEO becomes acclimated into the community. Parent community Social network	Talk with spouse about what she wants and help her become acclimated Activities to be determined	Board committee	 Outgoing CEO, community	Phone call in February. Other activities begin when appropriate. June

During the spring, the board and staff will get to know the new CEO and begin to feel confident and excited about the future.

Events/Activities	Who's Involved	Who's Responsible	Timing
Search committee presentation about the new CEO given to management team		Search committee	February 6
Search committee presentation about the new CEO is given to all staff	All Staff	Search committee	February 15
Letter to board and staff about the new CEO		Board president	February 20
E-mail message from new CEO to all board and staff communicating his excitement about the new job and the organization	New CEO	New CEO	February 28
Visit to organization by CEO (2 days)		Transition team	March
Monday memo update from transition team to board/staff after March visit		Transition team	March 2
Visit to organization by CEO (2 days)		Transition team	April 2
Monday memo update from transition team to board/staff after April visit		Transition team	April
Letter to staff from new CEO about Strategic Focus for upcoming fiscal year		New CEO	Early August

Members feel comfortable and confident that the new CEO is capable of leading the organization into the future.

Members believe that the CEO will be approachable, knowledgeable about the organization, and will honor their needs.

Events/Activities	Audience	Who's Responsible	Timing
E-mail message that new CEO was hired	Members	Board president	1/25
Information from newsletter article posted on the Web	Members/staff	Marketing Department	1/3
Letter articulating the new CEO's qualifications for the job and information about the transition team	Members	Board president	2/20
Post bio, photo, and letter on Web site	Members	Marketing Department	2/28
Letter outlining the transition plan	Members/staff	Board president	After 2/22
Update from transition team after March visit on Electronic Backpack	Members	Transition team	March
Update from transition team after April visit on Electronic Backpack	Members	Transition team	April
Letter to members from new CEO	Members	Administrative Assistant/new CEO	Summer packet distribution
Letter to members from new CEO about upcoming year Strategic focus for the year	Members	New CEO	Early August

Programs and initiatives that are time sensitive (for example, decisions need to be made between now and June 30) continue on course.

Outcomes	Events/Activities	Who's Involved	Who's Responsible	Timing
New CEO and senior staff are clear about what items need his input and what items don't need his input for next year	Identification of issues that need the new CEO's input Clarify which issues are FYI. Gain agreement with the new CEO.	Transition team	Senior staff	February
	Strategic plan is defined with CEO's input	Transition team and new CEO	Board and senior staff	June

The new CEO has built successful relationships and works well in the community.

Outcomes	Events/Activities	Who's Involved	Who's Responsible	Timing
	Identify an in-house mentor to acculturate the new CEO to the community	Transition team and others		August
Major donors Meet the inner circle of major supporters of the school (30 to 50 people)	Cocktail party Endowment campaign Lunches	Board president and others		August
Meet the inner circle of people who run the organization and make things happen, as well as community and members	Cocktail party	Board, Senior Staff		August
Organization council meeting	Phone call to ask them to welcome new CEO Letter to community leaders	Transition team/senior managers		June
Specific federation/agency CEOs	Agency CEOs meeting Letter	All agency CEOs Agencies		August
Community big shots who are supporters				
Outside relationships Foundations	Letter announcing selection of new CEO	Community Foundation Moore Foundation		
State Independent Schools and AAAIS	Letter announcing selection of new CEO			
Community calendar of events	List of everything new CEO needs to participate in	New CEO		
Political relationships with federation	Federation	New CEO		

Does the new CEO want to have one large party or two small ones?

Decide on criteria for major donors.

Public recognition/honoring of current CEO: Current CEO says goodbye to various groups at regularly scheduled end-of-the-year activities.

Outcomes	Events/Activities	Who's Involved	Who's Responsible	Timing
Community celebrates the past 20 years and Outgoing CEOs contribution	Day of learning	Members, community	Staff/board committee	February 4
Outgoing CEO has the opportunity to thank people	Annual dinner Thank-you event for Outgoing CEO end of year celebration	Members, community, staff Staff, members	Staff/board committee	May 30 End of year
People feel closure with Outgoing CEO and are ready to move into a new phase of growth	Staff appreciation luncheon Last board meeting	Members Board, staff	Fund Development committee Board of directors Board/senior staff Outgoing CEO	June 11 June 10
Money is raised for the school in Outgoing CEO's honor	Last staff meeting Letter from outgoing CEO to members	Board, Fund Development committee Fund Development Department Marketing Department	Board/Transition team Fund Development committee Outgoing CEO	June 13 June 14

New CEO is visible and accessible to staff and members during his first year as CEO.*

Outcomes	Events/Activities	Who's Involved	Who's Responsible	Timing
	Membership celebration	Board/Staff	Marketing Department	End of year
	New member event	Marketing Department	Director of Marketing	Beginning of new year
	New staff orientation	Senior Managers	Incoming CEO	Beginning of year
	Staff planning day (first day)	Senior Managers	Human Resources/Training Director	Within a week of incoming CEOs arrival
	New members orientation	Marketing Department	Human Resources/Training Director	Beginning months of new year
	Holiday party	Marketing Department	Senior Managers	December
	Program events	Direct Delivery staff	Program Director	Throughout the year

* Use planned events that are part of organization's calendar as much as possible.

Other Thoughts

The following sequence should guide all communication and events:

1. Executive committee/board of directors
2. Management team/board of directors
3. Staff
4. Members

First meeting with new CEO in March:

- Primarily focused on building relationships with staff managers
- Social get-together with staff (random assignment to groups) to meet new CEO:
  a. Senior managers to plan it
  b. Two mornings and two afternoons

Agenda for Senior Managers in March

Professional Development

Status Report (* = decisions need to be made)

Overall Outcome: Working relationship of departments

Outcome: Awareness and support of new initiatives for professional development:

1. Understanding by design
2. Differentiated curriculum
3*. New history program (input)
4*. Technology Intech or in-house training (April)
5*. Mentor program
6*. New staff evaluation formats (staff handbook change)
7. Learning for staff
8. Status report (current) State Univ.
9. Adding for next-year approval
10. Financial support for higher-level education

Structure: Interaction between new CEO and each department manager—opening door for conversation.

Curriculum Development

Outcomes: Understand how we plan, assess, and implement the programs.

Staff Recruitment and Retention

Outcomes: Understand the work done in salary scales and benefits (group structure).

Outcomes: Understanding the organization's calendar.

- Role of staff structure
- Work done on enhancing the organization's culture

Membership Education

Outcomes: Know the different programs that provide members with education/guidance.

- Policies and safety guidelines
- Lunch and learn
- Book clubs and chats
- Training of volunteer leaders
- Day and evening workshops

Other March Meetings

Outcomes: Establish communications between now and August 1; clarification of job role as CEO's assistant.

Outcomes: Help new CEO understand the past five years.

Big picture: How far the organization has come in the community. Role of CEO with relationship to the board. CEO utilized as the person who implements board policy and directs the operations toward achieving the mission.

Administrative Assistant

Outcomes: Expectation of responsibilities of board

Outcomes: Bylaws and the role of board committees

- CEO/board evaluation process
- The beginning of relationship building

Director of Advancement

Outcomes: Status report of where the organization is in terms of endowment, annual gifts, and so on.

- Plan for next fiscal year
- Understand challenges of the future

Chief Financial Officer

Outcomes: Buildings and grounds update

- Summer updates/workplan
- Understand the budget for the next fiscal year

Director of Technology

Outcomes: Web site

- Equipment
- Media center
- Future plans and dreams
- Membership communications (paperless)
- Social get-together

Second Meeting with New CEO in April

- Continue work with senior managers and board's transition committee
- Initial relationship building with department managers
- Meetings with the manager of each department

Sample CEO Job Descriptions

From Naava Frank, 2001, *The Jewish Day School Head Search Process: Strategies and Resources*. Partnership for Excellence in Jewish Education

Conservative Day School, K-8: Solomon Schechter Day School of Greater Boston, Massachusetts

Authority

The head of school operates under the authority of the board of trustees and reports to the president of the board of trustees. The president of the board of trustees and his designees conduct an annual performance and compensation review of the head of school. The head of school is a voting member of the board of trustees.

Responsibilities

The head of school is responsible for implementing the mission of the school and for implementing the plans and policies of the board of trustees.

The Board of Trustees

The head of school represents the professional staff and employees of the school to the board of trustees and represents the board of trustees to the professional staff and employees of the school.

In conjunction with the board of trustees, the head of school will develop, review, and periodically revise the short- and long-range plans of the school.

The head of school will consult and advise the president and officers of the board on the operation and development of the board.

Together, the president of the board and the head of school will ensure the appropriate and productive relationship between governance and operation.

Administration

The head of school is responsible for the organization, direction, supervision, and review of the staff and employees of the school.

He is responsible for the efficient and effective implementation of the policies and objectives of the school.

The head of school is responsible for the efficient and appropriate utilization of the school's resources. He will ensure that financial records, audit procedures, budgets, and financial planning meet the needs and standards of the school's operations.

He is responsible for the productivity and morale of staff and employees.

Academic

The head of school is responsible for the achievement of the academic goals of the school.

He will ensure that the most effective curricula available are being appropriately used in all subjects of general and Judaic studies.

Faculty relations, professional development, competency, and supervision are the responsibility of the head of school.

The communication of the school's academic mission and vision to the faculty, students, parents, administration, and wider community is the responsibility of the head of school.

The head of school will develop and maintain knowledge of and relationships with other independent schools and relevant education institutions and associations.

He will continue the process of integration of all general, Judaic, and Hebrew curricula.

He will be responsible for the continued accreditation of the school.

Development

The head of school in conjunction with the board of trustees will take a leadership role in all aspects of school development.

The development goals will include enrollment, annual and capital fund drives, alumni development, communications and public relations, board development, and community development.

He will serve as spokesperson for the school.

Environment

The head of school is the administrative, educational, and spiritual leader of the school community.

He will ensure an environment of trust, cooperation, and respect conducive to personal, professional, spiritual, and academic growth.

Reprinted with permission of the Solomon Schechter Day School of Greater Boston

Reform, Synagogue-Based School, K-6 (Expanded to K-8): Beth Am Day School, Miami, Florida

The head of school oversees the day-to-day operations of the Beth Am Day School and serves as a liaison between the school and Temple administration and related departments with regard to the management and operations of the school. This includes but is not limited to governmental agencies and other educational organizations. The Day School director functions within the operational organizational chart as approved by the board of directors.

Supervision

- Overall supervision of the following: administrative personnel, including preschool director, assistant director, Judaic studies director, office secretaries, school faculty
- Schedules and presides at regular school administrative staff meetings
- Defines parameters for student acceptance and resignation
- Selects and finalizes class placement of each student

- Maintains and develops an ongoing long-range plan and program to meet the future needs of the Beth Am Day School in conjunction with the Temple
- Development and supervision of general studies curriculum
- Management of the integration of the Judaic and general studies curricula
- Overseeing proper integration of all curriculum areas
- Staff assignment and scheduling
- Supervise teacher lesson plan and oversee the implementation of lesson plans
- Continuing educational programs and new-teacher training oversight including the maintenance of proper teacher certification or other requirements that may be mandated from time to time by related oversight and licensing agencies
- Hiring and dismissal of all school personnel in consultation with the executive director
- Coordinating and directing special projects, such as the yearbook, fairs, Jewish and secular holiday events, concerts, field trips, graduation, and more
- Develop, implement, and maintain school code of conduct and oversee all disciplinary matters
- Responsible for the cost effective purchase, use, and maintenance of all school supplies and equipment
- Development and implementation of educational philosophy and practices as an integral part of Temple Beth Am in partnership with the senior Rabbi
- Develop, implement, and maintain appropriate teacher standards to include regular observations and evaluations of classroom teaching and activities, including regular in-class observations and documented evaluation

Administration

- Define job descriptions and matters of policy related to school staff
- Prepare budget, and oversee, maintain, and supervise expenditures with the Temple executive director and school board

- Work in conjunction with the school board in setting school policies
- Maintain and oversee records dealing with the progress of each student regarding testing and placement, including tracking the performance and progress of each student in the school
- Maintain standards of education to ensure readiness of all students, including awareness of the programs in the local middle and high schools to ensure the proper readiness of all students in Beth Am Day School
- Support and represent the school at professional meetings, conferences, workshops, and accreditation bodies
- Be accessible to parents and guardians to meet and counsel
- Develop and maintain school safety standards
- Work closely with PATIO (Parents' Association) officers, assist and support PATIO projects, and support Temple-wide fund-raising projects
- Attend or arrange for representation of the school at all significant Temple meetings and events
- Work with the school board and the Temple board on matters of publicity and public relations
- Arrange the school calendar to synchronize with the calendars of both the Temple and local public school district, including attention to Jewish holidays, special events, state mandated requirements, teacher training workshops, and conferences

Curriculum

- Development, implementation, and supervision of curriculum; evaluating current curriculum and implementation of new trends in education to maintain excellence in general and Judaic studies
- Supervision of integration of Judaic and general studies curricula
- Staff development with regard to new trends in education and maintaining curriculum changes to meet new standards in education
- Keeping au courant with trends and developments in education

Reprinted with permission of Beth Am Day School

Brand New Community High School, 9 to 12: New Jewish High School of Boston, Massachusetts

Guidelines for the Head of School

The head of school is a professional leader imbued with visionary qualities and Jewish commitment that will establish the school as a community high school that provides its students with "knowledge about their dual heritage; appreciation of critical scholarship; and commitment to leading Jewishly informed and enriched lives."

(Extracted with changes from Mission and Philosophy of the school)

Summary of Job Description

The head of school will supervise, direct, and administer all the programs of the school. He will be responsible for supervising the development of both the general studies and Judaic studies curricula and activities that promote Jewish traditions and values. The head of school is the primary educational and administrative official of the school ultimately accountable to the board of directors. The head of school is responsible for the implementation of the school policies, programs, and ancillary activities. He will carry out policies and bylaws established by the board. His responsibilities and duties include, but are not necessarily limited to, the following.

Personal Qualities

- Being a Jewish role model for students

Vision

- Leading the school community in developing a coherent vision for the Academy
- Articulating the vision both internally within the school and externally in the community at large

Educational/Administrative and Support Personnel

- Recruitment, hiring, and firing of staff
- Regular supervision and written evaluation of personnel

- Providing opportunities for staff development, including internal and external in-service opportunities, staff meetings, workshops, and conferences
- Participation in ongoing personal and professional growth and development

Curriculum

- Developing the curriculum of the school
- Once curriculum is in place, leading the way to continually improving the curriculum
- Assisting all personnel in the implementation of the instructional program
- Giving special attention to the intersection, interaction, and whenever possible, integration of Jewish and general studies

Development

- Working cooperatively with other agencies
- Maintaining visibility within the community
- Serving as spokesperson for the school within the community
- Participating in the fund-raising efforts of the school

Parent-School Relations

- Developing procedures to facilitate appropriate communication among parents, teachers, support staff, and students
- Carrying out developed procedures

Supervision of Students

- Developing and maintaining educationally sound procedures with regard to admissions, retentions and withdrawals, placement, record-keeping, evaluation, special services, recruitment, health and safety codes, advising, and college placement

Budget

- Formulating, implementing, and monitoring an annual operating budget in conjunction with a board committee
- Expenditure on the budget

Board and Committees

- Contribute to leadership development to ensure continuity
- Provide guidance to lay organization
- Attend meeting with a clear head's agenda
- Work with the board to develop short- and long-range goals

Reprinted with permission of the New Jewish High School

Nonprofit CEO Job Description

Position Title: CHIEF EXECUTIVE OFFICER
Reports to: Board of Directors

Position Summary

The Chief Executive Officer (CEO) is accountable for working with the board of directors to provide leadership, strategic direction, and vision to this nonprofit organization which serves 48 counties in North Carolina. The organization will have a membership potential of 40,000 girls and 10,000 volunteers. Offices are located in Asheville, Greensboro, and Hickory. The CEO will be expected to lead throughout this jurisdiction.

The CEO will initiate operations with a $10M operating budget and $24M in assets. They will lead a staff of 100 experienced and committed professionals in implementing a strategic plan which includes: meeting the diverse needs of girls in all communities, restructuring service delivery to support strong volunteer leadership and providing high-quality program opportunities to girls at every age level. This will require the development of an expanded funding plan, strong fiscal management, and support of governance through a Board of Directors composed of prominent community leaders.

She will work closely with the Board of Directors and the senior management team to shape the organization's business strategy. She provides direction and guidance to the organization in the development of goals and objectives to execute and implement the strategy within the framework of the organization's policies and standards. The incumbent advises, recommends, and assists the organization's Board of Directors in the formulation of policies governing the organization and implements policies and directives of the board. The incumbent directs the organization's day-to-day operations through the senior management team.

The CEO works in partnership with the board to further the mission of Girl Scouting and facilitate the integration of the organization into the fabric of the jurisdiction. She promotes Girl Scout visibility and strengthens the Girl Scout image in the community. The incumbent works in partnership with the national organization to promote the Girl Scouts' public policy agenda and positions Girl Scouts as a premier voice for girls. She is a champion for girls and women.

The CEO ensures that organizations affairs are conducted in a manner consistent with corporate and charter requirements, as well as federal, state, and local laws and regulations. She works in partnership with the board chair to manage the due diligence process to ensure timely attention to critical issues.

The CEO serves as staff advisor to the council nominating committee and provides technical direction to the committee's chair and its members. Based on current and projected Council needs the CEO identifies qualifications of potential new Board members.

The CEO is responsible for stewardship of the organization's human, material, and fiscal assets. This individual is responsible for all hiring, release, retention, and management of employed staff and volunteers; for directing the management and development of the organization's physical resources; and for oversight of the organization's fiscal activities. The candidate should be able to leverage the use of technology to further the mission of Girl Scouting.

She partners with the national organization to carry out the mission of the organization, to address charter obligations, and to obtain advice or consulting services, information, and resources.

The ideal candidate must have at least five years of executive leadership experience in a multi-million dollar organization in the not for profit, for profit or government sectors. A master's degree is preferred. Significant fund development and asset building experience are required in this position.

Position Description

Chief Executive Officer

The chief executive officer (CEO) serves as the leader of the organization and its primary public representative, reporting to the board of directors. The CEO works in partnership with the board to ensure that the organization fulfills its mission and to create strategies that ensure its future success.

Functions

Planning

- Collaborates with the board to define and articulate the organization's vision and to develop strategies for achieving that vision
- Creates annual operating plans that support strategic direction set by the board and correlate with annual operating budgets; submits annual plans to the board for approval
- Develops and monitors strategies for ensuring the long-term financial viability of the organization
- Develops future leadership within the organization

Management

- Oversees the operations of organization and manages its compliance with legal and regulatory requirements
- Creates and maintains procedures for implementing plans approved by the board of directors
- Promotes a culture that reflects the organization's values, encourages good performance, and rewards productivity

- Hires, manages, and fires the human resources of the organization according to authorized personnel policies and procedures that fully conform to current laws and regulations
- Ensures that staff and board have sufficient and up-to-date information
- Evaluates the organization's and the staff's performance on a regular basis

Financial Stewardship

- Oversees staff in developing annual budgets that support operating plans and submits budgets for board approval
- Prudently manages the organization's resources within budget guidelines according to current laws and regulations
- Ensures that staff practices all appropriate accounting procedures in compliance with Generally Accepted Accounting Principles (GAAP)
- Provides prompt, thorough, and accurate information to keep the board appropriately informed of the organization's financial position

Fundraising

- Develops fundraising strategies with the board and supports the board in fundraising activities
- Oversees staff in the development and implementation of fundraising plans that support strategies adopted by the Development Committee
- Serves as a primary person in donor relationships and the person to make one-on-one fundraising solicitations
- Oversees staff in the timely submission grant applications and progress reports for funders

Community Relationships

- Serves as the primary spokesperson and representative for the organization

- Assures that the organization and its mission, programs, and services are consistently presented in a strong, positive image to relevant stakeholders
- Actively advocates for the organization, its beliefs, and its programmatic efforts
- Acts as a liaison between the organization and the community, building relationships with peer organizations when appropriate

Programmatic Effectiveness

- Oversees design, delivery, and quality of programs and services
- Stays abreast of current trends related to the organization's products and services and anticipates future trends likely to have an impact on its work
- Collects and analyzes evaluation information that measures the success of the organization's program efforts; refines or changes programs in response to that information

Leadership

- Serves as an ex-officio member of the organization's board of directors and all board committees
- Supports operations and administration of the board by advising and informing board members and interfacing between board and staff
- Advises the board in the development of policies and planning recommendations
- Assists in the selection and evaluation of board members and board leadership
- Makes recommendations and supports the board during orientation and self-evaluation
- Supports and participates in the board's evaluation of the CEO

Sample Evaluation Templates

Head-of-School Evaluation 1 (Johnson 1986: 45 to 49)

This form was developed by a metropolitan coeducational Friends day school of 1,000 students from age four through grade 12. The same form has been used with equal effectiveness by a small elementary school, demonstrating its wide applicability.

Directions: Read the entire questionnaire before answering any questions. Please note that you are asked to grade only at the end of each section. With regard to Section 6, "Personal Characteristics," if you have any areas of concern, please mark them with a C. If you have no opinion or knowledge of certain characteristics, mark them with an N.

Grade the head according to this scale:

5 = Consistently outstanding

4 = Generally above satisfactory performance

3 = Generally at satisfactory level

2 = Generally below satisfactory performance

1 = Unacceptable

? = I have no knowledge or opinion of this

1. Professional Skills

1.1 As an Educator
a. Inspires confidence and trust
b. Understands Quaker education
c. Has an interest in children

d.   Displays strong interest in improving the quality of the educational program
e.   Handles disciplinary cases/student problems
f.   Works on curriculum improvement
g.   Encourages introduction of new teaching ideas
h.   Formulates educational policy and goals
i.   Has good relations with students
j.   Inspires appropriate behavior and appearance

Section 1.1 grade: As an educator ____

1.2 As the Leader of the Faculty Working in Close Harmony with the Three Principals

a.   Inspires confidence and trust
b.   Gives clear direction as appropriate
c.   Displays initiative and creativity
d.   Effectively oversees the faculty and faculty evaluation programs of each division
e.   Hires good teachers
f.   Keeps good teachers and helps keep them motivated
g.   Involves teachers appropriately in decision making
h.   Supports teachers having difficulties
i.   Aggressively pursues solutions to problems
j.   Carries out the educational policy set by the board
k.   Knows what is going on in the school

Section 1.2 grade: Overall relationship with faculty and principals as their leader ____

2. Administrative Skills

2.1 Financial

a.   Inspires confidence and trust
b.   Understands budgeting and planning
c.   Communicates financial matters well
d.   Operates within budget
e.   Involves self in the school's financial affairs
f.   Helps to develop fund-raising objectives
g.   Helps in fund-raising

2.2 Plant
a.   Inspires confidence and trust
b.   Effectively oversees plant requirement planning
c.   Effectively oversees administration of maintenance functions

2.3 General Administrative
a.   Provides oversight of bookkeeping and billing
b.   Manages administrative staff
c.   Provides administrative staff with annual evaluations
d.   Spends appropriate amount of time on administration (versus education, parent, board, community relations)
e.   Pursues solutions to problems aggressively
f.   Handles school publicity well
g.   Makes sure school records are kept well

Section 2 grade: Overall as head of administration _____

3. Board Relations
a.   Inspires confidence and trust
b.   Keeps trustees appropriately informed
c.   Helps the board develop educational policy

Section 3 grade: Overall relations with the board _____

4. Parent Relations
a.   Inspires confidence and trust
b.   Makes self available
c.   Is helpful in difficulties
d.   Is helpful in counseling situations, as appropriate
e.   Is helpful in admission situations, as appropriate
f.   Aggressively pursues solutions to problems
g.   Deals with disagreements between parents and teachers or principals
h.   Puts parents at ease in conversation
i.   Explains the school's program and philosophy clearly
j.   Works effectively with parents in fund-raising activities
k.   Makes a good impression on prospective parents
l.   Counsels parents and students applying to the school
m.   Works effectively with the parents' association

Section 4 grade: Overall relations with parents _____

5. Community Relations

    a.   Is concerned about school-community relations

    b.   Aggressively pursues improvement in school-community relations

    c.   Contributes to parents' council and local, regional, and national independent school associations

Section 5 grade: Overall relations with community ____

6. Personal Characteristics

    a.   Accomplishment: Makes effective use of time

    b.   Quality of work: Is accurate and thorough

    c.   Dependability: Meets schedules and deadlines; adheres to instructions and policy

    d.   Acuteness: Is alert; understands instructions, explanations, unusual situations

    e.   Flexibility: Adjusts easily to changing situations, copes with the unexpected

    f.   Socialness: Makes friends easily, works "comfortably" with others, has sincere interest in people

    g.   Humor: Has an appropriate sense of humor

    h.   Attitude: Is enthusiastic, constructive, loyal; has good orientation to school, position, associates

    i.   Self-control: Is calm under pressure

    j.   Initiative: Is self-starting; seeks and acts on new opportunities

    k.   Drive: Is not easily discouraged; has basic urge to get things done

    l.   Self-confidence: Has assurance, inner security

    m.   Motivation: Willingly assumes greater responsibility; realistically ambitious

    n.   Objectivity: Has an open mind; is not distracted by emotional or personal interests

    o.   Verbal facility: Is articulate; generally understood at all levels

    p.   Intellectual ability: Adapts to new situations; can analyze and make judgments

    q.   Human relations skills: Can motivate people and get them to work together

    r.   Sensitivity: Is considerate; has a "feel" for people

    s.   Resilience: Learns from mistakes

    t.   Developing others: Recognizes others and encourages them to grow

u. Integrity: Is honest in dealing with people
v. Receptive: Handles criticism well
w. Decisive: Does not procrastinate in making decisions
x. Creative: Inquiring mind, fresh approaches
y. Consistent: Not erratic in judgment or in making decisions
z. Stamina: Capacity for hard work

Section 6 grade: Overall rating on personal characteristics as the *(sic)* relate to being head of a K through 12 coeducational independent school ____

7. Summary

7.1 What do you feel are the most important criteria in grading the head of the school, according to the following scale:

A = Very important

B = Quite important

C = May or may not be important

D = Hardly important

E = Not at all important

? = Don't know

	Importance	Your Grade of Head's Performance
As an educator (1.1)	_____	_____
As leader of principals and faculty (1.2)	_____	_____
As an administrator (2)	_____	_____
Relations with trustees (3)	_____	_____
Relations with parents (4)	_____	_____
Relations with the community (5)	_____	_____
Personal characteristics (6)	_____	_____

Please list what you believe are the head's main strengths in this position.

Please list any areas in which you would like to see the head focus increased attention or improve attention in the coming year.

As you think back on your review of the head's year, do you have any comments on areas of growth or of disappointment you have observed?

Head-of-School Evaluation 2 (Johnson 1986: 53 to 57)

This form, a composite of others, was used by a rural boarding school with an enrollment of 290 students that includes a small day population. Rating the head on the basis of personal knowledge as well as on general impression makes this form useful for trustees, whose daily contact with the school may be limited.

Please use the following scale in rating the head's performance (a) according to your personal knowledge, and (b) according to your general impression:

1 = Poor

2 = Improvement needed

3 = Satisfactory

4 = Excellent

5 = Outstanding

	Personal Knowledge	General Impression
1. Interpersonal relations		
a. Ability to relate to teaching staff	_____	_____
b. Ability to relate to students	_____	_____
c. Ability to handle difficult teachers, parents, children	_____	_____
d. Ability to convey criticism constructively	_____	_____
e. Ability to accept criticism Comments	_____	_____
2. Empathy		
a. Willingness to listen to problems	_____	_____
b. Willingness to help solve problems	_____	_____
c. Willingness to understand other points of view	_____	_____
d. Comments		
3. Administrative style		
a. Seeks opinions and ideas of colleagues	_____	_____
b. Listens to ideas and opinions of colleagues	_____	_____
c. Treats staff members as fellow professionals	_____	_____
d. Relates impartially with fellow professionals	_____	_____
e. Relates respectfully with fellow professionals	_____	_____
f. Makes decisions effectively	_____	_____

	Personal Knowledge	General Impression
g. Follows through effectively on decisions	_____	_____
h. Accepts responsibility for decisions	_____	_____
i. Deals promptly with matters referred to him	_____	_____
j. Comments		

4. Ability to communicate

a. Effectively communicates decisions and rationale for decisions	_____	_____
b. Ability to be clearly understood	_____	_____
c. Accessibility to others	_____	_____
d. Communications with groups and public	_____	_____
e. Communication on a one-to-one basis	_____	_____
f. Comments		

5. Organization, delegation of responsibility

a. Ability to delegate responsibility and authority effectively	_____	_____
b. Willingness to delegate responsibility and authority effectively	_____	_____
c. Ability to meet deadlines, appointments, commitments	_____	_____
d. Ability to establish priority for responsibilities	_____	_____
e. Comments		

	Personal Knowledge	General Impression
6. Appointments		
a. Ability to recruit outstanding people for the professional staff	_____	_____
b. Ability to recruit outstanding people for the nonprofessional staff	_____	_____
c. Ability to make key appointments within the professional staff for maximum use of talent available	_____	_____
d. Comments		
7. Curriculum		
a. Success in developing a curriculum commensurate with the purposes and objectives of the school	_____	_____
b. Ability to bring about regular changes in the curriculum when warranted	_____	_____
c. Success in making use of talents and ideas of the faculty in improving curriculum	_____	_____
d. Comments		
8. Overall school management		
a. Capacity for leadership in providing for smooth operation of the school's facilities and services	_____	_____
b. Success in working with trustees to provide an effective system of maintenance for the school plant	_____	_____
c. Comments		

	Personal Knowledge	General Impression

9. Discipline

a. Ability to bring about behavior patterns among children commensurate with their age level expectations as well as the purposes and objectives of the school   _____   _____

b. Success in leading the faculty in [its] role toward meeting these ends   _____   _____

c. Comments

10. Loyalty

a. Success in supporting faculty and staff in the face of unwarranted criticism from parents or other constituents   _____   _____

b. Success in supporting and aiding trustees in the performance of their role as a governing body without yielding the exclusive responsibilities of a head   _____   _____

c. Comments

11. Admission

a. Ability to recruit and hold students whose needs are best served by the purposes and objectives of the school   _____   _____

b. Success in attracting qualified financial aid candidates   _____   _____

c. Comments

	Personal Knowledge	General Impression
12. Secondary school placements		
a. Success in finding schools that appropriately meet needs of the individual student	_____	_____
b. Ability to provide thorough and comprehensive guidance to students and parents throughout the process of school search and application	_____	_____
c. Comments		
13. Personal characteristics: The total of the head's temperament or personality characteristics bearing on head's functioning		
a. Demonstrates convincing sincerity in dealing with people	_____	_____
b. Has a sense of humor appropriate to the occasion	_____	_____
c. Is resilient; can handle setbacks maturely and learn from mistakes	_____	_____
d. Has rapport with faculty	_____	_____
students	_____	_____
trustees	_____	_____
e. Has rapport with parents	_____	_____
others outside the school	_____	_____
f. Represents the school effectively in the community	_____	_____

	Personal Knowledge	General Impression
g. Can be empathetic with a number of alternatives to a problem yet be detached enough not to be caught up in the issue; able to come to an independent decision	_____	_____
h. Demonstrates balance between being a "humanist" and a manager	_____	_____
i. Comments		

E

Sample Board Evaluation Templates

Board Evaluation (Johnson 1986: 33 to 38)

This form is based on the excellent one produced in 1967 by the Association of Governing Boards and Universities, in Washington, D.C. The form shown here is a modification of the AGB form done by a state association of independent schools to make it apply more directly to schools; it is filled out by board members or anyone else concerned with evaluating the board's performance.

For the purpose of stimulating your thought about how a board of trustees should work and how its operations might be improved, there are set forth next ten basic fields of trustee responsibility and activity. You are asked either to use this form as provided or to let it suggest to you alternative forms of your own devising.

Please consider each of the fields and rate the performance of the board in terms of each statement and the field as a whole. Ignore statements that do not apply. Rewrite statements to make them more appropriate to your school. The rating system to be used follows:

5 = Very good performance; standard fully and completely met

4 = Good; standard met in all but minor respects

3 = Adequate; standard substantially met

2 = Poor; standard not met in significant respects

1 = Very poor; standard not met in any respect

0 = Object to or disagree with standard

A. School mission and policy should be jointly developed by the board and the school head, implemented by the head, and the implementation monitored by the board.

327

1. The school's statement of philosophy, purposes, and objectives is both clear and useful as a guide to planning, decision making, and recruitment of students and faculty.

2. The board keeps this statement in mind as it reviews policies and practices.

3. The school lives up to its stated mission.

4. The board periodically reviews—and, as necessary, revises—the statement of philosophy.

Overall rating of board performance in this field:

Comments and suggestions:

B. Institutional policy planning should be required, appropriately participated in, and reviewed by the board.

1. The board provides for satisfactory policy planning for the following:
   a. Enrollment
   b. Staffing
   c. Physical facilities and their use
   d. Availability of resources
   e. Educational programs
   f. Other

2. The school head is provided with an adequate staff organized to carry out board policy effectively.

3. The board's role in policy planning is clear and well-thought-out.

Overall rating in the field:

Comments and suggestions:

C. Physical plant is one of the resources whose adequacy and effective use must be ensured by the board.

1. The board has played its role in ensuring that there is a master plan for meeting plant needs.

2. The board gives the school head appropriate guidance and assistance in developing policy and procedures in this area.

3. The plan is well kept.

4. The potentials of the facilities and property are fully realized in both school year and nonschool year usage.

5. Board members avoid involvement in decisions on details that the administrative staff should properly make.

Overall rating in this field:

Comments and suggestions:

D. Financial support and management must be provided, both through the commitment of all trustees and through the application of the skills of the financial specialists among them.

    1. Each trustee participates in personal giving within his capacity, influencing other persons and organizations to give, and otherwise helps to raise funds.

    2. The board helps ensure that the school has competent and effective resource development capacity.

    3. The board has among its members sufficient expertise in the following:

        a.   Long-range fiscal planning

        b.   Investment practices

        c.   Fiscal management

        d.   Budget review

        e.   Analysis of auditors' reports

Overall rating in this field:

Comments and suggestions:

E. Board membership should be such that the needed skills, experience, perspective, and sensitivities are brought to bear during its deliberations while at the same time members perceive themselves as serving the school community as a whole rather than acting as advocates for particular constituencies.

    1. The size of the board is appropriate.

    2. The board contains a sufficient range of talents, experience, and attitudes to accomplish its purposes.

    3. The board takes adequate advantage of its members' skills and interests.

    4. Trustees serve the whole school, not a particular constituency.

    5. The board has developed appropriate policy with respect to the following:

        a.   Length of term

        b.   Number of successive terms

        c.   Age limits or honorary status

        d.   Age composition

        e.   Sex composition

       f.   Minority composition
       g.   Persons with educational expertise
       h.   Faculty representation
       i.   Student representation
       j.   Alumni representation
       k.   Geographic representation

6. The board has a satisfactory process for the review of its membership's composition and participation and for planning for future membership and leadership needs.

7. The nominating committee is effective in the following:
       a.   Identifying and recruiting new board members
       b.   Identifying potential officers
       c.   Identifying and developing candidates for committee membership, fundraising, and other volunteer activity

Overall rating in this field:
Comments and suggestions:

F. Board-head relations must be open and mutually supportive, fostering a total institutional perspective and good working relations.

1. The board gives the head the authority needed to run the school successfully.

2. The board has made clear to the head its expectations of the head.

3. The board assesses the head's performance in terms of those expectations.

4. The roles of board and head are well defined and understood by the trustees.

5. No trustee interferes improperly with the administration of the school.

6. The board gives the head adequate personal support and guidance.

7. The board assists the head by passing on concerns and problems that come to it *(sic)* its attention.

8. The search process that produced the present head was in all respects well conducted.

Overall rating in this field:
Comments and suggestions:

G. Board-faculty relations should foster mutual respect and trust and a cooperative working environment in the school.

1. Board members have sufficient opportunity to meet and know faculty members.

2. Satisfactory mechanisms are in place to inform board members of faculty concerns.

3. The board, through the school head, seeks the advice and recommendations of faculty members in formulating basic educational policy.

4. The board is well informed regarding processes and policies for faculty selection, evaluation, compensation, retention, and grievance.

5. Policies in this area are adequate.

Overall rating in this field:

Comments and suggestions:

H. Board-student relations require that trustees have a sufficient sense of student life to be able to understand issues with which the administration is dealing and to make some judgment as to how well the school is carrying out its mission.

1. The trustees have sufficient opportunity for contact with students and their activities.

2. The board has adequate policies for the protection of student health and welfare.

Overall rating in this field:

Comments and suggestions:

I. Board-community relations help determine the image of the school in the eyes of the community and significantly affect student and faculty recruitment as well as fundraising.

1. Trustees accept the responsibility of representing the school in the community.

2. Trustees exercise professional discretion in discussing the affairs of the school with members of the community.

3. Trustees take an active role as advocates of the school in the community.

Overall rating in this field:

Comments and suggestions:

Queries for Trustees (Johnson 1986: 43 to 44)

The head of a day school of 300 students founded in 1965 took the initiative in starting an annual evaluation of trustees' performance, which occurred after the head's evaluation was completed. The following queries for the board are the basis for a board self-evaluation, with comments from the head. The process is carried on during two meetings of the board, and then the board writes up and approves the essence of the evaluation.

Structure

1. Does the board operate under a clear and up-to-date set of bylaws with which all trustees are familiar?
2. Are members of and nominees to the board representative of the school's clientele, and do they have talents that qualify them to serve?
3. Is the board organized to deal effectively with its responsibilities (officers; committee structure; length, frequency, and format of meetings)?

Decision Making

4. How are board decisions made: Are all appropriate people involved? Is there a procedure for making decisions? If so, is it followed?

Responsibilities

5. Does each board member have a clear idea of the responsibilities involved in trusteeship? Does each trustee do his best to contribute time, energy, and resources to the school?
6. Has the board developed a philosophy of what kind of school it wants, what direction it wants the school to go, and a set of clear policy guidelines?

7. Is the board careful to observe the scope and limits of its responsibilities and those of the school's administration?

8. Is the relationship between the board and head such that each can communicate openly and frankly with the other when necessary?

9. Has the board collectively and individually done its best to provide sufficient financial resources for a high-quality K through 12 day school?

10. Has the board done the best it can to promote the school in the community?

11. Does each board member demonstrate a personal interest in the school and attempt to stay abreast of educational developments in the school?

12. Are new board members promptly and effectively oriented to their responsibilities and opportunities?

13. Does the board provide for a regular evaluation of its own performance as well as for evaluation of the head and the school program?

14. Does the board maintain good communication with its own constituents and with the school community?

15. Do board members exercise care and judgment in handling any complaints, grievances, or problems that may come to their attention?

16. Is the board responsible, careful, and forward-thinking in its financial management?

17. Does the board make an effort to know the employees of the school and take an interest in them as individuals?

Leadership America

Board of Directors Self Evaluation

July 2004

Please complete the following questions and send to the chair.

Name: _____ Date: _____

The board encourages and uses the unique abilities of all members?
___Yes ___ No

Examples:

Change and new ideas are accepted on their merits? ___Yes ___ No

Examples:

There is an effective relationship between the board and the CEO?
___ Yes ___ No

Examples:

The board members work at being productive and supporting one another to meet the board's responsibilities? ___ Yes ___No ___

Examples:

On a scale from 1 to 5 (5 being the highest), I feel that the board's performance during the past year was a _____. Why?

The following is the single greatest thing the board could do to improve its performance:

If I could make one change in how Leadership America's board operates, it would be:

Why?

I serve on the following committees for the Leadership America:

Please give examples of how each committee is, or is not, functioning:

I have contributed my leadership in the following ways:

I fulfill assignments carefully and within the desired time frame. ___ Yes ___ No

Comments:

I support and speak publicly about Leadership America. ___ Yes ___ No ____

Comments:

I contributed financially or was directly responsible for the following financial contributions:

On a scale of 1 to 5 (with 5 being the highest), I feel that my contribution to the board's performance during the past year was a ____.

The following is the single greatest thing I could do to improve my performance as a board member:

Is there anything else you would like the collective board to consider in this evaluation? If so, what?

Joint CEO and Board of Directors Evaluation

1. Challenging the Process

How did I/we seek opportunities to change the status quo? Choose a number.

1	2	3	4	5
Avoided Risk at Cost of Opportunity		Appropriate Risk/Opportunity		Took Risk for Opportunity at Cost of Mission

Examples:

2. Inspiring a Shared Vision

How did I/we envision the future and enlist others to share the future?

1	2	3	4	5
Avoided Vision		Shared Vision		Focused on Vision to Exclusion of Action

Examples:

3. Empowering Action

How did I/we empower achievement of goals and objectives?

1	2	3	4	5
Avoided Goals		Appropriate Goal		Pushed Goals Beyond Reason

Examples:

4. Taking Leadership Action

What catalytic actions did I/we take personally or together to move the organization's goals forward?

1	2	3	4	5
No Action		Appropriate Action		Acted Outside Roles and Goals

Examples:

5. Furthering the Mission of the Organization

When and how did I/we tell the organization's story to elicit broader community support?

1	2	3	4	5
Failed to Share Mission in Community		Appropriate Sharing of Mission		Abused Our Community

Examples:

References

Adams, A. (2002). How to keep your head: Great schools and long-term headship. *Independent School*, 62, 13–20.

Adams, T. (2002). Departing? Arriving? Surviving and thriving: Lessons for seasoned and new executives. *Nonprofit Quarterly*, 9(4). Retrieved August 4, 2003, from www.tsne.org/section/2.html/section/367.html.

Adams, T. (1998). Executive transitions: How boards and executives create their futures. *Nonprofit World*, 16(3), 48–52.

Adams, T. (1998). Transition success factors. *Nonprofit World*, 16(3). Retrieved August 4, 2003, from www.transitionguides.com/overview/success.htm.

Allison, M. (2002). Into the fire: Boards and executive transitions. *Nonprofit Leadership and Management*, 12, 341–351.

Andujar, G. (1993). Toward a successful transition: What to do once you've hired your new head of school. Excerpts from *The search handbook: A step-by-step guide to selecting the right leader for your school*, ed. by. B. Gilvar. *Independent School*, 52, 49–57.

Annie E. Casey Foundation (2003). *Community-Based Organizations and Executive Leadership Transitions*. Retrieved July 29, 2003, from www.transitionguides.com/resource/docs/aecf_grantees.pdf.

Axelrod, N. R. (2002). Chief Executive Succession Planning: The Board's Role in Securing Your Organization's Future. BoardSource.

Bencivenga, J. (2002). John Kotter on leadership, management, and change. *School Administrator*, 59, 36–40.

Bennis, W. (2003). On Becoming a Leader, Perseus Publishing, 2003, Revised 2009.

Boland, Peter, Carlo Jensen, and Bruce Meyers (2005). Addressing the Leadership Challenge, Nonprofit Executive Directors' Views on Tenure and Transition in Alberta, Calgary Center for Nonprofit Management, Calgary.

Brager, G., and S. Holloway. *Changing Human Services Organizations: Politics and Practice*, The Free Press, New York, 1978.

Bryson, John M. *Strategic Planning for Public and Nonprofit Organizations: A Guide to Strengthening and Sustaining Organizational Achievement*, Jossey-Bass Publishers, San Francisco, 1995.

Calder, F. C. (2002). Mentoring school heads: A semi-modest proposal. Independent School, 62, 56–58.

Carver, J. (1992). The founding parent syndrome: Governing in the CEO's shadow. *Nonprofit World*, 10(5), 14–16.

Dickey, M. (2002). Tips for making a leadership transition run smoothly. Chronicle of Philanthropy, September 26. Retrieved from http://philantrophy.com/jobs/2002/10/03/20021003-50885.htm.

Donohue, M. (2002). [Review of the book *Chief Succession Planning*]. *Charity Channel*, April. Retrieved August 4, 2003, from http://charity-channel.com/article_3943.shtml.

Drucker, P. (2001). *The Essential Drucker (Collins Business Essentials)*, HarperCollins Publisher, New York, 2001.

Dym, B. (2003a). El Dorado: A case study in school development and community integration in Jewish day schools. For Partnership for Excellence in Jewish Education.

Dym, B. (2001). Integrating entrepreneurship with professional leadership. *The Systems Thinker*, 12, 4.

Dym, B. (2003b). Organizational transitions: from grassroots to professional management. For Partnership for Excellence in Jewish Education.

Dym, B. (1999). Resistance in organizations: How to recognize, understand, and manage it. *The OD Practitioner*, 31(1).

Dym, B. (2003c). School development and community integration in Jewish day schools. For Partnership for Excellence in Jewish Education.

Dym, B. and H. Hutson (1998a). Is your organization ready to change? *Leverage* (Pegasus Communications).

Dym, B. and H. Hutson (1998b). Making change happen in your organization. *Leverage* (Pegasus Communications).

Dym, B. and H. Hutson (1997). Utilizing states of organizational readiness. *The OD Practitioner*, 29(2): 32–43.

Elkin, J. "Lay-professional relations in the Jewish day school." An article from the *Independent School Journal*.

Fish, T. (2002). Trout fishing from a trawler: Notes on head searches. *Independent School*, 62, 74–79.

Fram, E. H. and R. Pearse (1990). When worse comes to worst: Terminating the executive director. *Nonprofit World*, 8(6), 31–33.

Frank, N., ed. (2001). The Jewish Day School Head Search Process: Strategies and Resources. Preliminary Edition. Boston, Partnership for Excellence in Jewish Education.

Gibelman, M. and S. Gelman (2002). On the departure of a chief executive officer: Scenarios and implications. *Administration in Social Work*, 26(2), 63–82.

Grant, D. (1998). Goethe over Gates: The need for academic leadership. *Independent School*, 58, 22–30.

Guskin, A. (1996). Soft landings for new leaders. *Trusteeship*, 4, 12–16.

Hart, A. W. (1991). Leader succession and socialization: a synthesis. *Review of Educational Research*, 61, 451–474.

Hesselbein, F. (1997). The challenge of leadership transition. *Leader to Leader*. Retrieved August 4, 2003, from http://www.pfdf.org/leader-books/L2L/fall97/fh.html.

Hesselbein, F. (2002). Transition at the top: An ending is also a beginning. *Nonprofit Times*, December 1, 2002. Retrieved August 4, 2003, from www.nptimes.com/Dec02/onleadership.html.

Hesselbein, F. and Beckhard Goldsmith (1997). *The Organization of the Future*, The Peter F. Drucker Foundation for Nonprofit Management, New York.

Hesselbein, F. and Beckard Goldsmith (1996). *The Leader of the Future*, The Peter F. Drucker Foundation for Nonprofit Management, New York.

Hinden, D.R. and P. Hull (2002). Executive leadership transition: What we know. *Nonprofit Quarterly*, 9. Retrieved August 4, 2003 from www.nonprofitquarterly.org/section/368.html.

If your CEO departs, should a board member be appointed in the interim? (2003). *Board and Administrator Newsletter*, 19, 2.

Jenne, K. J. and Henderson, M. (2000). Hiring a director for a nonprofit agency: A step-by-step guide. *Popular Government*, Summer, 25–36.

Johnson, Eric W. (1986). *Evaluating the Performance of Trustees and School Heads. Revised Edition.* Boston, National Association of Independent Schools.

Karsten, R. (1998). Search, but not destroy: A head-hunting guide. *Independent School*, 58, 64–68.

King, M. and I. Blumer (2000). A good start. *Phi Delta Kappan*, January, 356–360.

Knight, C. (2000). Transition executive bridges the gap during change. *Nonprofit World*, 18(5), 11–16.

Kouzes, James M., and Barry Z Posner (1997). *Leadership Practices Inventory,* Jossey-Bass, San Francisco.

La Piana, David (2008). The Nonprofit Strategy Revolution, Fieldstone Alliance.

Lencioni, Patrick (1998). *The Five Temptations of a CEO: A Leadership Fable,* Jossey-Bass, San Francisco.

Linnel, Deborah, Zora Radosevich, and Jonathan Spack (2002). *Executive Directors Guide: The Guide for Successful Nonprofit Management,* The United Way of Massachusetts, Boston.

Littleford, J. Leadership transitions: Strategies to support a new head and maintain school stability. Retrieved July 29, 2003 from www.jlittleford.com/art-head-trans.html.

Marchetti, D. (1999). Managing turnover at the top. *The Chronicle of Philanthropy*, June 3. Retrieved August 18, 2003, from http://philanthropy.com/free/articles/v11/i16/16000101.htm.

Mathers, J. (2002). Succession: Insiders vs. outsiders. *School Administrator*, 59, 16–26.

McNamara, C. (2001). How corporations suffer and can recover (for nonprofit or for-profit organizations). Retrieved August 4, 2003, from www.managementhelp.org/misc/founders.htm.

Metzger, C. (1997). Superintendent involuntary turnover: Advice from survivors. *Trust for Educational Leadership*, 26, 20–22.

Miskel, C. and D. Cosgrove (1985). Leadership succession in school settings. *Review of Educational Research*, 55, 87–105.

Neighborhood Reinvestment Corporation (1998). *Managing Executive Transitions*. San Francisco, NeighborWorks. Retrieved August 4, 2003, from www.transitionguides.com/resource/docs/nrc_handbook.pdf.

Nemerowicz and Rosi (1997). *Education for Leadership and Social Responsibility*, The Falmer Press, Washington, D.C.

Online interview: Executive Transition: A powerful opportunity for change. *Nonprofit Genie*. Retrieved August 18, 2003, from www.genie.org/op_opinion_001.htm.

Orem, D. (2002). Leaders on leadership. What the recent NAIS survey reveals about school leadership today. *Independent School*, 62, 41–48.

Quinn, T. (2002). Succession planning: Start today. *Principal Leadership*, 3 (2), 24–28.

Ramsey, K. (2000). The interim superintendency. *School Administrator*, 57, 36–38.

Redington, Emily and Donn Vickers (2001). *Following the Leader: A Guide for Planning Founding Director Transition*, The Academy for Leadership and Governance, Columbus, Ohio.

Riede, P. (2003). The hard business of searching. *School Administrator*, 60, 14–19.

Rodd Jr., T. (2002, Fall). Trout fishing from a trawler: Notes on head searches. *Independent School*, 62, 64–72.

Rogers, J. J. and L. A. Safer (1990). Case study of an innovative superintendent succession plan. *The Clearing House*, 64, 136–140.

Santorra, J. C. (2001). CEO tenure in nonprofit community-based organizations: A multiple case study. *Career Development International*, 6(1), 56–62.

Sherrer, J. L. (1998). Executive follow-up: Boards and CEOs get a line on succession. *Trustee*, April, 20–26.

Tecker, Glenn H., Jean S. Frankel, and Paul D. Meyer. *The Will to Govern Well: Knowledge, Trust and Nimbleness*, American Society of Association Executives Foundation, 2002.

TransitionGuides and CompassPoint Nonprofit Services (2004). *The Executive Transitions Monograph Series*, The Annie E. Casey Foundation, Baltimore.

Wasley, P. (1992). When leaders leave. *Educational Leadership*, 50, 64–67.

Wildman, L. (1988). Against the grain: You should try a do-it-yourself superintendent search. *The American School Board Journal*, 175, 27–30.

Young, Dennis R., Robert M. Hollister, Virginia A. Hodgkinson, and Associates (1993). *Governing, Leading, and Managing Nonprofit Organizations*. San Francisco, Jossey-Bass Publishers.

The following books have helped provide a general background for the study of leadership transition:

Allison, M. and J. Kaye (1997). *Strategic Planning for Nonprofit Organizations*. New York, John Wiley & Sons.

Bennis, W. and B. Nanus (1985). *Leaders: Strategies for Taking Charge*. New York, Harper & Row.

Block, P. (1993). *Stewardship: Choosing Service Over Self-Interest*. San Francisco, Barrett Koehler Publishers.

Bridges, W. (1991). *Managing Transitions*. Reading, MA, Addison Wesley.

Bryson, J. M. (1995). *Strategic Planning for Public and Nonprofit Organizations*. San Francisco, Jossey-Bass Publishers.

Drucker, P. (1990). *Managing the Non-Profit Organization*. New York, HarperCollins.

Gardner, J. W. (1993). *On Leadership*. New York, Free Press.

Gilmore, T. N. (1989). *Making a Leadership Change*. San Francisco, Jossey-Bass Publishers.

Greenleaf, R. K. (1977). *Servant Leadership*, New York, Paulist Press.

Heifetz, R. A. (1994). *Leadership Without Easy Answers*. Boston, Belknap Press.

Herman, R. D and Associates (1994). *The Jossey-Bass Handbook of Nonprofit Leadership and Management*. San Francisco, Jossey-Bass Publishers.

Knauft, E. B., R. A. Berger, and S. T. Gray (1991). *Profiles of Excellence: Achieving Success in the Nonprofit Sector*. San Francisco, Jossey-Bass Publishers.

Kotter, J. P. (1996). *Leading Change*. Boston, Harvard Business School Press.

Letts, C. W., W. P. Ryan, and A. Grossman (1999). *High Performance Nonprofit Organizations*. New York, John Wiley & Sons.

Pava, M. (2003). *Leading with Meaning: Using Covenantal Leadership to Build a Better Organization*. New York, Palgrave MacMillan.

Northouse, P. G. (2001). *Leadership: Theory and Practice*. Thousand Oaks, CA, Sage Publications.

O'Connell, B. (1993). *The Board Member's Book*, The Foundation Center, USA.

Robinson, M. K. (2001). *Nonprofit Boards That Work*. New York, Joseph Wiley & Sons.

Rost, J. (1991). *Leadership for the Twenty-First Century*. Westport, CT, Praeger.

Sonnenfeld, J. (1998). The Hero's Farewell: What Happens When CEO's Retire. London, Oxford.

Stone, S. (1993). *Shaping Strategy: Independent School Planning in the 90s*. National Association of Independent Schools, USA.

Young, D. R., R. M. Hollister, and V. A Hodgkinson and Associates (1993). *Governing, Leading, and Managing Nonprofit Organizations*. San Francisco, Jossey-Bass Publishers.

Index